PRIVATE SCI

Geoffrey Walford is Lecturer in Education Policy and Management at Aston Business School, Aston University, where he is Course Organizer for the university's Society and Government course. He has researched and published widely, mainly on topics concerned with private education, research methods and higher education. He is author of *Life in Public Schools* (Methuen, 1985), *Restructuring Universities: Politics and Power in the Management of Change* (Croom Helm, 1987) and *Privatization and Privilege in Education* (Routledge, 1990). His edited books include *Doing Sociology of Education* (Falmer Press, 1987), *Private Schools in Ten Countries* (Routledge, 1989) and *Doing Educational Research* (Routledge, 1991). His recent research, *City Technology College* (Open University Press, 1991) was co-authored with Henry Miller.

PRIVATE SCHOOLING: TRADITION, CHANGE AND DIVERSITY

Edited by

GEOFFREY WALFORD

P·C·P
Paul Chapman
Publishing Ltd

Paul Chapman Publishing Ltd
144 Liverpool Road
London
N1 1LA

British Library Cataloguing in Publication Data

ISBN 1—85396—116—7

Typeset by Best-set Typesetter Ltd., Hong Kong
Printed and bound in Great Britain by
Butler & Tanner Ltd, Frome and London

A   B   C   D   E   F   G   7   6   5   4   3   2   1

CONTENTS

CONTRIBUTORS

Pauline Dooley is Senior Workshop Tutor and Principal Lecturer in Education at the Cheltenham and Gloucestershire College of Higher Education, Cheltenham. She previously worked at Aston University and, for three years, was Lecturer in Education at the University of the South Pacific, Fiji. She has researched and published on classroom observation, school effectiveness, comparative education and the experiences of educational researchers. She was principal author of *A Survey of Educational Researchers in Britain* (AEEM, 1981).

Tony Edwards is Professor of Education and Dean of the Education Faculty at the University of Newcastle upon Tyne. He previously taught at the Universities of Manchester and Exeter, and in secondary schools in London. His main publications have been in the sociology of language, on post-16 education and training and (more recently) on the politics of private education. His most recent books are *Investigating Classroom Talk* (Falmer Press, 1987, with David Westgate) and *The State and Private Education: An Evaluation of the Assisted Places Scheme* (Falmer Press, 1989, with Geoff Whitty and John Fitz).

Shirley Fisher is a Professor of Psychology at the Centre for Occupational and Health Psychology, University of Strathclyde. She was previously at the University of Dundee, and has conducted research into stress and health for many years. She has published widely in academic journals, is co-editor (with J. Reason) of the *Handbook of Life Stress, Cognition and Health* (Wiley, 1988) and (with C. Cooper) of *On the Move: The Psychology of Change and Transition* (Wiley, 1990), and is author of *Stress and the Perception of Control* (Lawrence Erlbaum Associates, 1984), *Stress and Strategy* (Lawrence Erlbaum Associates, 1986) and *Homesickness, Cognition and Health* (Lawrence Erlbaum Associates, 1989).

Sharon Gewirtz is Research Associate at the University of Newcastle upon

Tyne working with Tony Edwards and Geoff Whitty on an ESRC-funded study of city technology colleges. She previously worked with Jenny Ozga on an Open University project, investigating the role of élites in educational policy-making.

Janis Griffiths was educated at Barry Girls' Grammar School and Manchester Polytechnic and obtained an MEd in Education from the University of Wales College of Cardiff in 1986. She previously taught at one of the private schools in her study but is now working as a freelance journalist and a supply teacher.

Christine Heward holds a first degree in Social Anthropology from Edinburgh University, an MA in Social History from Warwick University and a PhD in Sociology from Birmingham University. She is a lecturer in the Department of Education at Warwick University. Her research interests are in the history of childhoods, families and education with a strong emphasis on gender and masculinities. Her publications include *Making a Man of Him: Parents and their Sons' Education at an English Public School, 1929–1950* (Routledge, 1988) as well as contributions to various academic books and journals. She is currently working on a book to be called *Reconstructing Childhoods in the Nineteenth Century*, for the Themes in Social Science series published by Cambridge University Press.

Máirtín Mac an Ghaill is a Lecturer in Education at the Faculty of Education and Continuing Studies, University of Birmingham. He previously taught Sociology and Economics at a State school in the Midlands. His main research interests include the sociology of 'race' and the sociology of education. He has a particular interest in Irish studies. He is author of *Young, Gifted and Black: Student–Teacher Relations in the Schooling of Black Youths* (Open University Press, 1988), and has also published work on teacher practices, post-16 education and the vocationalization of the curriculum. He is currently preparing for publication a co-edited book on teachers' work, and researching the construction of masculine identity.

Michael Rayner is a Lecturer in the School of Education, University of Leeds, where he teaches Philosophy of Education on higher degree courses and English to PGCE students. He has an interest in political philosophy, particularly of the New Right as it affects education, and epistemology in relation to the curriculum. He has recently co-edited *Curriculum Progress 5–16: School subjects and the National Curriculum* (Falmer Press, 1989).

Ivan Reid is Professor of Education at Loughborough University of Technology. He has spent nearly all of his career in teacher education, most recently at the University of Leeds where he was Pro-Dean of the Faculty of Education. He has written several books, including *Sociological Perspectives on School and Education* (Open Books, 1978), *Social Class Differences in Britain* (2nd edn, Blackwell, 1981), *Sex Differences in Britain* (Blackwell, 1982, with Eileen Wormald), *Teachers, Computers and the Classroom* (Manchester University Press, 1985, with James Rushton) and *The Sociology of School and Education* (Fontana, 1986). He is also an editor of the *British*

Journal of Sociology of Education and *Research in Education*. His current research interests include flexible learning development, education for mutual understanding and the role and function of project work in GCSE.

David Scott is a Research Fellow at the Centre for Educational Development, Appraisal and Research (CEDAR), University of Warwick. From January 1988 until December 1989, he worked on a project sponsored by the Midland Examining Group on coursework and coursework assessment in the GCSE. His most recent work is sponsored by the Training Agency, and is an investigation into language teaching in universities, polytechnics and colleges of higher education in the UK. For thirteen years, before he joined CEDAR, he was a school teacher in an 11–16 comprehensive school in the Midlands. He has published in the fields of assessment and curriculum is a number of journals, including *Forum*, *Curriculum* and the *Journal of Education Policy*. He has also published *The GCSE: An Annotated Bibliography and an Introductory Essay* (CEDAR Papers 1, University of Warwick, 1990).

Geoff Whitty is the Goldsmiths' Professor of Policy and Management in Education at the University of London. He previously taught at Bath University and King's College, London, and was Professor and Dean of Education at Bristol Polytechnic. He has published extensively in the fields of sociology of education, curriculum studies and education policy studies. His most recent books are *Sociology and School Knowledge: Curriculum Theory, Research and Politics* (Methuen, 1985) and (with Tony Edwards and John Fitz) of *The State and Private Education: An Evaluation of the Assisted Places Scheme* (Falmer Press, 1989).

Ralph Williams is a Lecturer in the School of Education, University of Leeds. He taught in secondary schools and a college of education. His research and teaching interests range over the sociology of education, school management and curriculum evaluation. Currently he is directing a project evaluating a local-authority-wide scheme to enhance the secondary curriculum. He has a particular interest in the governing of educational institutions, and is Chair of Governors of a large high school and Vice-Chair of Governors of an FE college.

1

PRIVATE SCHOOLING INTO THE 1990s

Geoffrey Walford

In Britain there is surprisingly little research on private schooling, and debate is often conducted more in terms of polemic than rational argument. Many of those on both the political left and the political right seem to believe that the high quality of private schooling is so evident that research is redundant. They differ only in their reactions to that supposed superiority – the left arguing that such élitism in education should be abolished and the right claiming that parents should be able to pay for whatever form of schooling they wish for their children. Debate proceeds largely in ignorance of the changing present-day nature of private schooling and of the wide diversity of provision within the sector. Of even greater concern is that few of the critics or advocates appear to wish to move beyond their fixed prejudices about private schooling, and increase their understanding by studying the little research work that is available.

This book is designed for those few who do wish to find out more about present-day private schooling in Britain. It gathers together ten specially written chapters, which explore the diversity of schools within the private sector (including the traditional élite schools) and examine the continual rapid change within the sector as a whole. All of the chapters are firmly based on research and all are previously unpublished.

TRENDS IN PRIVATE SCHOOLING

Within this book the terms 'independent' and 'private' are used interchangeably to describe the whole range of schools not maintained by the State. In Britain, these schools are officially designated as independent schools, which encourages the idea that they are not dependent upon local or central government for financial or other support. However, in practice, many of these schools now derive a large proportion of their funding from the State through such means as the Assisted Places Scheme and the Aided Pupils Scheme, and are also highly dependent on the government's ideological support, which sustains the idea that they are almost automatically superior to maintained schools. In many cases, their degree of independence is less than they might wish their customers to recognize. In practically every other country, such schools are designated as private schools, a term that, in Britain, carries with it associations of exclusivity and the profit motive, but does not necessarily do so elsewhere. Over the last decade, however, the government has shown itself keen to support privatization and all forms of private enterprise, which means that it is now more acceptable both within the schools and outside to use the term 'private' without too great a chance of misunderstanding. Luckily, the misleading term 'public schools' that historically has been applied to the major schools and, in particular, to the boys' boarding schools whose headmasters are in membership of the Headmasters' Conference, has now largely fallen into disuse. The various private-school organizations have tried to replace this 'public school' designation with the idea of independence, and the former term is now mainly used only in historical discussions.

Whichever terms are used, one of the most important facts to note is that the distinction between State and private schools is now less clear than it was even a few years ago. An increased number of private schools receive substantial funding from the State through arrangements such as the Assisted Places Scheme and the Aided Pupils Scheme, while many parents with children in maintained schools are increasingly expected to contribute to their children's education. The introduction of city technology colleges, which are independent schools funded jointly by industry, commerce and the State, and grant-maintained schools, which are State-maintained schools outside the LEA system, adds to the confusion. Such a blurring of the boundaries and the development of a range of schools can be regarded as an important part of the government's privatization strategy for schooling (Walford, 1990).

The various chapters in this book set out to explore some of the great diversity of schools that exists within the range of those officially designated as independent. There are some obvious ways in which schools differ, in terms of clearly observable variables such age range, gender of pupils, size, religious denomination and geographical location. Some, for example, are small, isolated boarding schools attached to Roman Catholic religious houses, while others are large day schools set in the centre of busy cities. But the schools also differ greatly in their culture, history and traditions and in the experience of private schooling the pupils receive. While some are heavily academic and highly selective by academic ability, others are more comprehensive in their intakes or may cater for children with learning difficulties, such as dyslexia.

In 1987–8 there were 2,548 registered independent or private schools in the UK. They educated just over 621,700 children, representing about 6.9 per cent of the school-age population, excluding those in special schools (DES,

1990a). Within England, in January 1989, there were 2,270 independent schools (including one city technology college) teaching 532,500 pupils, representing 7.3 per cent of the school population (DES, 1990b). Although private schools are currently experiencing a slight increase in pupil numbers, it is important to recognize that the previous century was one of gradual decline. Before 1870 all schools were private schools, for it was only then that the government of the day began to establish State-owned and maintained schools to fill the gaps in voluntary and charitable provision. By the start of World War Two over 90 per cent of the appropriate school-age population were being educated in State-maintained elementary schools. The majority of the formerly private Roman Catholic and Church of England schools were included within a broader State-maintained sector following the Education Act 1944, thus reducing the number of private schools still further. This was an important move, for in most other countries the percentage of children within private schools is higher than in Britain simply because the denominational schools are still part of the private sector. In Britain, the major existing denominations of the day were able to retain some control over their schools, yet be maintained by the State. As several of the chapters in this book indicate, that decision now has important implications for the schooling of ethnic-minority children in the far more multicultural 1990s Britain.

Table 1.1 indicates how the proportion of children in private schools has varied since 1951. A full analysis is given in Halsey, Heath and Ridge (1984), but it is clear that the general picture is one of continuous contraction of the private sector's share until the late 1970s, then an upturn by 1981 for most age-groups, followed by a gradual increase throughout the age range to the present time. Interestingly, at the primary level for the early part of the period, there was a decline in the absolute numbers in private schools, despite the fact that until the mid-1970s this age-group was increasing. Halsey, Heath and Ridge (*ibid.*) argue that this decline indicates the popularity of educationally progressive State-maintained primary schools during this period. However, the later increase would suggest a growing dissatisfaction with State primary schools as the 1970s and 1980s progressed. Throughout the entire period a lower percentage of children were in private primary schools than in private secondary schools. This may show a greater satisfaction with maintained provision at the primary level, but could also be due to the absence of private primary schools near enough for parents to use for these younger children. The percentage of children in private primary schools has risen considerably in the last decade, and the primary level is the major growth area for the private-school sector as a whole.

At the secondary level, if the direct-grant schools are counted within the private sector, the absolute number of private-school pupils remained relatively steady over a thirty-year period from 1951. The decline in the proportion of privately educated secondary children is due to the two 'baby booms' of 1946 and 1961 and the raising of the school leaving age in 1973. It

Table 1.1 Full-time pupils, by age and type of school. Direct-grant schools are included under private schools (excluding maintained and private special schools) (%)

Year	Type of school	5–10	11–15	16+	All 5+
1951	Maintained	93.1	88.9	62.1	90.8
	Private	6.9	11.1	37.9	9.2
1956	Maintained	94.0	89.5	67.2	91.7
	Private	5.9	10.5	32.8	8.3
1961	Maintained	94.3	91.2	71.9	92.2
	Private	5.7	8.8	28.1	7.8
1966	Maintained	95.1	91.2	77.7	92.7
	Private	4.9	8.8	22.3	7.3
1971	Maintained	96.0	92.3	81.8	93.9
	Private	4.0	7.7	18.2	6.1
1976	Maintained	96.2	93.3	86.2	94.4
	Private	3.8	6.7	13.8	5.6
1981	Maintained	95.3	93.4	82.2	93.8
	Private	4.7	6.6	17.8	6.2
1986	Maintained	95.0	92.6	82.0	93.2
	Private	5.0	7.4	18.0	6.8
1987	Maintained	94.8	92.2	81.1	92.9
	Private	5.2	7.8	18.9	7.1
1988	Maintained	94.7	91.9	80.2	92.7
	Private	5.3	8.1	19.8	7.3

Source: DES *Statistics of Education.* For 1951 and 1956 the figures for private schools not recognized as efficient are estimates. Figures for 1981 onwards relate to England only, not England and Wales, as for earlier years.

is interesting to note that the size of the private sector did not markedly increase to take account of this larger potential market. Over the last decade or so there has been a small increase in private secondary-pupil numbers even though there has been a large decline in the overall secondary-school age population. Nationally, the number of 13-year-olds reached its peak in 1978 and declined by over 30 per cent from that year until 1990. That the secondary schools have been able to maintain their pupil numbers and actually increase their market share might at first seem to indicate a major growth in popularity. However, the decline in secondary-school age population has been predominantly to parents of social classes III to V (Registrar General's classification), while the number of 13-year-old children of social classes I and II has remained far more constant (Smithers and Robinson, 1989). Since children from these top-two social classes dominate the private sector, the private schools have not experienced the same decline in potential customers as has the State sector. The proportion of the population in social classes I and II has also risen over the years with changes to the social structure. There have thus been more upwardly mobile families than those going in the downward direction, and it is to be expected that an increased number of parents would thus be in a position to consider private education. Both of these factors have protected the schools from the decline in enrolments experienced in maintained schools, such that the proportion of children aged 11–15 within the private sector has risen from 6.7 per cent in 1976 to 8.1 per cent in 1988. While most of this percentage rise is attributable to the decline in the maintained sector, some of the increase is the result of a growth in the absolute number of pupils in the private sector, and indicates that a growing number of parents are prepared to pay highly for their children's education.

An interesting pattern can be detected in post-16 provision. In the private sector, absolute numbers of those staying on at school past 16 increased by over one third in the thirty years from 1951, but the corresponding increase in the State sector was nearly 300 per cent. This led to the proportion of post-16 pupils in the private sector plummeting, even though the absolute numbers increased. In the last decade or more, there has been a dramatic turnaround, such that the proportion of sixth-form pupils in private schools has now risen to nearly one fifth again by 1988.

Table 1.2 gives a more detailed time series for the whole of the English

Table 1.2   Full-time primary- and secondary-school population, England, 1970–89 (000s)

Year	Total (all ages)	Private	Percentage private
1970	7,998	521	6.5
1971	8,188	515	6.3
1972	8,378	516	6.2
1973	8,521	521	6.1
1974	8,864	528	6.0
1975	8,915	530	5.9
1976	8,960	523	5.8
1977	8,955	519	5.8
1978	8,861	510	5.8
1979	8,755	512	5.8
1980	8,593	517	6.0
1981	8,377	516	6.2
1982	8,147	510	6.3
1983	7,905	503	6.4
1984	7,717	500	6.5
1985	7,569	501	6.6
1986	7,441	504	6.8
1987	7,332	515	7.0
1988	7,211	523	7.3

Source: DES, 1989.

private sector. It shows in more detail that the total school-age population steadily declined by about 20 per cent from 1976 with a corresponding, if irregular, decline in the private sector until 1984. After that date there has been a gradual rise in the numbers in the private sector, such that the 1976 figures have now been regained.

DIVERSITY WITHIN THE PRIVATE SECTOR

The previous discussion of the whole of the private sector is only partially illuminating. It inevitably gives the impression of homogeneity within the sector, when this is far from correct. In practice, the private sector in Britain is highly diverse and, as the chapters in this book illustrate, the study of this variety is unexpectedly fascinating. Existing research is patchy, incomplete and focused on a narrow range of experience within the sector. The chapters in this volume go some way towards rectifying these omissions.

Much of the limited research available on the private sector has been concerned with the major schools and, in particular, the boys' boarding schools. For a private-school headmaster to be a member of the Headmasters' Conference (HMC), which was formed in 1871, was for many years used as an indicator of the status of a school. The total number of members was limited, at first to 50, but now stands at 231. As the number of schools grew, so did the diversity of schools involved. The range is now from well-known names, such as Eton and Winchester (which are of ancient foundation and provide a full boarding life for highly academic boys at very high cost) to several day schools that cater for children of more moderate abilities at about a quarter of the cost of the historic schools. The HMC group includes both day and boarding schools, but only about 29 per cent of pupils are either full or weekly boarders. Day pupils predominate. Day schools usually take the age range 11–18, while boarding schools often start at the later age of 13, although they increasingly have their own linked preparatory schools to take younger children. Until the 1960s, all HMC schools were for boys only, but the decision of Marlborough to admit girls meant that the HMC was forced to change its policy. By 1990 about two thirds of the HMC schools admitted some girls, with about half of these schools only having girls in the sixth form but, increasingly, girls are admitted throughout the entire school. This has been a fundamental change, and has been the result of varying reasons and circumstances in different schools. For some schools, the 1970s brought a need to expand numbers to keep them economically viable, yet there was a shortage of boy applicants. This was often a particular problem in boarding schools. Other schools introduced girls to act as a 'civilizing' influence on the boys, while yet others wished to enhance or maintain their academic standards. More recently, schools have become co-educational as a result of parental pressure within a changing social environment where mixed schooling is seen as more 'natural' and acceptable than single-sex schooling.

Lastly, some schools have admitted girls for genuine equal-opportunities reasons at a time when parental demands for the education of their daughters has grown to more nearly match those for their sons (Walford, 1986).

The HMC schools form the largest group of private schools in terms of pupil numbers, but they still only educate about a quarter of all privately educated children. Yet it is these schools that have been the subject of the majority of academic research. In part this can be justified because of their historic position in educating the nation's élite. The chapter in this volume by Reid, Williams and Rayner indicates that a large proportion of present-day judges, civil servants, diplomats, directors of major banks and other similar highly prestigious and powerful occupations, were educated at HMC schools. These positions are more open to non-privately educated candidates than when Boyd (1973) conducted his similar study of élite occupations, but the HMC schools are still heavily over-represented. Additionally, together with the prestigious girls' private schools, they still provide about 25 per cent of university undergraduates and more than 50 per cent of Oxford University's home under-graduates. Given the HMC schools' important historic role in the generation and reproduction of our class- and gender-divided society, it is inevitable that much of the research that has been conducted on private schools should have concentrated on these schools. There are numerous historical studies of the system and of individual schools, and sociological studies including Wilkinson (1964), Weinberg (1967), Wakeford (1969) and Walford (1986). Lambert (Lambert and Millham, 1968; Lambert, 1975), who has published extensively on boarding schools, also includes much information and discussion about HMC schools.

The chapter by Christine Heward in this volume is a fascinating account of the processes by which these traditional HMC schools construct various masculinities, and the way that gender and power interact in these schools. She draws upon a historical case study of one HMC school and supplements this with present-day material to describe both the traditional masculinities of the public schools during the first part of this century and the changes that have occurred since that time.

There has been less research work on private schools for girls, where the organization taken to be roughly analogous with the HMC is the Girls' Schools Association (GSA) and the related Governing Bodies of Girls' Schools Association (GBGSA). In 1990 there were 267 schools in membership of GSA/GBGSA, with an even wider range of size, academic emphasis, geographical location, religious affiliation, and so on, than in the HMC. There is less variation in the date of foundation as growth in the number of girls' schools was linked to the greater emancipation of women in the nineteenth century. Of greatest importance was the work of Frances Mary Buss, who started the North London Collegiate School in 1850, and Dorothea Beale, who developed Cheltenham Ladies College after she became head in 1858. These schools served as models for many others.

Fewer girls attend private schools than do boys and there are fewer girls in

GSA/GBGSA schools than boys in HMC schools, even though there are more schools in membership. In England, in January 1988, 46.5 per cent of private-school pupils were girls. The proportion of girls being privately educated has increased faster than that for boys, which has enabled the girls' schools to expand, even though some of them have suffered a considerable loss of girls to the HMC schools as the latter have become co-educational. The few former girls' schools that have attempted to become co-educational have been markedly unsuccessful. About 20 per cent of girls in GSA/GBGSA are boarders, but both day and boarding schools tend to start at age 11 rather than 13. The important sociological studies of girls' schools include Ollerenshaw (1967), Wober (1971) and Delamont (1976, 1984). A collection of research studies that concentrates on girls' private schools and girls experience of private schooling is due to be published (Walford, 1992).

The moves towards greater co-education are just part of the rapid change occurring in the private sector in response to wider structural changes within society and developing educational practice. The schools have also had to respond to changes in the quality of facilities parents demand for their children, to a wider range of curriculum choices and to major changes in public examinations. The implementation of GCSE, in particular, reflects a dramatic restructuring of the role of the private sector within public examinations. Where, traditionally, the leading private schools had played a major part in structuring the curriculum and public-examination process for State-maintained schools (Walford, 1985), the introduction of GCSE largely reversed this role. Many commentators predicted that the private schools would find great difficulty in adapting to the change.

In this volume, the chapter by David Scott looks in detail at one co-educational day and boarding school and one day girls' school, and the ways in which they dealt with the change from GCE to GCSE examinations. The prediction was that the more coursework-based assessment procedures used in GCSE would prove difficult for private schools more used to traditional examination methods, but Scott shows that the reality is more complex.

Separate private schools for children below the age of 11 or 13 are often called preparatory schools. Traditionally, these schools have also been single sex. However, the moves towards greater co-education at this age were great and led, in 1981, to the amalgamation of the two separate preparatory schools associations into the Incorporated Association of Preparatory Schools (IAPS), which was formerly the name of the boys' association. The new body now has 540 schools in membership. All pupils must leave these schools by age 14, but most boys leave by 13, usually to the various HMC schools, while girls may leave at any time between 11 and 13. Most of these schools are far smaller than the secondary schools, and about 20 per cent of the pupils are either full or weekly boarders. Although there is now a good history of the preparatory schools (Leinster-Mackay, 1984), there have been no sociological studies. It is in this preparatory-school age range that the main recent increase in private-school pupil numbers can be found, particularly at the pre-school and pre-prep school levels. In 1990, about 11 per cent of IAPS pupils were under age 5. Schools within other groupings have also moved to exploit this market and some 8 per cent of HMC pupils were under 11 in 1990.

About two thirds of all private-school pupils are in schools within these three major groups, but there are several other small groups of schools worthy of consideration. For example, the heads of 47 of the boys' and co-educational senior schools together form the Society of Headmasters of Independent Schools (SHMIS). These schools are smaller than those in the major associations, and generally have a higher percentage of boarders. The list includes some unusual schools, such as the Jewish Carmel College and Chetham's School of Music. The heads of a further 279 private schools catering for all ages come under the umbrella of the Independent Schools' Association Incorporated (ISAI). The majority of these schools are for day pupils only, and fees are usually considerably lower than those of the other groups. Only a few pupils leave from these schools to go to university or other forms of higher education. Finally, some 15 schools hold membership of the Governing Bodies Association (GSA) and not of any other organization, and hence are often categorized together.

All of the schools in the groups described above are members of the Independent Schools Information Service (ISIS) and the Independent Schools Joint Council (ISJC), which represent about 80 per cent of the private-school population. Far more is known about these pupils and schools than the rest of the private sector. Indeed, it is ISIS *Annual Census* figures that are yearly paraded in the Press and media, and that many commentators take to be indicative of the entire private sector. Table 1.3 provides some statistical information on the numbers of schools and pupils in each of the member associations, together with information on the number of children who board.

Table 1.3 Pupils in schools in the major private-school associations

Association	No. of schools	No. of pupils	Percentage girls	Percentage boarding
HMC	230	153,179	16.7	29.2
GSA	244	111,734	98.6	20.0
GBGSA	23	9,144	90.9	8.0
SHMIS	47	16,960	24.1	43.5
GBA	15	6,420	31.3	32.6
IAPS	540	115,223	29.7	19.8
ISAI	279	61,543	50.7	7.9
Total	1,378	474,203	45.5	22.2

Source: ISIS, 1990. One HMC school failed to return the census form. A very few schools in Ireland are included in these numbers. These associations include about 80 per cent of private-school pupils in the UK.

It can be seen that, while the most highly prestigious schools are generally boarding schools, the percentage of children who board is not uniformly high throughout the private sector. Within the HMC 29 per cent of children are boarders, while the figure drops to 20 per cent for GSA schools. Overall, 37 per cent of boarders were girls in 1988. Moreover, there has been a steady decline in the total number of children who board over the last two decades. There are some differences between girls and boys, with a gradual increase in the proportion of girls who board, but this has been overwhelmed by the decrease in boy boarders of a regular 2 or 3 per cent each year. The 1960s brought with them a change in parental attitudes towards the desirability of boarding, and vastly increased boarding fees. The result is that many schools, even some of the well-known names, now find it difficult to attract enough pupils of sufficiently high academic ability to fill their boarding places. There have also been changes in boarding arrangements such that, even within those classified as boarding pupils, some 10 per cent are actually weekly boarders and return to their homes each weekend. In this book, the chapter by Shirley Fisher investigates some of the effects of boarding in terms of homesickness. Her research, which has been conducted over many years, gives numerous insights into the problems children may face when living away from their own homes.

The ISJC member schools publish their own census material every year, and it is often assumed that these figures can be taken to be representative of the whole of the private sector. However, this is far from being always a correct assumption, for there is a great diversity of experience for the remaining 20 per cent of private-sector pupils who are accommodated in about 40 per cent of the total number of private schools. These pupils' experience is usually within smaller schools, which are often very different from the larger and longer-established schools. However, while it is known that there is a wide diversity of schools in the remaining part of the private sector, there has been practically no published research that examines such schools.

The number of smaller private schools is increasing rapidly, predominantly through the growth of religious schools, such as Evangelical Christian schools and Muslim schools, but also through the growth of low-fee schools responding to local demand. Many of the religiously based schools are run by parents who argue that the State-maintained sector does not offer an educational experience to their children that is congruent with their group's religious beliefs. They believe that the State-maintained system has become secularized, while education should centre around religious and moral teaching.

Several of the chapters in this volume concentrate on this highly neglected segment of the private sector. The chapter by Janis Griffiths describes the pattern of provision of private schooling within an area of South Wales. She shows that most of the schools in the area lack the prestige often associated with private schools. She describes the way these schools promote themselves and raises questions about their everyday workings and organization. In her chapter, Pauline Dooley tackles the highly controversial topic of private

Muslim schools. She examines the reasons why some Muslim parents feel the need to establish separate Muslim private schools for their children and describes three examples of such schools. This chapter is closely linked to the following chapter by Geoffrey Walford, which considers a range of small private schools that wish to obtain funding from the State. He gives some examples of a heterogeneous group of private schools, which includes Evangelical Christian schools, small schools and Muslim schools that are attempting to move from the private sector into the State sector. This is an important example of the blurring of the boundary between the State and private sectors of education, for these various groups that have established their own schools wish to retain authority over various issues of crucial importance to their religious or philosophical beliefs, but be at least part financed by the State.

A further group of schools that makes the boundary between private and State provision less distinct is the black voluntary schools discussed by Máirtín Mac an Ghaill. The pupils at these early-evening hours and Saturday schools also attend local maintained schools, but their parents believe that the level and nature of education provided for their children is inadequate and does not reflect black culture to a sufficient degree. Instead of starting their own schools in opposition to the maintained sector, these parents have established supplementary schooling, so that their children can benefit from what is provided by the State, but also move beyond it. These schools are not officially recognized as independent schools for they offer only part-time teaching to children who already attend other schools. Those who attend are charged no fees and the teachers are unpaid, but these schools represent an important response to the racism black children often experience in schools, and illustrate further the growing complexity of schooling provision.

Since its election in 1979 the Conservative government has gradually encouraged a privatization process for schooling, by supporting existing private schools, both ideologically and financially, and by reducing the psychological barrier between the State and private sectors. The Education Act 1980, for example, introduced the Assisted Places Scheme to enable some selected children to attend academically selective private schools, their parents paying no fees or only a part of the fees on a means-tested scale. The scheme has acted as a firm financial and ideological support for the private sector. The Education Reform Act 1988 further softened the dividing line between the maintained and private sectors by legislating for the introduction of city technology colleges (CTCs) and grant-maintained schools. The CTCs are designated as independent schools, but are funded jointly by the State and industry and commerce, while the grant-maintained schools are still officially within the State system, but are funded directly by the DES rather than through the LEA system. Both of these new types of schools were designed to increase competition between schools and to deepen the privatization process. The chapter by Tony Edwards, Sharon Gewirtz and Geoff Whitty is based on recently completed research on the origins, implementation and workings of the Assisted Places Scheme, and on similar ongoing research on CTCs. It examines the relationship between the Assisted Places Scheme and the emergence of CTCs, and describes some of the ideological conflicts between the two ideas.

The final chapter by Geoffrey Walford also looks at these newest additions to the private sector, and explores the tensions between the private-school and magnet-school natures of the CTCs. His chapter is based upon a period of ethnographic fieldwork in the first CTC at Kingshurst, Solihull, and he describes and discusses the ways in which that CTC has exploited and been constrained by these two somewhat opposing rhetorics of justification.

The collection of chapters presented in this book does not cover the whole range of private education provision, for there are still many topics and areas or interest where no research work has been conducted. It also focuses on private provision within schools and does not consider the rapid expansion of private education and training within further and higher education, or the major growth in private pre-school provision. However, the chapters presented here indicate the continuing importance of the private sector of schooling, and show that these schools have rapidly adapted to changing social, financial and practical circumstances. The chapters show that there is considerable diversity within the sector, and that recent changes within both the private and the State-maintained sectors have led to a greater blurring of the boundary between State and private provision. If this is correct, an understanding of the nature and diversity of the private sector becomes an important factor in attempting to understand the State-maintained sector. This book aims to increase understanding by presenting new research work in this key area.

REFERENCES

Bamford, T. W. (1967) *The Rise of the Public Schools*, Nelson, London.
Boyd, D. (1973) *Elites and their Education*, NFER, Slough.
Delamont, S. (1976) *Interaction in the Classroom*, Methuen, London.
Delamont, S. (1984) Debs, dollies, swots and weeds: classroom styles at St Luke's, in
    G. Walford (ed.) *British Public Schools: Policy and Practice*, Falmer Press, Lewes.
DES (1989) *Statistics of Education*, London.
DES (1990a) *Statistical Bulletin 4/90. Education Statistics for the United Kingdom 1989
    Edition*, London.
DES (1990b) *Statistical Bulletin 6/90. Statistics of Schools in England – January 1989*,
    London.
Halsey, A. H., Heath, A. F. and Ridge, J. M. (1984) The political arithmetic of public
    schools, in G. Walford (ed.) *British Public Schools: Policy and Practice*, Falmer
    Press, Lewes.
ISIS (1990) *Independent Schools Information Service. Annual Census 1990*, London.
Lambert, R. (1975) *Chance of a Lifetime? A Study of Boarding Education*, Weiden-
    feld & Nicolson, London.
Lambert, R. and Millham, S. (1968) *The Hothouse Society*, Weidenfeld & Nicolson,
    London.
Leinster-Mackay, D. (1984) *The Rise of the English Prep School*, Falmer Press,
    Lewes.

Ollerenshaw, K. (1967) *The Girls' Schools*, Faber & Faber, London.

Smithers, A. and Robinson, P. (1989) *Increasing Participation in Higher Education*, BP Education Service, London.

Wakeford, J. (1969) *The Cloistered Elite. A Sociological Analysis of the English Public Boarding School*, Macmillan, London.

Walford, G. (1985) The construction of a curriculum area: science in society, *British Journal of Sociology of Education*, Vol. 4, no. 1, pp. 39–54.

Walford, G. (1986) *Life in Public Schools*, Methuen, London.

Walford, G. (1990) *Privatization and Privilege in Education*, Routledge, London.

Walford, G. (ed.) (1992) *The Private Schooling of Girls: Past and Present*, Woburn Press, London.

Weinberg, I. (1967) *The English Public Schools*, Atherton Press, New York, NY.

Wilkinson, R. (1964) *The Prefects. British Leadership and the Public School Tradition*, Oxford University Press.

Wober, M. (1971) *English Girls' Boarding Schools*, Allen Lane, Harmondsworth.

2
THE EDUCATION OF THE ÉLITE

Ivan Reid, Ralph Williams and Michael Rayner

This chapter reviews some aspects of the relationship between the educational and social structures of Britain. In particular, it is concerned with the relationship between what might be seen as élite education – schools other than those provided as free at point of use by the government and the universities of Oxford and Cambridge – and those people who can be recognized as belonging to a, or the, social élite. A first task is to clarify and define both the terms and the approach we have adopted here in order to replicate and extend some of the empirical work in this field.

PRIVATE SCHOOLING AND ÉLITE EDUCATION

Academic interest in the role of 'public' schools in the education of the élite can be conveniently placed as following the 1960s' Labour government's interest in private schooling, which lead to the publication of the two reports of the Public Schools Commission (1968, 1970). There can be little doubt that the consensus over the existence, if not the legitimacy, of social-class differences in Britain has lead to the acceptance that social institutions involve separation and segregation (Reid, 1986; 1989). This is well witnessed in respect to education and particularly schooling. Not only, as Silver (1973) has recorded, were two types of schooling produced following the 1870 Act – secondary for the middle classes and elementary for the working classes – but there were also private schools for the upper classes, the more prestigious of which were known as 'public' schools. More than surprisingly, public schools have rarely been the centre of political controversy. They survived intact the Education Act 1944, together with Butler's remit to the Fleming Committee of 1942 to come up with a plan to bring them into closer association with the 'State' system, and its report, which proposed they should be open to all who could benefit irrespective of parental income.

Figures such as Tawney (1931) and Crosland (1956) appear as relatively lone antagonists. Crosland clearly affected Labour Party thinking with statements such as 'a system of superior private schools open to the wealthier classes, but out of reach of poorer children, however talented and deserving...much the most flagrant inequality of opportunity, as it is cause of class inequality generally, in our educational system' (*ibid.*) It was he who led the Labour government of the 1960s to the commitment to comprehensive schools (i.e. schools for all) and the setting up of the Public Schools Commission with the explicit brief for a plan for integration – which together with a clear statement that such schools were 'socially divisive' it duly presented. Apart from removing direct-grant schools in 1974, the commission's recommendations were ignored, or at least not implemented.

Current Labour Party thinking accurately enough states 'Attendance at a private school means something far more than education. In Britain it is the basic requirement for membership of the hierarchy which still dominates so many positions of power and influence' Labour Party (1981). It is interesting that this so closely echoes the sociological commentary of Giddens (1979) that they 'continue to play a dominant role in the self-perpetuation of recruitment to élite positions'. The Labour Party is presently committed to a policy that would see the rapid abolition of public schools' charitable status. However, in the meantime, the Conservative governments of the 1980s introduced and extended an Assisted Places Scheme. Public opinion when last measured in the mid-1970s showed more support across all social classes for public than for comprehensive schools, and only minorities wanting the former to be abolished (Gallup Polls, 1973 and 1975, cited in Reid, 1981).

PRIVATE, PUBLIC, OR INDEPENDENT

There is no commonly accepted set of definitions of any type of school in Britain, and perhaps nowhere is this more confusing than in the private sector or non-maintained sector. Private schools, the catch-all category, encompasses the complete range not only of quality and social exclusivity but also of age range. Independent is now the preferred term, assumed by the schools to be more socially acceptable (Rae, 1981), but is misleading to the extent that while the schools may be free from government control they receive considerable direct and indirect financial support from that source (Glennerster and Wilson, 1970; Edwards, Fitz and Whitty, 1985; Griggs, 1985; Pring, 1986, 1987; Walford, 1987).

Like other commentators we are concerned primarily with the prestigious boys' schools, whose products inhabit in disproportionate numbers the higher ranks of professions and élite occupations, commonly referred to as public schools. As a working definition and to enable the replication we have accepted public as those schools whose heads belong to the Headmasters' Conference (HMC – founded in 1869 as an exclusive 'club'), even though some of these in the past have been direct-grant grammar schools (see below) and it fails to distinguish the élite schools of the Clarendon or Great Schools, as Rae (1981) calls them. The Public Schools Commission (1968) illustrated that influence of this particular group in that two third of the Conservative cabinet of 1963 were products of only six public schools – Charterhouse, Eton, Harrow, Marlborough, Rugby and Winchester. We have used the term independent to refer to private schools other than public in our replication of Boyd's (1973) work and elsewhere to refer to all private schools including public. This use is clearly indicated in text and tables.

ÉLITE OR ÉLITES

There is a considerable literature concerning the concept 'élite', most of which is not of direct relevance to our discussion. Our use of the term in this chapter follows the basic form identified by Pareto (1935) who, having suggested that in every branch of human activity each person could be given a score (10 to 0) to represent their capacity, concluded, 'So let us make a class of people who have the highest indices in their branch of activity, and to that class give the name of élite'. Pareto, like Mosca before him, was almost exclusively concerned with the governing (in the political sense) élite. The identification of a ruling élite, the ways in which it operates, its relationship with democracy and equality, need not be examined in any detail here. The occupational groups, and the levels within them examined below, are apparently influential and are generally recognized in the literature as at least representative of the British élite (for example, Boyd, 1973; Crewe, 1974; Stanworth and Giddens, 1974; Giddens, 1979). However, it is obvious that, by definition and operation, we are concerned in this chapter with occupational élites.

In effect, then, Pareto's initial concept of élite provides two separate models. The first is to take only those in each sphere of activity who are scored as the highest. The second is to see a tapering heirarchy in each sphere (a pyramid) from 1 through to 10. Boyd (1973) appears to be subscribing to the former in that he takes, for example, only high-court and appeal judges as the élite of the judiciary (see Tables 2.2 and 2.3), though taking both bishops and assistant bishops in the Church élite he might be seen to go somewhat lower than ten. In our study of the occupation of education we have used most of the available range of the second model.

PROCESS OR ASSOCIATION

There appears to be two main ways in which public and/or independent schools help to furnish occupational élite groups: first, by providing a particular education for the children (until recently almost exclusively male) of élite parents, thereby sustaining parental status; and, second, in providing élite access for certain non-élite parented children. Much has been written on the nature of this particular education, often along the lines of a 'public school ethos' of expressive goals, service to the community and leadership (Weinberg, 1967; Public Schools Commission, 1968, 1970; Lambert, 1975; Gathorne-Hardy, 1977).

A more rigid analysis is that by Scott (1982), who identifies three aspects. First, academic achievement (but for which he quotes the Oxford Mobility Study to show that maintained grammar schools have provided this at least as well – holding family background and leaving age constant and making (in our opinion) not uncontroversial assumptions about the distribution of IQ across school types – Halsey, Heath and Ridge, 1984). Second, the promotion of a common set of values, beliefs and ideological commitments, which unify the élite regardless of origin. Again he argues that public schools do not have a monopoly. Third, and for Scott the crucial one, is the old-boy network, consisting of a distinctive lifestyle with useful social contacts.

Our analysis does not afford comment on, or examination of the above processes, but simply concentrates on the association of public schooling and élite occupations. Indeed, we are concerned with but one side of that association – output as opposed to input. That independent and public schools recruit predominately from the upper-middle classes is beyond dispute and very well documented (see, for example, Kalton, 1966; Public Schools Commission, 1968, 1970; *General Household Survey 1976*, 1978; Halsey, Heath and Ridge, 1980, 1984; Griggs, 1985; Fox, 1985, 1989). Similarly, both the social origins of Oxbridge undergraduates and their likelihood of public schooling (52 per cent were from independent schools in 1983 – Reid, 1986) have been more than well displayed over time (see, also, Halsey, Heath and Ridge, 1980, 1984).

ÉLITES AND THEIR EDUCATION

As has been shown above, the relationship between attendance at a public school and Oxford or Cambridge University, with entry into occupations having high status, power and financial rewards, is part of both the reality and folklore of British educational and social life. Empirical investigations of the precise nature of this relationship are relatively, and perhaps surprisingly, rare and somewhat dated. One study that received a good deal of attention, and continues to do so, is Boyd's (1973) perhaps none-too-aptly entitled book, *Élites and their Education*. While this book received criticism (see, for example, Glennerster, 1974; Szreter, 1975; Abrahams, 1976), few have since taught or written on the subject without making reference to it (recent examples include, among many, Walford (and contributors), 1984; Salter and Tapper, 1985; Cookson, 1989; Fox, 1989; Whitty, Edwards and Fitz, 1989).

Basically, Boyd's study involved identifying the educational experience of eight 'élite' occupational groups (listed in Table 2.2) by reference to their entries in *Who's Who*. In replicating the study we do not subscribe to the view implicit in his work that we have a view of the education of the élite in our society, but only some selected part of it, which may or may not be typical or the most important. We are conscious that the criticisms levelled at studies of the élite by Crewe (1974) apply. That they:

1. do not approach the whole élite, only parts;
2. select élite groups on the grounds of accessibility of data, rather than importance;
3. focus on a group's collective biography/origins – who they are rather than their ideology or roles; and
4. conceive élite groups as those in the top parts of clearly marked social organizations, and hence the élite as the aggregation of groups.

Without meeting these criticisms, what our study does provide is a comparison of the situation of 1970–1 with that in 1984, allowing for the identification of change. Further, it extends Boyd's survey, providing a view from 1939 to 1984, allowing for a consideration of the trends identified by him.

In exploring Boyd's methodology we were drawn to make some minor modifications. We used his definition of public schools as those whose heads were members of HMC and of independent schools as other schools at which fees were paid. However, membership of HMC does change and we were initially concerned that he had used the HMC list for 1971, when the schooling of the samples stretched over a considerable period. Consequently, we analysed our 1984 data using HMC and other school listings on the basis of date of birth plus thirteen years, together with current ones and that for 1971. However, the variations produced were of such a small order that we decided that, rather than re-work Boyd's data, we would use the same base as he. Of much greater concern was Boyd's assumption that where schooling was not specified in a *Who's Who* entry it should be assumed that it was not public. This we saw as unwarranted and probably misleading; consequently, we excluded such persons from our analysis and re-worked Boyd's figures in that manner (in both cases the numbers involved were very small). Hence the data presented here include only those members of élite occupations whose schooling was fully recorded. We have not differentiated, as did Boyd, 'well-known' from 'other' public schools, since we considered his criterion 'various writers have considered the best known' as both subjective and subject to change.

In viewing the data a number of considerations have to be made. The representation of particular types of educational background in any given occupational group is clearly dependent upon three main, interrelated factors:

1. The proportion of the population receiving a particular form of education.

2. The recruitment and promotion policies and practices within the occupation.
3. The predisposition of those receiving particular forms of education to enter the given occupation.

These factors are dynamic, extremely complex and our knowledge of them limited. It is only in respect to (1) that we have any clear evidence. The proportion of 14-year-olds attending HMC schools remained constant in the previous quarter decade to our study at around 2.5 per cent (Higher Education, 1963, and our computation of data supplied by ISIS, 1984). Consequently, if recruitment (2) and disposition (3) had remained constant it might be anticipated that the proportion of public-school-educated members of élite occupations would have remained stable. On the other hand, the percentage of all British first-degree graduates who came from Oxbridge has markedly declined from around 20 per cent in 1950–1, with a peak of 22.2 per cent in 1960–1 to 7.8 per cent in 1982–3 (see Table 2.1). While the number of Oxbridge graduates increased by two thirds between 1950–1 and 1982–3, those from other universities increased fivefold. At the same time it has to be appreciated that 52 per cent of Oxbridge entrants in 1984 were from independent schools (Reid, 1986) and that on graduation they are proportionately more likely to enter accountancy (a fifth more), law (over twice), commerce (a third more) although, of course, in numerical terms they are but a small fraction of those entering these fields of employment (*University Statistics 1982–83*, 1983; *Annual Report of the University of Cambridge Careers' Service Syndicate*, 1984; *University of Oxford Appointments Committee Report 1983–84*, 1984).

To assess these facts properly and in particular the effect of these changes on the composition of élite occupations, or entry into those forms of employment from which they emerge, would require analysis of recruits over time that falls well outside the scope of this chapter. Obviously, too, some holders of élite positions in 1970–1 appear in the listing from 1984. However, it seems reasonable to assume that both in respect to public schooling and to Oxbridge

Table 2.1   Percentage of first-degree graduates* from Oxbridge and other British universities, 1950/1–1982/3

	1950–1	1960–1	1970–1	1982–3
Oxbridge graduates	19.6	22.2	10.1	7.8
Other university graduates	80.6	77.8	89.1	92.2
Total (nos.)	17,337	22,426	51,189	72,225

Note
* Includes overseas students.
(*Sources:* 1950–1 – Cmd 8638, 1952; 1960–1 – Cmnd 1855, 1962; 1970–1 – *Statistics of Education*, 1971; 1982–3 – *University Statistics 1982–83*, 1983.)

graduation the comparison to hand should indicate, rather than measure, change if it is occurring.

ÉLITES AND PUBLIC SCHOOLING

Table 2.2 shows that during the 14-year period, between Boyd's study and ours, the proportion of the élites educated at public schools declined overall by 13.8 per cent, composed of a 12-per-cent increase of those attending other (mainly LEA) schools and 1.9 per cent from independent schools. In each élite group with the exception of the judiciary, there was a decline, from an extremely marked one of 34 per cent in the RAF to 8.4 per cent among ambassadors. In the cases of bankers, army and RAF officers and bishops, the decline is reflected in an increase in the proportion educated in other schools, whereas among civil servants, ambassadors and the navy some of the decline is accounted for by an increased percentage from independent schools – in the case of the navy the percentage moved from nil to 7.5.

Some change is therefore clearly indicated. In 1970–1 almost three quarters of the élite groups were public school educated, and half the groups (the army, ambassadors, judiciary and bankers) had more than 80 per cent so schooled. Only in the navy had more than half been educated outside public and independent schools. By 1984 public-school-educated members of the same groups accounted for three fifths; only the judiciary had more than 80 per cent and both the navy and RAF had more than 60 per cent educated in other schools. Over a third (36.7 per cent) of the élite had attended other schools and some 3 per cent independent ones.

Such changes can be viewed in a number of ways. Bearing in mind we are viewing whole groups and not recruits, one view would be that they indicate a fairly severe change in recruitment policy and promotion prospects in favour of those educated in the LEA sector. This is most dramatically apparent in the case of the RAF, somewhat less so for the army, civil servants, bankers and bishops, and barely so for the judiciary and ambassadors. The contrary view is that the data continue to display extremely large advantage for those educated at public school given their representation in the general population. The over-representation of public-school-educated élites as compared with the population has merely declined from 28 times to 23 times – not, perhaps, a major change. In absolute terms it is clear that those educated in independent schools have gained the greatest opportunity from the changes in respect to entry into the élites reviewed. Between 1970–1 and 1984 the representation of public-school-educated products in the groups declined by 18 per cent, that of other schools increased by 48 per cent, while that of independent schools increased by 158 per cent.

It is fairly obvious that the groups vary in the extent of change. The armed forces have changed fairly dramatically, perhaps reflecting changing roles, and demands on them, of a greater degree than for other groups. The civil service, bankers and bishops represent a middle grouping, where change while visible is not so marked. Finally, ambassadors and the judiciary, whom many would regard as the highest part of the establishment élite represented among the groups, display the least and very little change.

Table 2.2 Type of school attended by members of élite occupations,* 1970–1[†] and 1984

	1970–1		1984		%
	No.	%	No.	%	
Ambassadors[1]					
Public[‡]	66	86.8	58	78.4	−8.4
Independent	—	—	4	5.4	+5.4
Other	10	13.2	12	16.2	+3.0
Judiciary[2]					
Public	73	83.9	90	84.1	+0.2
Independent	3	3.4	2	1.9	−1.5
Other	11	12.6	15	14.0	+1.4
Bishops[3]					
Public	87	77.7	90	65.7	−12.0
Independent	—	—	—	—	—
Other	25	22.3	47	34.3	+12.0
Bankers[4]					
Public	107	81.7	73	69.5	−12.2
Independent	4	3.1	2	1.9	−1.2
Other	20	15.3	30	28.6	+13.3
Civil servants[5]					
Public	177	65.8	168	49.4	−16.4
Independent	—	—	13	3.8	+3.8
Other	92	34.2	159	46.8	+12.6
Army[6]					
Public	99	90.0	59	73.8	−16.2
Independent	2	1.8	2	2.5	+0.7
Other	9	8.2	19	23.8	+15.6
RAF[7]					
Public	50	70.4	20	36.4	−34.0
Independent	2	2.8	2	3.6	+0.8
Other	19	26.8	33	60.0	+33.2
Navy[8]					
Public	27	39.1	13	24.5	−14.6
Independent	—	—	4	7.5	+7.5
Other	19	26.8	33	60.0	+33.2
All					
Public	686	74.0	571	60.2	−13.8
Independent	11	1.2	29	3.1	+1.9
Other	228	24.7	348	36.7	+12.0

Table 2.2   (cont.)

	1970–1		1984		%
	No.	%	No.	%	
All non-armed services					
Public	510	75.6	479	62.8	−12.8
Independent	4	1.0	8	2.8	+1.8
Other	158	23.4	263	34.5	+11.1
All armed services					
Public	176	70.4	92	49.7	−20.7
Independent	4	1.6	8	4.3	+2.7
Other	70	28.0	84	46.0	+18.0

Notes
*Figures and percentages are of those whose education was recorded; [†]1970–1 data are from Boyd (1973) adjusted to exclude those whose schooling was not recorded; [‡]HMC schools; 1. heads of embassies and legations; 2. high-court and appeal judges; 3. assistant bishops and above of Church of England; 4. directors of clearing banks; 5. under-secretary and above; 6. major-generals and above; 7. airvice-marshalls and above; 8. rear-admirals and above.

ÉLITES AND OXBRIDGE GRADUATION

Table 2.3 shows that over the same 14-year period the percentage of Oxbridge graduates in the élite groups declined by 11.5 per cent while that of other graduates rose 9.6; the difference, interestingly enough, being accounted for by a rise of 1.9 per cent in non-graduates. The largest decreases, around 13 per cent, were in the army and among bankers. Both these groups exhibited the greatest growth in non-graduates (around 7 per cent) that, given that the number of university graduates rose by a third between 1950–1 and 1960–1 and doubled in the following decade (Table 2.1), might be viewed as surprising. The largest increases in other graduates were in the RAF – which also displayed it in respect to all graduates with a corresponding, large drop in non-graduates – and among civil servants and bishops – where the increase was matched by a decrease in Oxbridge graduates. As in the case of public schooling, least change occurred among ambassadors, which was the only group to display an increase in Oxbridge graduates (2.2 per cent) and the judiciary, whose 2-per-cent decrease in such graduates was made up by an increase of non-graduates.

Again, these changes can be viewed in a number of ways and within the context of a rapid overall decline in the proportion of graduates from Oxbridge (Table 2.1). In view of this latter change, the fact that the decrease in Oxbridge-educated élite members was smaller than that of the public school educated (11.5 compared with 13.8 per cent) might be seen as a relative increase in the importance of Oxbridge in élite recruitment and/or promotion. At the same time, such a difference might be taken to indicate the fact that the proportion of Oxbridge entrants from public schools has also declined over the same period. Hence the opportunity for Oxbridge graduates to enter élite groups has simply been maintained.

Table 2.3 University attendance by members of élite occupations,* 1970–1[†] and 1984[‡]

	1970–1		1984		%
	No.	%	No.	%	
Ambassadors[1]					
Oxbridge	64	80.0	69	82.2	+2.2
Other	9	11.3	7	8.4	−2.9
None	7	8.7	8	9.4	+0.7
Judiciary[2]					
Oxbridge	77	84.6	90	82.6	−2.0
Other	9	9.9	11	10.1	+0.2
None	5	5.5	8	7.3	+1.8
Bishops[3]					
Oxbridge	100	77.5	109	69.4	−8.1
Other	18	14.0	36	22.9	+8.9
None	11	8.5	12	7.6	−0.9
Bankers[4]					
Oxbridge	81	60.4	51	47.2	−13.2
Other	13	9.7	17	15.7	+6.0
None	40	29.9	40	37.0	+7.1
Civil servants[5]					
Oxbridge	119	69.3	216	60.8	−8.5
Other	50	17.4	99	27.8	+10.4
None	38	13.2	41	11.5	−1.7
Army[6]					
Oxbridge	28	24.3	9	11.0	−13.3
Other[8]	64	55.7	50	61.0	+5.3
None	23	20.0	23	28.1	+7.9
RAF[7]					
Oxbridge	14	17.5	5	8.3	−7.2
Other[8]	27	33.8	31	51.7	+17.9
None	39	48.8	24	40.0	−8.8
All					
Oxbridge	482	57.6	549	57.4	−0.2
Other	190	22.7	251	26.3	+3.6
None	165	19.7	156	16.3	−3.4
All non-armed services					
Oxbridge	440	68.5	535	65.7	−0.8
Other	99	15.4	170	20.9	+5.5
None	103	19.7	109	16.3	−3.4

Table 2.3   (cont.)

	1970–1 No.	%	1984 No.	%	%
All armed services					
Oxbridge	42	21.5	13	9.2	−12.3
Other	91	46.7	81	57.4	+11.3
None	62	31.8	47	33.3	+1.5

Notes
*Figures and percentages are of those whose education was recorded; †1970–1 data are from Boyd (1973) adjusted to exclude those whose schooling was not recorded; ‡HMC schools; §includes services' colleges; 1.   heads of embassies and legations; 2.   high-court and appeal judges; 3.   assistant bishops and above of Church of England; 4.   directors of clearing banks; 5.   under-secretary and above; 6.   major-generals and above; 7.   air vice-marshalls and above; 8.   rear-admirals and above.

PRE-WAR AND POST-WAR CONTINUITY AND CHANGE

Tables 2.4, 2.5 and 2.6 display Boyd's and our data for 1939, 1950, 1960, 1970–1, 1984 and the overall average in respect to public-school, Oxbridge-educated and non-graduate members of the occupational élites. In making observations (let alone drawing conclusions) about change and trends it is necessary to bear in mind the strictures spelt out above. In particular, we have no measure of the delay between possible changes in recruitment and their subsequent effect on these figures.

Between 1939 and 1984 the overall proportion of the élites educated at public school declined from a little over 4 in 5 to 3 in 5 (Table 2.4). The most dramatic drops occurred in the RAF and navy. Among the non-services élites the overall proportion dropped from almost 9 out of 10 to just over 6 out of 10, or a fall of 26 per cent. In round terms the judiciary barely changed, ambassadors were less than average, bishops on the average, bankers and, most markedly, civil servants above the average. Interestingly enough, the most marked changes took place either between immediately pre and post-war or between 1970–1 and 1984. There is a clear difference between Boyd's figures and ours.

In the same period the overall proportion of Oxbridge graduates increased by some 11 per cent from just less to just over half, though it stayed much same in the non-service élite (Table 2.5). A dramatic rise took place among ambassadors, from 49 to 82 per cent, while the bishops reversed the trend, falling from 90 to 69 per cent. Civil servants also recorded a decline from a little over three quarters to three fifths. It is also noticeable that the overall percentages peaked in 1970–1 at the time of Boyd's study and for 1984 have returned to the levels for 1960.

Table 2.4   Percentage* of public-school educated members of élite occupations,[†] 1939–84

	1939	1950	1960	1970–1	1984	1939–84
Ambassadors	95	82	86	87	78	85
Judiciary	90	92	88	84	84	87
Bishops	91	84	80	78	66	78
Bankers	92	90	84	82	70	84
Civil servants	91	68	69	68	49	64
Army	84	83	91	90	74	85
RAF	85	79	68	70	36	69
Navy	42	18	23	39	25	27
All	83	74	74	74	60	73
All non-service	89	80	78	77	63	76

Notes
* Rounded; [†] see notes to Table 2.1.

Table 2.5   Percentage* of Oxbridge-educated members of élite occupations,[††] 1939–84

	1939	1950	1960	1970–1	1984	1939–84
Ambassadors	49	66	84	80	82	74
Judiciary	78	74	75	85	83	80
Bishops	90	85	77	78	69	79
Bankers	45	52	53	60	47	51
Civil servants	77	56	70	69	61	65
Army	3	9	12	24	11	11
RAF	18	14	19	18	8	15
All	46	48	55	61	57	54
All non-service	64	62	68	72	66	67

Notes
* Rounded; [†] see notes to Table 2.1; [‡] Boyd (1973) excluded analysis of navy because of very small numbers of graduates.

Table 2.6 illustrates, or at least reflects, the general move towards graduate entry requirements for many top jobs. In 1939 a third of the élites were non-graduates, in 1984 less than 1 in 6. The corresponding figures for ambassadors are 47 per cent. Only in the case of bishops was the trend different, though even in 1984 only 8 per cent were non-graduate.

Putting the increase in Oxbridge graduates with the decrease in non-graduates together suggests that, despite the more marked increase in graduates from universities other than Oxford and Cambridge (Table 2.1), graduates of Oxbridge are more than holding their own in attaining occupational

Table 2.6   Percentage* of non-graduate members of élite occupations,[‡‡] 1939–84

	1939	1950	1960	1970–1	1984	1939–84
Ambassadors	47	21	6	9	9	16
Judiciary	18	15	17	5	7	11
Bishops	2	6	3	5	8	5
Bankers	46	41	38	30	37	39
Civil servants	11	22	9	13	12	14
Army	46	27	16	20	28	28
RAF	36	64	38	49	40	47
All	33	29	19	17	16	22
All non-service	28	24	17	13	13	18

Notes
* Rounded; [†]see notes to Table 2.1; [‡]see note [‡] to Table 2.5.

élite status. Indeed, it is even reasonable to speculate that the Oxbridge degree may have replaced public schooling as the most important entry/success requirement in these spheres of activity. However, as we saw above, these are not unrelated attributes and our knowledge and database are limited.

THE EDUCATION OF THE EDUCATIONAL ÉLITE

We had several reasons for choosing education as an occupational group to analyse in terms of education. First, it is not normally seen as an élite, though it is associated in many people's minds with the production of élites. Second, as an occupation it has a sufficient number of interrelated levels of operation to fit into Pareto's (1935) initial concept of élites. Consequently, it appeared as suitable to extend Boyd's range of élites – and there were no readily available references such as *Who's Who*. Third, it might well be argued that if there was one branch of human activity where education would be critical in terms of achievement it would be education. Finally, because we are all educationalists we were not only close to and part of education but also fascinated to find out whether public schooling and Oxbridge degrees operated within, as without, education.

The groups we selected to represent the prestigious in the range of sectors in the education service were university vice-chancellors, directors of polytechnics, parliamentarians who had served with the DES, HMIs of schools, LEA chief and deputy education officers, LEA advisers and/or inspectors and headteachers of independent and LEA secondary schools. With the exception of the first three, all these groups normally require school-teaching experience as a qualification for entry. While the role and status of most of these groups are relatively well known, this is least true of HMI and LEA staff.

HMI are government-employed professional inspectors who advise the Secretary of State for Education on the basis of their monitoring work in schools and colleges and on other aspects of the quality of the education service. They are based at the DES but take some pride in their independence from it. Few would question their influential position in the contemporary educational system.

Each of the local authorities in England and Wales are bound by law to have a CEO, sometimes called director of education. LEAs are charged with the responsibility of providing schooling and some forms of further education and, until recently, have enjoyed a fairly high level of autonomy in educational policy. Consequently the principal professionals in the local educational service should be expected to form part of any consideration of élites within education. Elsewhere we have shown that the CEOs and DEOs surveyed were so similar in educational background as to allow them to be treated as one group (Rayner *et al.*, 1986).

It is not so easy to identify the nature and influence of LEA advisers and/ or inspectors. In many ways their work is, at local level, similar to that of the HMI at the national level. However, they have a closer relationship with the schools they serve. Since World War Two the relationship between their inspectoral and advisory functions has had various changes in emphasis. This has been reflected in the different labels that have been attached to their role – some LEAs use 'adviser', some 'inspector', a few both and, in some local authorities, certain aspects of their work is carried out by other educational officers. LEA advisers and/or inspectors are paid on headteacher-related salaries, which probably indicates their level of influence and prestige.

The Survey

In 1985 and 1986 we sent a postal questionnaire to all HMI and CEOs in England and Wales and to a 10-per-cent sample of LEA DEOs, LEA advisers and/or inspectors and LEA and independent secondary-school headteachers. From within fairly extensive data concerning the social, educational and professional backgrounds of these educational personnel, we have extracted here that on secondary schooling and university education. Other than in the case of LEA advisers and/or inspectors (43 per cent) the response rate was above 50 per cent, which, while low, may be regarded as satisfactory for this sort of inquiry. We are grateful to the Chief HMI for providing addresses for all HMIs, since public lists do not exist. The sample frames for the population of the three LEA-sector and the independent groupings were derived from the 1986 *Education Authorities' Directory and Annual*. The data in respect to vice-chancellors, directors and parliamentarians were collected along similar lines to that of Boyd's investigation. As a consequence, the data in respect to these groups were not always directly comparable and so we begin our analysis of all the groups using Boyd's categories.

Public Schools and Educational Élites

As can be seen from Table 2.7, the proportion of public-school-educated educational personnel varies from 56 per cent among DES parliamentarians and 43 per cent of independent-school headteachers to 10 and 12 per cent of the various grades of LEA staff. Putting these proportions together with those whose schooling was independent makes few changes to the range, though it greatly increases the proportion of independent-school heads who were educated in the public or independent sector (two thirds). Interestingly enough, in each and every case, the proportion of public- or independent-school educated is markedly higher than would be expected in a random sample of the population (overall, 2.8 and 7 per cent respectively). It is noticeable that there is a very clear distinction between public and independent education among university vice-chancellors (almost a third) and polytechnic directors (17 per cent).

Given that until recently HMC schools catered exclusively for boys, a related, though complex, factor is variation in the proportion of the sexes in any élite group – the higher the proportion of women in any group the lower the percentage of public-school-educated members may be expected to be. For example, at the time of our study there were no female university vice-chancellors or polytechnic directors and only a single female DEO. However, 17 per cent of the HMIs who responded to our questionnaire were women and they were less likely than their male colleagues to have attended either an independent school – 5 compared with 21 per cent – or a direct-grant grammar school – 8 compared with 13 per cent.

Table 2.8 displays the schooling of our educational élites, taking into account direct-grant schools (these were semi-independent schools, phased out in 1976, when virtually all the non-Catholic schools became fully independent) and respondent's age. With the exception of independent-school headteachers,

Table 2.7 The secondary schooling of senior educational personnel using Boyd's (1973) classification (%*)

	HMC	Independent	Other
DES parliamentarians	56	4	40
University VCs	29	3	68
Poly. directors	13	4	83
HMIs	16	14	70
LEA officers	12	6	83
LEA advisers/inspectors	10	9	81
LEA heads	12	8	80
Independent heads	43	25	33

Note
* Rounded.

the vast majority were educated at LEA secondary schools – HMI at 70 per cent overall slightly less frequently than LEA staff and heads at 80 per cent. Such a change as is indicated through the age-groups is relatively minor and not always of a clear direction. What is noticeable is that the proportion of LEA-educated independent-school headteachers, together with similarly educated LEA advisers and inspectors, is somewhat higher in the youngest age-group but lower in the case of LEA-school headteachers.

The most obvious point to arise from our analysis is the importance of the direct-grant grammar school's (a few of which were HMC) contribution to the education of senior educational personnel. When viewing column 3 in Table 2.8, bear in mind that such schools catered for only around 2.3 per cent of the secondary-school population in 1972 (*Statistics of Education*, 1972).

Table 2.8 The secondary schooling of senior educational personnel by age-group* (%[†‡])

	HMC[‡]	Independent[‡]	Direct grant[‡]	LEA
HMIs:*				
Under 44	15	20	10	70
46–51	19	23	11	65
52+	13	13	12	74
All	16	18	12	70
Lea officers:				
Under 45	16	12	8	80
46–54	10	3	14	83
55+	22	13	9	78
All	15	8	12	81
LEA advisers/inspectors:				
Under 45	9	—	18	82
46–54	11	5	10	84
55+	8	9	17	74
All	10	5	14	80
LEA heads:				
Under 45	9	7	16	77
46–54	15	10	13	76
55+	8	6	6	88
All	12	8	12	80
Independent heads:				
Under 45	50	27	36	36
46–54	45	55	18	27
55+	33	55	18	27
All	43	46	22	28

Notes
*note that the age-groups for HMI are slightly different from the others; [†]rounded; [‡]these categories of school are not exclusive. HMC includes some direct-grant, but not independent, schools, outside membership.

Oxbridge Education and Education Élites

Table 2.9 shows the proportion of each élite who were Oxbridge or other graduates or non-graduates. It is clear that university vice-chancellors were by far the most Oxbridge educated (58 per cent). While this figure is not as high as that found in some of the groups in the replication of Boyd's work, it is still about three times what would be expected from a random population of graduates of that age. To the extent that universities may be regarded as the most prestigious and influential level of the educational system and their vice-chancellors as their most significant members, then Oxbridge can be seen as having a very dominant influence in their education. In marked contrast, of polytechnic directors only 12 per cent had a first degree from Oxbridge.

It might be expected that the frequently asserted link between independent schools and Oxbridge would be reflected in the educational background of their headteachers. As can be seen, this was confirmed in that independent teachers were three times more likely to have an Oxbridge first degree than were LEA secondary-school headteachers. Indeed, independent-school heads were much more likely to have been Oxbridge educated than any of the other groups surveyed. It might be argued that the association and/or influence of Oxbridge appears to diminish as one moves nearer the day-to-day activity of LEA secondary schools.

It is important to bear in mind while viewing these data that there is a variety of training routes into teaching. For the age-groups represented here, a major route was the non-graduate teachers certificate, which was a particularly important entry into primary-school teaching and also for some secondary-school subjects – PE, Domestic Science and Craft, for example. Among HMI and LEA advisers and/or inspectors those with responsibility for such aspects of schooling might well have been recruited from among the pool of non-graduate teachers. This would account for the relatively high percentage in those groupings without a first-time degree. Comparing the data in Table 2.9 with the proportion of Oxbridge graduates in the total gradu-

Table 2.9   The university education of senior educational personnel (%*)

	Oxbridge	Other	None
DES parliamentarians	46	30	23
University VCs	58	42	—
Poly. directors	12	92	—
HMIs	26	46	28
LEA Officers	36	57	7
LEA advisers/inspectors	12	36	52
LEA heads	15	64	21
Independent heads	46	41	13

Note
* Rounded.

Table 2.10   Percentage* of graduate senior educational personnel with Oxbridge degrees, by age-group[†]

	45 years and under	46–54	55 years and under
HMIs[†]	29	38	43
LEA officers	48	31	48
LEA advisers/inspectors	8	22	50
LEA heads	19	21	15
Independent heads	60	62	44

Note
*Rounded; [†]HMI age-groups are 44 years and under, 45–51 and 52 and over.

ate population (see Table 2.1) shows that all education élites surveyed here are over-represented, and this is particularly true in the case of independent-school teachers, HMIs and CEOs.

The data in Table 2.10 show that, in general, the percentage of Oxbridge first-degree holders declines over the age-groups. The most apparent drop in the proportion is among LEA advisers/inspectors – from half of those 55 years and over to but 8 per cent for those under 45 – though it can also be discerned among HMI. The opposite trend can be seen in the case of independent-school headteachers. Save for the youngest group of LEA advisers/inspectors, the percentage of Oxbridge degree holders for each age and occupational group is much higher than that to be found in the relevant graduate population.

CONCLUSIONS

This chapter has shown that public, or independent, school- and Oxbridge-educated persons continue to be over-represented in variously defined high-status occupations or élites in British society. In common with other work in the field, what it does not show is anything of the nature of this relationship. Such an education can be viewed simply as an indication of social class and gender rather than necessary or instrumental in the success of given fields of endeavour. That the association exists and persists is clear; to explore it further would require cohort studies of very considerable depth and breadth. They would need to isolate both entry into, and subsequent selection up-wards, of variously educated personnel.

This association, though at lower overall levels, was maintained in our study with respect to what we called educational élites. We suspect that studies in a variety of other fields of endeavour would reproduce our findings. Hence, it is interesting to speculate as to the extent in terms of type and level of oc-cupation at which the representation of public-school and Oxbridge-educated personnel is over-represented, equal to or falls below that of the proportion so educated in the population at large.

Obviously, any such view would be affected by educational and social change. For example, our study showed something of the importance of direct-grant schools. The subsequent movement of the majority of such schools into the independent sector may well have enhanced the role of these schools. Change will also occur if women continue to penetrate, and do so significantly, what have been exclusively male élite groups, while at the same time HMC schools remain predominately a male experience (in the mid-1980s 4.4 per cent of male 14-year-olds were at such schools, compared with 0.5 of females). It is open to speculation as to whether this change would enhance the representation of the LEA-school educated, or that of the other independent schools, which are currently experiencing growth.

Perhaps the general lack of knowledge and the need for extensive further research is suprising to some. That so little is known of the general situation and processes involved is perhaps indicative of a socially stratified society, which is viewed by its members as legitimate. In such a society educational status differentials may be thought as important, or more important, than educational achievement. And where achievement is similar, or required, the institution in which it was gained may be a critical factor in occupational placement and advancement.

NOTE

The research reported in this chapter benefited from some financial assistance given by the School of Education, University of Leeds and from Helen Krarup and Angela Mulvie who worked as part-time research assistants.

REFERENCES

Abrahams, F. F. (1976) Review of D. Boyd, 1973, *International Review of Education*, Vol. 22, pp. 39–40

Annual Report of the University of Cambridge Careers' Service Syndicate (1984) Cambridge University Press.

Boyd, D. (1973) *Elites and their Education*, NFER, Slough.

Boyd, W. L. and Cibulko, J. G. (eds.) (1989) *Private Schools and Public Policy*, Falmer Press, Lewes.

Cmnd 8638 (1952) *Returns from Universities and University Colleges in Receipt of Treasury Grant (1950/1)*, HMSO, London.

Cmnd 1855 (1962) *Returns from Universities and University Colleges in Receipt of Treasury Grant (1960/1)*, HMSO, London.

Cookson, P. W. (1989) United States of America: contours of continuity and controversy in private schools, in G. Walford (ed.), op. cit.

Crewe, I. (1974) *British Political Sociology Yearbook, Vol. 1, Elites in Western Democracy*, Croom Helm, Beckenham.

Crosland, C. A. R. (1956) *The Future of Socialism*, Jonathan Cape, London.

Education Authorities' Directory and Annual (1986), Longman, London.

Edwards, A., Fitz, J. and Whitty, G. (1985) Private schools and public funding: a comparison of policies and arguments in England and Australia, *Comparative Education*, Vol. 21, pp. 29–45.

Fox, I. (1985) *Private Schools and Public Issues*, Macmillan, London.

Fox, I. (1989) Elitism and the British 'public' schools, in W. L. Boyd and J. G. Cibulka (eds.), op. cit.

Gathorne-Hardy, J. (1977) *The Public School Phenomenon, 597–1977*, Hodder & Stoughton, London.

General Household Survey 1976 (1978) HMSO, London.

Giddens, A. (1979) An anatomy of the British ruling class, *New Society*, 4 October.

Glennerster, H. (1974) Happy families, *Higher Education Review*, Vol. 7 no. 1, pp. 89–90.

Glennerster, H. and Wilson, G. (1970) *Paying for Private Schools*, Penguin Books, Harmondsworth.

Griggs, C. (1985) *Private Education in Britain*, Falmer Press, Lewes.

Halsey, A. H., Heath, A. F. and Ridge, J. M. (1980) *Origins and Destinations*, Clarendon Press, Oxford.

Halsey, A. H., Heath, A. F. and Ridge, J. M. (1984) The political arithmetic of public schools, in G. Walford (ed.), op. cit.

Higher Education (1983) *Robbins Report on Higher Education* Cmnd 2154, HMSO, London.

ISIS (1984) *Annual Census*, ISIS, London.

Kalton, G. (1966) *The Public Schools: A Factual Survey*, Longman, London.

Labour Party (1981) *A Plan for Private Schools*, TUC–Labour Party Liason Committee, London.

Lambert, R. (1975) *The Chance of a Lifetime?*, Weidenfeld & Nicolson, London.

Pareto, V. (1935) *The Mind and Society*, Jonathan Cape, London.

Pring, R. (1986) Privatization of education, in R. Rogers (ed.), op. cit.

Pring, R. (1987) Privatization in education, *Journal of Education Policy*, Vol. 2, no. 4, pp. 289–99.

Public and Preparatory Schools Year Book (1971), A. & C. Black, London.

Public Schools Commission (1968) *First Report*, HMSO, London.

Public Schools Commission (1970) *Second Report*, HMSO, London.

Rae, J. (1981) *The Public School Revolution*, Faber & Faber, London.

Rayner, M., Williams, R., Reid, I. and Krarup, H. (1986) The educational backgrounds of LEA chief and deputy officers in England and Wales, *Research in Education*, Vol. 36, pp. 13–17.

Reid, I. (1981) *Social Class Differences in Britain* (2nd edn), Blackwell, Oxford.

Reid, I. (1986) *The Sociology of School and Education*, Fontana, London.

Reid, I. (1989) *Social Class Differences in Britain* (3rd edn), Fontana, London.

Rogers, R. (ed.) (1987) *Education and Social Class*, Falmer Press, Lewes.

Salter, B. and Tapper, T. (1985) *Power and Policy in Education: The Case of Independent Schooling*, Falmer Press, Lewes.

Scott, J. (1982) *The Upper Classes: Property and Privilege in Britain*, Macmillan, London.

Silver, H. (1973) *Equal Opportunity in Education*, Methuen, London.

Stanworth, P. and Giddens, A. (1974) *Elites and Power in British Society*, Cambridge University Press.

Statistics of Education (1971) Vol. 6, HMSO, London.

Statistics of Education (1972) Vol. 2, HMSO, London.

Szreter, R. (1975) Review of D. Boyd, 1973, *Educational Review*, Vol. 27, no. 2, pp. 210–11

Tawney, R. H. (1931) *Equality*, Unwin, London.

Universities Central Council on Admissions (1984) *Statistical Supplement to the Twenty-first Report*, Cheltenham.

University of Oxford Appointments Committee Report for 1983–84 (1984) Oxford University.

University Statistics 1982–83 (1983) Universities Statistical Record, Cheltenham.

Walford, G. (ed.) (1984) *British Public Schools: Policy and Practice*, Falmer Press, Lewes.

Walford, G. (1987) How dependent is the independent sector?, *Oxford Review of Education*, Vol. 13, no. 3, pp. 275–96.

Walford, G. (ed.) (1989) *Private Schools in Ten Countries: Policy and Practice*, Routledge, London.

Weinberg, I. (1967) *The English Public Schools*, Atherton Press, New York, NY.

Whitty, G., Edwards, T. and Fitz, J. (1989) England and Wales: the role of the private sector, in G. Walford (ed.), op. cit.

Who's Who (1971, etc.) A. & C. Black, London.

3

PUBLIC-SCHOOL MASCULINITIES – AN ESSAY IN GENDER AND POWER

Christine Heward

LEADERSHIP

The public schools are 'the chief nurseries of our statesmen' – so the Clarendon Commission memorably crystallized the role of the public schools in 1864. That Britain's commanding world position was due to the high quality of its political and governmental leadership, selected and educated in its unique system of public schools, was a widely held opinion in the second half of the nineteenth century (Wilkinson, 1964; Mangan, 1986). It rested on a series of pervasive and important assumptions about the interrelations of gender, power and social class. Preparing for power was about producing a particular sort of masculinity, first, through rigorous selection of the recruits on social-class criteria, followed by prolonged socialization through harsh processes of psychic hardening in a competitive hierarchy in which the fittest survived, the weak suffered silently and the weakest were eliminated (Mangan, 1987; Heward, 1988, p. 193).

Gender was conceived as a polarity in terms of power. Since femininity was about subordination and weakness, the antithesis of power, appropriate preparation for its exercise was first of all exclusively masculine. The public schools were boys' schools, from which girls were excluded. Similarly, power was seen as directly proportional to social-class position, the higher the class the greater the power. Consequently, the public schools restricted their selection of boys to be prepared as leaders to the minute fraction of the population, who could pay their very high fees and had a suitable preparation in the classics. Rigorous selection was followed by an even more rigorous training. Much of the justification of traditional public-school hardening, through such experiences as team games, the prefect system and corporal punishment, was that it induced courage and the subordination of self and individuality to the group – necessary in future leaders. It was through the struggle up the competitive hierarchy from grub to senior to prefect, obedient follower to responsible authority, that leadership qualities were developed and tested. The self-confident plucky public-school boy accustomed to the command of subordinates remains one of the most prestigious models of masculinity associated with success and the exercise of power in British society (Norwood, 1929; James, 1951). Using case material from two schools, this essay examines the notion that public schools are homogeneous with a single model of masculinity – the leader. The evidence of letters written by parents to the Headmaster of Ellesmere College in Shropshire between 1929 and 1950 is compared with oral evidence from a small sample of boys from the same school and a northern public school in the 1980s (Heward, 1984; 1988).

The Clarendon Commission (1864) approved the role and the regime of stern discipline, Spartan living conditions, dedication to team games and the classical curriculum through which boys were toughened into leaders at the public schools. Their recommendations for reform reflected their worries about the schools, which were concerned mostly with the widespread illegal peculation of endowments and a little bit, at the insistence of T. H. Huxley, with the lack of interest in science.

This straightforward association of power with uni-dimensional notions of gender and social class, which are mutually reinforcing and reproductive, has considerable theoretical allure. The model of élite boarding schools in perpetuating social-class and power relations underlay the recent study of American boarding schools, *Preparing for Power*, by Cookson and Persell (1985). It concentrated on the 'preppy crucible', the process of psychic hardening, loneliness and the suppression of emotion, and the school's rigorous preparation for the academic competition to enter élite colleges as the means whereby the pupils are prepared for leadership positions in business, the professions and public life. Despite the fact that some of the schools were single sex and some co-educational, the study ignored gender. Any possible complexities in the relationship of gender to social class and power was thus rendered unproblematic and invisible.

This view supports the malestream orthodoxy in the long sociological tradition of studies of social class, mainly about social mobility in terms of the male occupational structure with power as an integral but less popular focus. Halsey, Heath and Ridge's (1980) study, *Origins and Destinations*, which provided valuable data on HMC schools as élite reproducers, excluded women from the sample. It would seem that such writers can still cling to their view that gender may be conceptualized as an epiphenomenon of labour-market and social-class position at least with the support of theories and evidence about the educational reproduction of élite class and gender relations, however ironically uncomfortable that may be (e.g. Lockwood, 1986).

In recent years concern has grown in a number of academic disciplines with the tautology of these conceptualizations and attempts are being made to coin understandings and explanations for the way power is associated with certain groups of men – white upper-class heterosexuals rather than blacks and gays.

Accounting for the consistent exclusion of women from power has been the subject of much feminist work and attempts are now underway to forge more satisfying explanations than the universality of patriarchy (Connell, 1987).

The role of the public schools and their traditional masculinities, their continued dominance in the education of men in élite positions, is important in Britain today. The success of the public schools in preparing men for power and leadership is demonstrated by the large numbers of public-school men in powerful positions in late twentieth-century Britain. In 1982 42 per cent of MPs had been to a public school. In 1984 49 per cent of top civil servants, 78 per cent of ambassadors, 84 per cent of the judiciary, 66 per cent of the episcopate and 70 per cent of the director of the clearing banks were public-school men (see Chapter 2).

DIVERSITY

Yet the public schools are far from a monolithic structure of leadership factories; rather, they are a heterogeneous and complex hierarchy of organizations that are constantly adapting and changing, sometimes in very different ways. The present system had its origins in the nineteenth century when the group of great Clarendon schools were reformed and a much larger number of new schools were founded in response to the expansion and reform of the State and the professions and the consequent rising demand for an education for sons that would prepare them for examinations and entry to the professions. By the end of the nineteenth century the public schools formed an established hierarchy, cemented by membership of the Headmasters' Conference, formed in 1869 as a pressure group to resist the Clarendon reforms and realized for the boys in the etiquette of who competed against whom at rugger, cricket and rowing (Honey, 1977). The importance of examinations was greater in the schools catering for the less secure social groups, who were also seeking to establish their own positions in the lower echelons of the hierarchy. While the great schools continued to celebrate the games cult until World War One and beyond, Ellesmere College, founded in 1884 and admitted to the Headmasters' Conference in 1933, was a competitive hierarchy dedicated to academic achievement, career preparation and prowess in games (in that order) by the end of the nineteenth century (Mangan, 1981; Heward, 1984).

The schools varied in the social composition of their clientele. When it opened in 1884, the majority of the pupils at Ellesmere College were the sons of local farmers, while its prestigious neighbour, Shrewsbury (a Clarendon school) was drawing increasingly from a national clientele and excluding local boys (Shrosbree, 1988). Schools lower down the hierarchy modified their goals, attempting to produce leaders for the communities they served. They also recruited a small number of boys from lower social groups, often scholarship boys selected for their academic ability, whose parents were helped to pay the fees. Rubinstein (1986) has assembled a formidable array of biographical evidence to show that the public schools were the means whereby a number of sons of clerks, commercial travellers and shop-keepers entered Oxford and Cambridge and had meteoric careers into very powerful positions thereafter.

While they strove to create a uniform type ('the leader'), the effects of the very intense socialization in the public schools upon the boys was always uncertain. The results of the schools' attempts at moulding boys into a type, such as the Wykehamists' 'mint mark', were often far from perfect (Dilke, 1965). Even at its zenith in the period before World War One, it could produce rebellion and criticism among a significant number of boys. In Alec Waugh's case, his heretical views were defined before the experience of the trenches called into question everything he knew and understood, the cause of Robert Graves' apostasy (Waugh, 1917; Graves, 1929).

There was a great variety of models of masculinity throughout the public schools. Within the schools masculinities were negotiated, contested and changing. Masculine identities were forged in peer groups with the immediate end of surviving in the competition in boarding houses for friendship, influence and power. It was here that early masculine identities were negotiated. It was in the intense, insulated society of boarding houses that bullies could find their prey – who had few hiding places. Bullying is a power struggle in which those seeking to dominate demonstrate their superior power by successfully designating themselves strong and another individual or group weak, and then ensure these designations are accepted by the rest of the house.

Bullying, found in many large, predominantly male organizations, notably the army and prisons, has a long dishonourable history in the public schools, immortalized in *Tom Brown's Schooldays*. Bullying is particularly destructive in boarding schools, prisons and the armed services because there is no escape (Tattum, 1989; Walford, 1989). The study of Ellesmere during the war suggested that bullying was experienced by boys with no adequate models of masculinity and few resources from their previous experience to deal with the initial competitive struggles of the toughening process through which neophyte public-school boys were transformed into self-confident leaders. Lionel Mason was an orphan, brought up in the company of adults, who arrived at Ellesmere in 1941, a timid, serious-minded boy with no tactics to deal with life in the company of other boys. His school fellows made Lionel's early days at the school such a torment that he finally resorted to the school doctor, whose 'prescription' was a course of boxing. In the public schools, games were about toughening as much as health and enjoyment and boxing was seen as an ideal way of increasing boys' assertiveness. When Lionel's uncle finally returned from Palestine in 1945, he was 'impressed with the remarkable increase in Lionel's self confidence' (Heward, 1988, p. 126–7).

The competition for power was also about the labelling and valuing of groups and their definitions of masculinity. In the school there was a variety of such groups whose masculinities were precisely valued in relation to each other and notions of the always inferior femininity. At Ellesmere College between 1929 and 1950, the Captain of the Rugby XV was the most pre-stigious model of masculinity celebrated in the school. But this was a lonely and, for many, a hopelessly unattainable model for the aspirations of groups of boys. Whilst physically tough team captain was an ideal for individuals, there never seems to have been a group with that identity. Among the models other than tough rugger player, competing for allegiance and power in the school-boy community were pious, future priest, busy polymath and the most popular among the C-class boys, rebel and prankster. 'Churchy' boys spent their Friday afternoons in the Scouts under the Chaplain's leadership, while the majority opted for the rigours of the Officer Training Corps. Most boys formed groups whose identity was based on male sociability and reasonable, but certainly not over, conformity to the school's model requirements. The ideal was to have a group of 'pals', and to be good, but not excel, in the school's main activities, academic work, games and house social life. Those who had failed in the school's main activity, academic work, were all in the C forms where, as in other schools, a rebel culture thrived (Hargreaves, 1967; Lacey, 1970). In the valuation of masculinity in the school-boy culture, rebel-lion, particularly smoking, was considered manly; being 'churchy' was cissy.

   The school was a male community where women were marginalized and femininity despised. The few women within its portals were in subordinate, menial positions, dedicated to the domestic service of men. Its social and spatial organization emphasized the significance of age and gender as the principles on which seniority and authority were distributed. The women domestics, mainly from Welsh villages, some as young as 14, were isolated in a corridor called the Warren. The masters were almost all bachelors with rooms in the school. The Headmaster, the only married man on the premises, lived in a house separate from the school.

THE WAR

World War Two brought a number of changes to the public schools in general and Ellesmere in particular. First of all it increased the demand among parents for public-school education, boosting the schools' self-confidence and prosperity. The country's need for young men to lead all aspects of its war effort at the battle front, in the development laboratory and in home food production, was urgent. Young men were conscripted from the age of 18. Leadership potential, officer material, was anxiously sought among the con-scripts. The public schools buckled to their task vigorously.

   With the disruption of many grammar schools and rising incomes with few consumer goods available, the numbers of parents able to afford a public-school education for their sons expanded to fill the schools. After a lean time in the 1920s and 1930s the public schools 'had a good war'. This was especially true of such schools as Ellesmere, whose inaccessible position in rural Shrop-shire had hitherto been a disadvantage. As a school in a safe area it was sought after. As those in the prestigious public-school belt on the south coast had to evacuate to whatever rambling and unsuitable premises they could find in a safe area, there was a temporary disruption of the hierarchy of schools. The flagship of the Woodard schools, Lancing, was evacuated to Ellesmere in the summer of 1940 and had to endure the ignominy of camping on their rugger pitches – an experience made tolerable only by the simple expedient of ignoring each others' existence (Derry, 1980). Greater social mixing and a sense of facing a common enemy together, which some commentators have seen as an effect of the war, did not affect Ellesmere. While social-class relations in the schools were little affected by the war, gender relations and identities changed in a number of interesting ways. During World War Two conscripted masters were replaced by retired men and the first women joined the staff. One of the most profound changes in the gender relations of the labour market brought about by the war was the permanent eclipse of domestic service as the largest single employer of women. At Ellesmere College the departure of the maids for better-paid jobs and greater independence in local factories and farms caused a crisis solved only with some ingenuity. Eton collars, an uncomfortable way of distinguishing junior boys from their superiors, were abolished to reduce the work of the harassed laundry staff. More controversially, the boundaries of gender definitions were redrawn as the boys themselves took over many domestic tasks, such as laying tables and making beds. The most arduous of the women's tasks, for example, floor cleaning, became punishments for recalcitrant school boys imposed by prefects. Reactions among the boys were mixed. Some welcomed the greater independence this encouraged; others considered such mundane tasks should not be part of a public-school boy's education. Not surprisingly women saw things differently; one mother thought it made good husbands of the boys (Heward, 1988, p. 116).

To many British people the experience of war was not about heroism but one of all-pervasive restrictions, endless irritations, long hours of work, food queues and severely limited pleasures (Calder, 1971). Both the heroism and restrictions of war subtly affected masculinities in the school, for masculinities are constructed in many sites with inextricably related structures and meanings (Douglas, 1972). Petrol rationing meant the suspension of all away matches. Despite the dimming of his lustre because he could no longer prove his superiority in Titanic struggles with other schools, the Captain of Rugger continued to reign supreme in models of masculinity at Ellesmere. The war also brought a wealth of new heroes to the school-boy culture. After the Battle of Britain in the summer of 1940, the saviours of the nation, the RAF, 'the few', became the heroes of every British school boy. The school also had its own particular war heroes – its Victoria Cross, J. C. Brunt, won his battle honours in the Italian campaign in 1943 in which he died.

Schools, even public schools designed to be hermetically sealed, were never completely insulated. The impact of the war demonstrates the way in which social change and outside influences were important in the construction of masculinities within the school. There is an important paradox here. Parents wanted their sons to have 'the best start in life' and to be prepared for successful careers, in the professions, it was hoped. They sent their sons to the school in the belief that they would have a more effective socialization there than at the local grammar school, since the school could direct their every waking moment effectively and they would be insulated from any undesirable influences from the 'wrong sort' of boys or girls. The school often saw the parents as a negative influence. Mothers' inclination to indulge their sons was seen as inimical to the central characteristic of all masculinities: independence. Not all masculinities are about power and its exercise. While the adoption of some masculine identities is much more likely to presage the and attainment of power than others, whether individuals become powerful is determined by their subsequent careers.

Masculinities are actively constructed in families, schools and occupations. Such complex biographical processes can never be confined to a single institution, moulding boys in particular ways, however thoroughly insulated. While their time in a prestigious boarding school may have more importance for public-school boys in constructing a masculine identity than the school days of other boys, masculinities in public schools mediate those already encountered and internalized in their families. Boys' ideals of adult masculinities are derived from many sources. Their gender identities are their own active creations, forged biographically in families, schools and their peer groups. Changing social structures and families and parental models are of crucial importance in these processes (Willis, 1977; Walford, 1986; Connell *et al.* 1982, 1989).

FATHERS AND SONS

The study of Ellesmere between 1929 and 1950 showed that fathers were crucial models for their sons. Fathers managed and directed their sons' careers. In many cases their long-term strategies involved a considerable commitment from the family budget over many years. Clergy and others with limited means used ingenuity in their strategies to ensure that their sons were prepared for a suitable profession. A number followed their fathers into the priesthood. Fathers were the principal models for their sons bestowing a variety of heritages, including pugnacious business success, failure with lost honour to be regilded and shining Christian faith, enabling a little to go a long way (Heward, 1988, pp. 87–9). This framework of expectations and sacrifice could cause conflicts between fathers and sons. Some fathers complained that the emphasis on sport in the school-boy culture conflicted with their desire for examination success. Many parents worried about the war and their sons' desire for battle honours. Parents wanted their sons to have a career they could pursue after the war. Mothers, survivors of World War One, sometimes saw little but carnage where their sons saw heroism. The conflicts were particularly sharp for the farmers' sons. They were not conscripted; most were withdrawn from the school early to help in the home production of food, which became such an important feature of the war effort. For some this brought recrimination and regret that their education had finished so early, but their frustration at not being able to join the forces, the RAF of which so many dreamed, was the cause of greater bitterness for some (*ibid.* pp. 148–51).

It was in this context of intra-family relations, particular economic conditions and the changes brought by the war that these boys forged their gender identities within the school and then embarked upon a career. We simply do not know why certain men among them gained powerful positions in later life and others did not. Ellesmere has a number of illustrious sons, not all of whom were bright or indeed conformist. The war-time hero, J. C. Brunt, was described by one of his contemporaries as 'bit of a duffer, but bags of guts' (*ibid.* p. 54). It was my impression when I interviewed a number of Old Ellesmerians for my book that in the words of the school's favourite master, 'the C boys all made money'. It seemed to me that the boys who failed in the system and were relegated to C forms (a stigma they deeply resented) internalized the school's emphasis on competitive success and became very successful in business, which the school disdained, rather than the professions, which was the school's preferred career. What is it that makes some public-school men successful and others less so? While the way in which Bill Beaumont, former Captain of the British Lions, presently TV personality, acquired his highly successful gender identity at Ellesmere is clear; how Sir Paul Dean MP, Deputy Speaker of the House of Commons, acquired a means to a different sort of distinction and power is more difficult to discern. The significance of their school days, the gender identities they acquired there and their subsequent adaptation must remain speculative.

RECENT CHANGES

Since 1950, the end of the published Ellesmere study (Heward, 1988), the public schools have undergone profound change. The model of producing leaders by rigorous social selection and gruelling psychic hardening has been replaced by that of well-rounded university entrants, survivors of a rigorous academic selection and training (Salter and Tapper, 1981; Walford, 1986). Whereas in the period of the previous study, HMC schools were predominantly boys' boarding schools, the proportion of day pupils among them has risen steadily to 70 per cent in 1989 and 64 per cent of HMC schools now admit girls. A century after its zenith in the last decade of the nineteenth century, the supremacy of the games cult as the dominant value in public schools has been officially replaced by fierce individual academic competition, the 'examination mill'. Oxbridge scholarships, all now won in open competition, places in higher education and A-level grades are the currency of the schools' success, celebrated by headmasters and parents at speech days. The schools have espoused Maths, Science and Technology, taking the lead in such curriculum developments as Nuffield Science.

The constituents of the psychic hardening process – harsh discipline, insulated house society and team games – have also changed in the intervening period. A variety of individual sports, such as squash and skiing, have been introduced, challenging the supremacy of rugger. Large dormitories, where sleep is an intermittent luxury and social life a constant political contest, have been replaced by study bedrooms for small groups and individuals. The schools have attempted to 'humanize' their discipline, abolishing fagging and beating by prefects. The presence of girls as pupils and women staff is also seen as desirable in providing sympathetic ears, helping to reduce the effects of the suppression of emotion so important in the production of inhibited and emotionally stunted public-school men renowned for their 'stiff upper lips'. Community service and other attempts to reduce isolation and improve relations with local communities are another recent innovation in public schools. Ellesmere is the home of a local arts centre built with money from the Gulbenkian Foundation on school land. It brings many local people into the school for cultural events. Many of the changes, notably the provision of new buildings for smaller dormitories, girls' houses and new subjects, have been expensive to introduce. Philosophical commitment by governors, pressure from parents and staff and money have produced considerable variety in the nature and pace of change (Walford, 1986).

The homogeneous pattern of élite boys' boarding schools has changed to a more heterogeneous one, with some schools such as Bromsgrove being completely co-educational, while other take girls into the sixth form, as Ellesmere has done and others remaining exclusively boys' schools. Schools in the lower echelons of the hierarchy have been more enthusiastic about girls than the Clarendon schools. The apex of the hierarchy remains almost exclusively male. Vacancies in senior teaching posts in the schools are invariably filled by men. While from this perspective the public schools still appear to reproduce a male power élite as they did in the 1930s and 1940s, reproduction of a single masculinity within them is as uncertain now as it was then. The processes of constructing masculinities and the ways in which they have changed are patchy, uneven and problematic. Certain schools have remained largely 'traditional', introducing few of the changes other than an increased academic competition. Others, for example, Ellesmere, have introduced a range of innovations, new subjects such as Economics, Business Studies and Technology, individual games, abolition of fagging, outlawing bullying and the admission of girls. The relationship of masculinities and power has also changed in a number of interesting ways.

THE CONTEMPORARY PERIOD

At Ellesmere in the 1940s and the late 1970s the differentiation of the powerful dominators from the dominated began in Waiting Dorm (Heward, 1988,

p. 72). This dormitory housed almost fifty boys and was completed just before World War Two to extend the capacity of the school. Until it was closed
in 1982 it housed all the new entrants to the school, who could not be placed
immediately in the self-contained boarding houses in the various wings of the
school. Crucial initial contests for individual hegemony took place here in the
competition for friendships, territory and the ablution facilities. There were
two forms of intimidation in the dormitory, among the neophytes themselves
and from the prefects in charge of the dormitory. Bullying of younger Tom
Browns by the bigger and stronger Flashmans and the right of prefects to beat
younger boys have always brought opprobrium on the public schools (Walford, 1989). For the prefects, controlling Waiting Dorm was always a difficult
task. They had to sleep at the end of the serried ranks of creaking and uncomfortable beds of youngsters, many of whom were miserable and some even
wretchedly homesick. The dorm was gloomy, cold and institutional. There
were no showers, only baths and wash basins in inadequate supply. Instilling
fear, making an example of the weakest, sarcasm, humiliation and a cuff on
the ear were all at the service of prefects, anxious to ensure order by any
available means. By 1983 Waiting Dorm and the right of prefects to beat and
control by fear had both become fading memories, swept away by a tide of
change. While parental pressure has been largely responsible for replacing
such inhospitable living conditions, it was a newly installed reforming headmaster who outlawed beating and fear by prefects.

While the authority (the power of prefects legitimated by the school) can
be changed by the higher authority of the headmaster, it is not so easy to
legislate away the differentiation of a large group of boys into the powerful
dominators and the dominated. The physically weak, disadvantaged in the
survival of the fittest, are often the victims of ragging and baiting (Walford,
1986, p. 81). At Ellesmere between 1979 and 1982 a boy who did not play
games for medical reasons was isolated and ragged. Those who affected a
superior moral authority themselves, or who threatened to involve the school
authorities to overturn dormitory tyranny, invariably found themselves in an
endless cycle of more or less vicious japes. One small boy, no sporting hero,
who frequently lost out in the competition for ablution facilities in Waiting
Dorm in 1979 'always made a fuss and threatened to go to the masters and
that just encouraged the bigger boys to throw him out of his bath water' (AJH,
oral evidence, 1990). As in the earlier period it was boys with no previous
experience of boarding-school life who were more likely to be ragged.

The majority of public schools have been changing and adapting and there
is considerable diversity. Many have adopted a range of innovations similar
to Ellesmere. A smaller number have retained a more 'traditional' image and
organization, taking few day pupils and no girls, 'modernizing' the curriculum
cautiously and retaining the emphases on team games, rigorous discipline and
character training. At a northern 'traditional' school at the beginning of the
1980s, the strong insulation of the house life and prevailing view among
housemasters that boys learn important lessons in finding their feet and

battling it in the house, ensured that housemasters rarely intervened in what they saw as the prefects' bailiwick and bullying, which attracted no official attention or sanction. A common way of conveying an identity as an isolate in prisons, boarding schools and the like, is through the use of a nickname conveying a negative and stigmatized meaning, which arouses immediate ridicule and disgust, ensuring the individual's society is shunned by his peers (Kelly and Cohn, 1988). Such nicknames were often the focus of ragging and bullying at the northern 'traditional' school. One boy attracted the attention of the powerful members of his house because of his religious beliefs and, in consequence, became 'Eddie', a symbol drawn from the world of pop music.

Since World War Two, pop music has become increasingly important as a symbol of individual and group identity among adolescents seeking to assert their identity in relation to their parents' generation and each other. In the early 1980s heavy metal had emerged as a type of extremely loud and discordant pop music, associated with working-class greaser and biker groups. Iron Maiden, a Cockney greaser group, became the most popular symbol of rebellious aggressively masculine youth. (They were 'crowned kings of British heavy metal in August 1988 when they topped the bill at the Castle Donnington Monsters of Rock Festival and deafened a crowd estimated at 100,000' – *Insight*, 1990, p. 18.) Their mascot, the centre of their greatly prized album sleeves, is a horrifically ugly, snarling monster, with blood-red eyes called Eddie.

The unceasing use of this nickname conveyed a wealth of meaning in the school-boy culture, where acceptance into friendship groups and the power structure of the house depended on conformity to its rigid set of norms. The aim of baiting the victim was to exploit his weaknesses to the point where he broke down and showed any sort of emotion, anger, fear, distress or pain. Such outbursts were then ridiculed as those of Eddie, the hideous monster, so that finally the use of the name in the corridor aroused sniggers (BJB, oral evidence, 1990).

As well as the differentiation of the isolates in the processes of forming gender identities and their power relations, group identities were also forming around different masculinities. Both at Ellesmere and the nothern 'traditional' school, the important characteristics in the most valued masculinities were sociability and success at games. At Ellesmere, having a rich and successful father, with its associated self-confidence and possessions, seemed to help in becoming the leader of a group. At both schools the ideal masculinity was popular sportsman, competent but not over-zealous in academic work. At the 'traditional' school, the higher value attached to games than work was evidenced in the regular housemasters' discussion of boys' progress, recalled typically as 'mmm. . .Maths could do with more attention. What about that game on Saturday?' (BJB, oral evidence, 1990). At Ellesmere the importance of sport in the school's values and notions about leadership were seen in the way sports captains were the favourite choice for house captains. In one house in 1984 the house captain was a noted sportsman, who had entered the school at the end of the era when prefects could beat. His sporting prowess had given him few means of gaining the respect of younger boys other than physical force and fear, by that time proscribed. The other house prefects thus found themselves frequently in fire-fighting situations (AJH, oral evidence, 1990).

The replacement of sport by the 'examination mill' in the public schools appears to be an aspect of the official account that is somewhat modified in the realities of school-boy cultures. Sport may not be as significant in those cultures as it was in the 1930s and 1940s but it still retained a greater attraction than academic work even in the fierce academic competition of the 1980s.

PUBLIC-SCHOOL MASCULINITIES: CONTINUITIES AND CHANGE

In his theory of gender and power, Bob Connell (1987) refers to the most prestigious and powerful masculinities as hegemonic masculinities. According to oral evidence from a small sample of boys at Ellesmere in the first half of the 1980s, the popular sports captain, who had attracted the most prestigious or 'dolly' girl as his girlfriend was the ideal, the hegemonic masculinity, lionized by the younger boys, and the subject of much common-room gossip. If the importance of sport is the significant historical continuity of public-school masculinities in the 1980s with those of the 1930s and 1940s, then that of heterosexual relations is the most significant change. Contrary to the official account it was not the introduction of girls that reduced the most adverse effects of the hardening process. This was achieved, as we have seen, by the new headmaster. He also introduced a new sort of housekeeper, with some of the characteristics of a housemother. The boys were encouraged to talk to her about their problems. 'Well, you would hardly admit to the housemaster that you were homesick. The housekeepers were a good idea, someone you could talk to' (AJH, oral evidence, 1990).

The advent of girls greatly increased the importance of sexualities in the masculinities in the school, making success in heterosexual relations a crucial criterion in valuing those masculinities. Only a small number of girls entered the school and they immediately became a source of attention. The boys divided them into two groups, the 'dollies', who were chased after, and the 'swots', who were not (cf Delamont, 1984). There was some resentment among the boys of the attention lavished on these few girls. The new girls' house christened 'Fort Knox' was a focus for these sentiments. The girls had to learn to conform to the boys' expectations of them as dollies who could 'take it'. The most isolated girl was a physically unattractive swot who was known to cry, apparently because she was not being pursued. Most of the girls appeared to be from wealthy backgrounds and were thought by many of the boys to be at the school in search of wealthy boyfriends rather than as a means to independent careers. Their commitment to academic success was considered poor. 'Rather than putting in the work to get good A-levels, they spent a lot of time socializing and watching the telly with the boys' (AJH, oral evidence, 1990). The accuracy of these boys' perceptions about girls is open to question, but such statements are indicative of the continuities and changes in public-school masculinities.

In both the northern 'traditional' school and at Ellesmere, the rebel was a popular masculine identity, with smoking as its most prominent symbol as in the 1930s and 1940s. However, in contrast with the earlier period, there were no well-defined rebel groups in the C forms, setting by subject ability having replaced rigid streaming. Rather, rebellion was individualized, an active response of individuals to the school's requirement for conformity. Pop music, as we have seen, has become a pervasive symbol of identity among boys. An expensive stereo system on which the music with which he identifies is played extremely loudly is often the first thing a public-school boy attempts to import into his study. Personal stereos are a poor substitute for such a public statement of identity. Clothes and music may be integrated into a very elaborate statement of identity. In the first half of the 1980s, bikers and greasers were associated with heavy-metal music and black leather jackets (CM, oral evidence, 1990). Clothes have a special significance in public schools, the expensive and distinctive nature of the uniform symbolizing the élite social status. During the war the headmaster of Ellesmere's determination to maintain the uniform in the way he considered appropriate in a public school gave rise to regular circulars loftily reminding parents of his expectations. The files for the period are full of letters from mothers cataloguing the difficulties involved with weary resignation (Heward, 1988, pp. 95–6).

In the later period, subtle but studied variations to the uniform were a frequent sign of a rebel. At the northern 'traditional' school rebels smoked and played heavy rock music as loudly as possible to signal their defiance. The uniform for the lower school was a blazer and blue shirt, the collar of which was worn outside. Prefects had to enforce this rule, remonstrating with offenders among the lines of younger boys in the corridors. It was 'very cool' to wear your collar in and to be insouciantly deliberate in getting it out when the prefects were insisting 'Get your collars out!' In 1984 the uniform was changed to sports jackets, ties and flannels during the week and suits on Sundays, and this form of rebellion disappeared. Although rebels were found in all ability groups they were more common among the less able. In both schools there were small groups of 'weirdos' – boys who did not fit in. Some were very extreme rebels who risked expulsion by mounting a violent, anti-social challenge to the system. At the northern 'traditional school' such a group damaged the cricket square, which resulted in ostracism by the rest of the school. Others were conformists as far as the school rules were concerned but their social behaviour was unacceptable to their fellows. At Ellesmere, physical weakness and homosexuality were the stigmatized forms of masculinities, taunts and innuendoes of 'wimp' or 'poofta' being the commonest among the boys. The northern 'traditional' school also had a group of 'trendies', sharply dressed over-conformists who constantly sought the approval of masters (AJH and BJB, oral evidence, 1990).

There is now much greater emphasis on social and sexual success and more variety among the competing gender models, masculinities and femininities than there was at Ellesmere in the period of my earlier study. Then the war was the most important agent of change suddenly promoting the RAF into the premier position as every school boy's dream of becoming a national hero. Changing gender relations in the family and labour market, the promotion of competing gender models and stereotypes in the media, rapidly changing labour markets, greater sexual freedom and openness mean that public-school boys and girls meet a variety of masculinities and femininities in all areas of their school lives – games, academic achievement, sexualities and social relations (Connell *et al.*, 1982; Connell, 1989). The extensive data for the war-time period demonstrated the precise nature of the contexts of intra-family relations and the way that backgrounds of farmers, clergy, businessmen and professionals had differing effects on their sons' careers and masculinities. In the contemporary period, many schools have come to terms with the insistent influence of the media and pop culture. Some see the alienation of the schools from their local community as a loss for both parties. Decorating, gardening and just talking to local old people provides another focus of caring and positive emotional relations at Ellesmere, fondly referred to as 'granny bashing' by the boys and girls involved.

The process of forming gender identities and the emergence of hegemonic masculinities are extremely complex and it is clear that even in a comparatively insulated school, such as the northern 'traditional' school, the meanings of the pop youth culture and media are pervasive influences and sexualities are prominent among them. While success in heterosexual relations has not established itself in the definition of hegemonic masculinities in that school in the way it has at Ellesmere, monthly discos with local girls' schools were established in the early 1980s, suggesting that the school had begun to realize the importance of heterosexual relations in the future well-being of its pupils. At Ellesmere the very small number of girls were viewed within the conventional heterosexual relations of dominant males and subordinate females. The girls had little influence as a group. 'It was a boys' school with a few very privileged girls in it' (AJH and BJB, oral evidence, 1990).

While the power relations in the schools and the system demonstrate an unreconstructed patriarchy, the process of negotiation and contest between gender identities, models and individuals for power within the schools cannot be so easily taken for granted and simply read off from the evidence of those officially in power. Despite the patriarchal superstructure, some of the girls in public schools may be learning how to get and maintain power, hitherto held exclusively by their male schoolmates. It is also possible that some public-school boys brought up alongside these public-school girls regard them not as inferior and future subordinates, but as of equal worth and power, potential future bosses and superiors.

It is in their subsequent careers that the public-school boys and girls of the 1980s will or will not gain power, and the relation of this to their earlier school experience remains as problematic as it was for the boys at Ellesmere during the war. Since the war the occupational structure and family relations have changed markedly. Manual occupations continue to decline and professional, administrative and managerial to expand. Women form an increasingly large proportion of the labour-force, which is segregated into men's and women's work with many women in low-paid and part-time work. Family relations are changing, with divorce and cohabitation increasing and the birth rate continuing to fall. These changes are the context for the formation of the pupils' gender identities within the school and of their subsequent careers. The previous study (Heward, 1988) showed the importance of fathers' legacies for their sons. We do not know the effects of these wider contexts on the formation of gender identities in the more recent period but it is already clear that the careers of more recent public-school boys and girls will be constructed in a rapidly changing labour market with a falling number of young people and increasing number of women. Whether or not more of them will get to the top and whether a public-school education will help them to do so is an open question. However gender relations in the labour market and elsewhere change, it is clear that masculinities in public schools are negotiated, contested and changing and that the processes of change and their effects on masculinities are patchy, uneven and problematic. While at a superficial level the malestream view of social class, gender and, by implication, power relations is supported by the evidence of élite education, on closer inspection, Connell's notions of hegemonic masculinities and Crompton's argument about the potential impact of rising educational credentials among women are a great deal more apposite (Crompton, 1986; Connel, 1987).

ACKNOWLEDGEMENTS

The Headmasters and Governors of Ellesmere College gave generous access to their archives. Ben Butlin, Angus Heward and Christopher Morgan, whose oral evidence is noted in this chapter, spent time answering my questions about their schooling, thoughtfully and fully. I am also indebted to Bob Connell whose stimulating ideas and encouragement have been invaluable, and to Geoffrey Walford for his patience and editorial advice.

REFERENCES

Calder, A. (1971) *The People's War: Britain 1939–1945*, Granada, London.
Clarendon Commission (1864) *Report of Her Majesty's Commissioners Appointed to Inquire into the Management and Revenues of Certain Schools Pursued and Instruction given therein* (the Clarendon Report, 3288). HMSO, London.
Connell, R. W. (1987) *Gender and Power*, Polity Press, Cambridge.
Connell, R. W. (1989) Cool guys, swots and wimps: the interplay of masculinity and education, *Oxford Review of Education*, Vol. 15, no. 3. pp. 291–303.
Connell, R. W., Ashenden, D. J., Kessler, S. and Dowsett, G. W. (1982) *Making the Difference: Schools, Families and Social Divisions*, Allen & Unwin, Sydney.

Cookson, P. W. and Persell, C. H. (1985) *Preparing for Power: America's Elite Boarding Schools*, Basic Books, New York, NY.

Crompton, R. (1986) Women and the 'Service Class', in R. Crompton and M. Mann (eds.) *Gender and Stratification*, Cambridge University Press.

Delamont, S. (1984) Debs, dollies, swots and weeds: classroom styles at St Luke's, in G. Walford (ed.) *British Public Schools: Policy and Practice*, Falmer Press, Lewes.

Derry, Canon W. (1980) The Provost's farewell address, *The Ellesmerian*, Vol. 92, no. 317.

Dilke, C. (1965) *Dr Moberly's Mint-Mark: A Study of Winchester College*, Heinemann, London.

Douglas, M. (1972) *Rules and Meanings: An Anthropology of Everday Knowledge*, Penguin Books, Harmondsworth.

Graves, R. (1929) *Goodbye to All That*, Jonathan Cape, London.

Halsey, A. H., Heath, A. F. and Ridge, J. M. (1980) *Origins and Destinations: Family, Class and Education in Modern Britain*, Clarendon Press, Oxford.

Hargreaves, D. (1967) *Social Relations in the Secondary School*, Routledge, London.

Heward, C. M. (1984) Parents, sons and their careers: a case study of a public school, 1930–50, in G. Walford (ed.) *British Public Schools: Policy and Practice*, Falmer Press, Lewes.

Heward, C. (1988) *Making a Man of Him: Parents and their Sons' Education at an English Public School 1929–50*, Routledge, London.

Honey, J. R. de S. (1977) *Tom Brown's Universe: The Development of the Public School in the Nineteenth Century*, Millingham, London.

Insight (1990) Iron Maiden, no. 18, BBC Publications, London.

James, E. (1951) *Education and Leadership*, Harrap, London.

Kelly, E. and Cohn, T. (1988) *Racism in Schools: New Research Evidence*, Trentham Books, Stoke-on-Trent.

Lacey, C. (1970) *Hightown Grammar: The School as a Social System*, Manchester University Press.

Lockwood, D. (1986) Class, status and gender, in R. Crompton and M. Mann (eds.) *Gender and Stratification*, Polity Press, Cambridge.

Mangan, J. A. (1981) *Athleticism in the Victorian and Edwardian Public School*, Cambridge University Press.

Mangan, J. A. (1986) *The Games Ethic and Imperialism: Aspects of the Diffusion of an Ideal*, Viking, Harmondsworth.

Mangan, J. A. (1987) Social Darwinism and upper class education in late Victorian and Edwardian England, in J. A. Mangan and J. Walvin (eds.) *Masculinity in Britain and America, 1800–1940*, Manchester University Press.

Norwood, C. (1929) *The English Tradition of Education*, John Murray, London.

Rubinstein, D. (1986) Education and the social origins of British elites, 1880–1970, *Past and Present*, Vol. 112, pp. 163–7.

Salter, B. and Tapper, T. (1981) *Education, Politics and the State*, Grant McIntyre, London.

Shrosbree, C. (1988) *Public Schools and Private Education: The Clarendon Commission, 1861–64, and the Public Schools Act*, Manchester University Press.

Tattum, D. P. (1989) Violence and aggression in schools, in D. P. Tattum and D. A. Lane (eds.) *Bullying in Schools*, Trentham Books, Stoke-on-Trent.

Walford, G. (1986) *Life in Public Schools*, Methuen, London.

Walford, G. (1989) Bullying in public schools: myth and reality, in D. P. Tattum and D. A. Lane (eds.) *Bullying in Schools*, Trentham Books, Stoke-on-Trent.

Waugh, A. (1955) *The Loom of Youth*, Richards Press, London (first published 1917).

Wilkinson, R. (1964) *The Prefects. British Leadership and the Public School Tradition*, Oxford University Press.

Willis, P. (1977) *Learning to Labour*, Saxon House, Farnborough.

4

THE IMPACT OF GCSE ON PRACTICE AND CONVENTIONS IN PRIVATE SCHOOLS

David Scott

This chapter focuses upon curriculum change in two independent schools in response to the introduction of the General Certificate of Secondary Education (GCSE). Kingdon and Stobart (1988) suggest that independent schools that had previously followed traditional academic and examination paths would find the transition from the old to the new difficult to make. The reality is more complicated than this and ignores the multiplicity of organizational structures that co-exist within the independent sector (Walford, 1984, p. 2). Two case studies of such schools have been made. The first is of a mixed day/boarding school, the second of a single-sex (female) day school. The research was conducted using the condensed fieldwork methods of multi-site case study (Walker, 1974; Stenhouse, 1982), and it fits broadly within the ethnographic research tradition (Hammersley and Atkinson, 1983; Burgess, 1984; Woods, 1986). A number of data-collection methods were adopted, though the main techniques used were unstructured interviews and observation. To support the descriptive techniques employed here, use will be made of transcribed evidence from the interview material.

After a lengthy gestation period, the GCSE finally replaced O-level and CSE as the principal means of examination for 16-year-olds. The final versions of the national and subject criteria were published in March 1985, and the first cohort of students sat the examination in June 1988. The most innovative element in the examination is the introduction of coursework and its assessment by teachers, though this is not totally new (Beloe Report, 1960).

Coursework and coursework assessment in the GCSE can be characterized in the following way (Scott, 1990). Different subjects have adopted different models of coursework organization and different ways of assessing that coursework. Though syllabus requirements restrict teacher choice as to where and when they should set coursework, subject departments and teachers within them still have to make important decisions about coursework settings. As a result, variation exists in the following: timing of coursework during the two years; where it is completed; the type of exercises done; the amount and quality of teacher input; and the availability of resources and the degree of parental and 'other' help. The introduction of coursework has therefore meant that though the public examination system is now a more valid and in some ways more reliable system (Torrance, 1987), in other ways it is a less reliable assessment instrument (Kingdon and Stobart, 1988).

This variation in coursework practices has implications for sociological explanations of educational disadvantage, in that those pupils who are not incapacitated by their home circumstances, nor denied access to educational opportunities (Mortimore and Blackstone, 1981), may still be handicapped because the methods used to assess them place them at a disadvantage in comparison with their contemporaries. In the context of the independent sector, Halsey, Heath and Ridge (1984) suggest that inequality of provision between the State and independent sectors is not the most important contributor to inequality of outcome and, indeed, that school 'effects' have in the past been exaggerated. Despite this, coursework provides opportunities to increase school 'effects' (Scott, 1989), and these opportunities relate not to actual learned outcomes but to the way those outcomes are assessed.

Within that multiplicity of organizational structures that characterize the independent sector, decisions about curriculum and examination matters are an important determinant of the differences between the various institutions. This chapter will, through close examination of the two cases cited above, suggest five ways by which curriculum decision-making may be conceptualized in the independent sector. Curriculum policy and curriculum practice within specific sites is always the result of contestation (Giroux, 1983; Ball, 1987). Indeed, Foucault (1986) argues that 'discourse is the power to be captured'. Furthermore, within institutions that devolve power and decision-making, outcomes are never comprehensive; that contestation will have different outcomes at different moments within the history of each institution. The introduction of the GCSE has given teachers an opportunity to re-assess curriculum practice within their schools and within their classrooms, and to implement new organizational strategies that best fit their conception of the curriculum. By focusing on a critical moment in that process of policy formation, we are in a better position to examine those conflicting and contested ideologies that, when seen in the context of external constraints and personal histories (Ball, 1987), account for curriculum change within institutions.

Those five ways of conceptualizing the curriculum debate are as follows:

Humanism – this corresponds, though is not identical with, Williams' (1961) categorization of 'old humanism', which considered education to be more than mere training. Its proponents see themselves as guardians of a cultural heritage. They are élitist only in so far as practical and not ideological constraints restrict access. They stress rationalist epistemologies and notions of intrinsically worthwhile knowledge (Peters, 1965; 1966). Breadth, balance and depth of curriculum provision would be considered important criteria. The conceptualization of the curriculum advocated here is a non-vocational entitlement version.

Élitism – a major concern is to effect the maximum penetration of an élite into the power structures of society (Arnold, 1932; Eliot, 1948; Bantock, 1968). Though élitist views of education have traditionally been humanist in orientation, Skilbeck (1976, pp. 15–16), for instance, argues that 'the tradition has shown itself capable of change, but the principle of continuous adjustment and adaptation to circumstances has never been admitted'. This is its most abiding characteristic. Its purpose is therefore avowedly political. Curriculum-making is a pragmatic exercise in that it is acknowledged that the means by which entry is gained to positions of power within society change over time. It is therefore important to adapt and change to meet such new requirements. Though they advocate policies designed to maximize examination results and to attract large numbers of students into their sixth forms, the intention is above all to maintain and increase the numbers of their pupils who go to university and in particular Oxford and Cambridge. Thus the narrow recruitment base they serve is sustained in power regardless of the levels of educational expertise they are dealing with. Academic knowledge is seen as a desirable goal, whereas the acquiring of practical skills is seen as less important.

Pastoralism – this focuses on the specific concerns of small numbers of students whose needs are not being met either elsewhere in the independent sector or within the State system. Their focus is frequently on the social needs of their clientele (both parents and students) and academic success is not considered to be a priority. At the micro-level subject departments and subject teachers adopt policies geared in part to the social and pastoral needs of their pupils.

Accountability – their major concern is to satisfy the needs and demands of their clientele, both student and parent. Thus choice of subject, range of options, types of syllabus and other related curriculum matters have to satisfy parental approval. Education and accreditation are seen as commodities to be exchanged for money in the market place. The consumer has to be seen to be getting full value for their investment. The emphasis is therefore on the maximization of examination results and the acquiring of cultural capital (Bourdieu, 1973). Access to the sixth form and institutes of higher education is considered an essential goal, though many parents' aspirations may be satisfied at a lower level.

Professionalism – Decisions about curriculum and academic matters are made in terms of a professional ethic, whose key notion is fairness. Thus coursework and examination settings are controlled so that no pupil may gain an unfair advantage. Proponents of this view see their brief as being wider than the school they teach in or the sector they work in.

LAMPTON SCHOOL

The first case, which has been given the name of Lampton School, is an independent day/boarding school. It caters for pupils from 3–18 years of age. In the last five years it has increased its roll by a third. There are a number of possible explanations for this. The growing dissatisfaction with the State sector and, in particular, teacher industrial unrest, has persuaded more parents to choose an independent education for their children. The rapid expansion of the local industrial base within the last five years has meant that more people are able to afford the fees. Furthermore, the headteacher, who has only recently taken up his appointment, has adopted more effective marketing strategies, which have persuaded more parents to send their children to his school.

The school itself has a number of unique features in comparison with its local competitors. It is co-educational right throughout its three levels. There are no other fee-paying co-educational secondary schools in the immediate locality. The equal stress on boarding and day attendance means that provision for day-pupils to stay at school for the full working day is readily available. In the end the school has built its reputation on its academic record and its ability to achieve consistently high examination pass rates (see Table 4.1). The school's Examinations Officer comments on this aspect of their performance while describing a visit by a team of HMIs doing a full inspection of the school:

> The second time they arrived they said. 'You must have made a mistake in your O-level results', and we said, 'Well, why?'; and they said, 'They can't be that good, not with that IQ of intake, not with that quality of intake'. . . we didn't think that we were that good, but we were very good at bashing kids through O-level.

This is not to suggest that the school is not selective. In the first place the selection is made in terms of the ability of parents to pay fees. In the second

Table 4.1 Lampton School. Percentage of total candidates who achieved grades A–C by subject at GCSE level, 1989

	No. of A–C grades achieved	No. of total candidates	%
Biology	35	56	62.5
English	105	109	96.3
English Literature	80	103	77.7
French	78	105	74.3
Geography	49	83	59.0
History	50	58	86.2
Mathematics	81	110	73.6
RE	44	124	35.5

Notes
1. Only MEG subjects included; 2. only subjects with more than 55 candidates included; 3. RE candidates are fourth years.

place various assessment procedures are gone through to sift out those pupils without obvious academic potential. As the Examinations Officer explains:

> We are not equipped for remedial teaching. The lower school tests for basic skills at 8 and 11. The upper school, having abandoned the common entrance examination many years ago, sets their own tests in verbal reasoning, mathematics and English before entry is gained. Though the school's results at GCSE and A-level compare favourably with the national picture, they do not compete with the performance of a small number of more highly selective independent schools.

Lampton is able to offer a traditional academic curriculum, with a wide range of options (see Table 4.2). It is subject-driven, though with the school having made the decision to follow the National Curriculum, there will be a move towards both the teaching of general areas of the curriculum (Balanced Sciences, Integrated Humanities) and the rationalization of option choices. At present the school offers its examination pupils a core of four subjects (English, Mathematics, French and RE – the latter is examined at fourth-year level). Pupils are then required at the end of their third year to choose four options from a list of fourteen. No attempt here is made to balance a pupil's

Table 4.2   Choice of options by gender – upper fourth year at Lampton School, 1988–9

	Total (% of sample)	Male pupils (% of male sample)	Female pupils (% of female sample)	Male pupils (% of option)	Female pupils (% of option)
Latin	21.1	10.0	14.6	45.5	54.5
Geography	70.3	68.0	73.2	53.1	46.9
German	20.9	8.0	36.6	21.1	78.9
History	56.0	56.0	56.1	54.9	45.1
Roman Civilization	15.4	20.0	9.8	71.4	28.6
Physics	69.2	82.0	53.7	65.4	34.9
Biology	54.9	44.0	68.3	44.0	56.0
Business Studies	34.1	42.0	24.4	67.7	32.3
Chemistry	38.5	46.0	29.3	65.7	34.3
Art and Design	24.2	22.0	26.8	50.0	50.0
Music	5.5	2.0	6.7	20.0	80.0
Graphic Communication	6.6	8.0	4.9	66.7	33.3
Technology	3.3	6.0	—	100.0	—

Notes
1. Total sample was 91 fourth-year pupils; 2. male sample was 50 pupils; 3. female sample was 41 pupils; 4. English, Mathematics, French and RE are not option subjects; 5. 89% (81 pupils) of the sample have chosen four options; 6. 9.9% (9 pupils) of the sample have chosen five options; 7. 1.1% (1 pupil) of the sample have chosen six options.

timetable formally by restricting choice, though balance of subjects between the sciences, the arts and the humanities is one of the factors taken into consideration when choices are made. Indeed, this emphasis on free choice is considered to be an important principle to follow: 'That choosing the subjects in which they have prospects or interests or whatever is the main objective' (Director of Studies). Each pupil will take a battery of aptitude tests in their lower fourth year, which will help guide pupils in their choices. The key figure in this process is their housemaster or housemistress. As the Director of Studies explains: 'They retain a very important advisory level here'.

A further element in the decision is the traditional relationships, as the school sees it, between subjects and between subject and ability level. It would be suggested to each pupil that in order for them to do Physics they would need to be reasonably adept at Mathematics. Likewise, in order for them to choose History they would need to have reasonably good writing skills. Furthermore, as the Director of Studies explains, some subjects are considered more suitable for academically inclined pupils: 'I think a bright child would probably be suggested to them that they did Latin or Physics'.

Though the intention is clearly a differentiated curriculum, Table 4.3

Table 4.3   Choice of options by gender – upper fourth year at Lampton School, 1988–9

	Total (% of sample)	Higher-setted pupils (% of sample)	Lower-setted pupils (% of sample)	Higher-setted pupils (% of option)	Lower-setted pupils (% of option)
Latin	12.1	17.6	5.0	81.8	18.2
Geography	70.3	62.7	80.0	50.0	50.0
German	20.9	27.5	12.5	73.7	26.3
History	56.0	56.9	55.0	56.9	43.1
Roman Civilization	15.4	5.9	27.5	21.4	78.6
Physics	69.2	72.5	65.0	58.7	41.3
Biology	54.9	39.2	50.0	60.0	40.0
Business Studies	34.1	25.5	45.0	41.9	58.1
Chemistry	38.5	45.1	30.0	65.7	34.3
Art and Design	24.2	25.5	22.5	59.1	40.9
Music	5.5	7.8	2.5	80.0	20.0
Graphic Communication	6.6	9.8	2.5	83.4	16.6
Technology	3.3	3.9	2.5	66.6	33.3

Notes
1.   Total sample was 91 fourth-year pupils; 2.   sample of higher-setted pupils was 51 (in at least one of the top-two setted groups for English, Mathematics and French); 3.   sample of lower-setted pupils was 40; 4.   English, Mathematics and French are not option subjects.

provides evidence that, though some subjects continue to attract the majority of their pupils from the higher-ability levels within the school, such a differentiated approach is not as marked as one would expect. Physics, for instance, is chosen almost equally by pupils from the higher and lower core-subject sets in the school (see Table 4.3). This emphasis on pupil choice has other consequences. Though the upper school is able to stream in English, Mathematics and French at examination level, other subjects are not able to. The Examinations Officer argues that the eventual introduction into the school of a curriculum format based round the National Curriculum proposals would enable more departments to set and stream their pupils: 'One of the advantages I think of Baker and the National Curriculum is that the choice will go just like that and we'll stream, so that we'll actually have something we've never had in my subject, History, here, which is streaming'.

Gender differentiation is a marked feature of the option-choosing process (see Table 4.2), and also conforms to the pattern experienced in both State and independent sectors of the educational system (Kelly, 1981; Equal Opportunities Commission, 1982). Reference was made at the beginning of the chapter to a number of different ways of perceiving the curriculum that, it was argued, are in constant competition with each other as the curriculum unfolds historically. The continuing decision to exclude girl-friendly subjects and combinations of subjects that may prove more attractive to girls (HE: Food; HE: Child Development) reflects the inability of those advocates of such a change to provide a powerful-enough expression of them to influence policy. On the other hand, the recent introduction of Business Studies, the continuing support given to 'male' craft subjects, shows how at different points in the process of curriculum-making different themes are emphasized, different conceptualizations of the debate win out.

The introduction of Drama into the examination timetable, which coincided with the introduction of the GCSE, shows how a different examination ideology has strengthened the hand of those advocating the study of practical and expressive subjects in the curriculum. Craft subjects have become craft, design and project orientated – with a consequent diminution of craft skills and an elevation of theoretical and written elements. It therefore more closely conforms to academic notions. Drama, in a similar way, is now examined both by practical elements (coursework 50 per cent) and also by investigative project (25 per cent) and examination (25 per cent). Furthermore, the introduction of coursework into most examination syllabuses at GCSE level has in effect given greater status to those subjects such as Drama that naturally and more efficaciously may be assessed by continuous assessment throughout the course. Since subjects with a traditionally high status are now being assessed, at least in part, in this way, subjects that have always been assessed like this are no longer being stigmatized as practical or low-status subjects. It should be said here that this destigmatization of practical subjects has, first, not come about exclusively as the result of the introduction of the new examination system and, second, that historical conceptualizations of the importance of different subjects continue to exert a powerful counter-acting force. Jonathan, for instance, describes his timetable in the following way: 'generally academic. I have chosen mainly academic subjects, in that I am not doing CDT or Art'.

The introduction of Drama, then, into the curriculum at examination level provides us with an account of how subjects that are essentially pastoralist in orientation, and have been introduced as a counterbalance to the more traditional aspects of the curriculum, can gain a foothold in that curriculum. The Head of Drama explains the rationale for his subject:

> In a sense we were quite early in introducing CDT and Drama and the less academic subjects, and the headmaster was very supportive of Drama as a curriculum subject as opposed to Theatre and Performance, and we felt it had so many ways in which it fed into other academic subjects in terms of broadening experience and self-awareness, that they were very supportive of introducing it and still are.

But he also makes the point that the way practical and expressive aspects of the curriculum are now treated at examination level has made it more acceptable: 'My subject is changing. It's not just theatre and play-acting. It's serious study in its own right. GCSE has helped'. Curriculum policies within the school itself, then, are subject to constant change. The introduction and encouragement of Drama is one example of this; but with the forthcoming National Curriculum – and Lampton is committed to its implementation – it is going to be increasingly difficult to find a place on the timetable for Drama at examination level.

It has been suggested that independent schools that previously followed traditional academic curriculums would have the greatest problems with adapting to the GCSE examination (Kingdon and Stobart, 1988), and that schools that had previously run 16+ and CSE syllabuses with their emphasis on project work and assessed practicals would be able to make the transition from one examination to the next without too many difficulties. Lampton, it has been argued, is therefore one of those schools without such obvious bridging potential. In fact, the change from O-level to GCSE was made without too much stress. The Director of Studies comments: 'We anticipated major problems here and in practice there haven't been any'. In some subjects GCSE actually meant a reduction in coursework. The O-level History syllabus the department used to follow was assessed 50 per cent by course-work. The present GCSE syllabus's coursework is only weighted at 30 per cent. Other subjects have had to make only minimal changes anyway: 'Certainly I heard a lot of scientists say there's no difference between O-level and GCSE, they think it's all very much the same as before' (Examinations Officer).

One problem anticipated was overload of work on pupils. The Director of Studies devised a schedule that attempted to accommodate all the course-work demands individual departments would make on pupils. Though this schedule was in the end imposed on subject departments, in fact most of the decisions made were made by the teachers concerned and the Director of Studies only made minor adjustments to fit the whole schedule together. The Examinations Officer explains what happened:

> Yes, what we do is we've sat down and got all the departments who have course-work. Our Director of Studies said, 'Right, what do you want, what's your ideas? When do you want the coursework coming in from kids?' We all put it down; and he got a chart and left it as it stood. No child is now going to have to hand in five pieces of coursework on the same day. . .and all he's done is acted, first of all he tried to be nice, and then gave up trying to be nice and said, 'You may not change it, it stays like that', and everybody accepted; there's been no grumbling. So we haven't had that problem which was anticipated.

The minor adjustment the Director of Studies made, and in the end imposed on the staff, were to do with rescheduling coursework submission dates by at the most two or three weeks.

The negotiation process included a number of interesting accounts of coursework from individual subject departments. The English department, for instance, wanted to be considered as a department that did not set course-work. Their reasoning was that, to be described as a department that set a large amount of external coursework, would put in jeopardy the strategy they were adopting whereby coursework would be integrated as closely as possible into classwork and homework. Such a strategy has the advantage that course-work is not then seen by pupils as extraneous work, an extra demand they have to face up to in addition to their ordinary work. It melds more closely together assessment and learning strategies, so that the formative process of drafting, reviewing and re-drafting of work can be a genuine one. It suffers from the disadvantage that coursework is seen as an ordinary part of class-work and cannot therefore act to motivate pupils because it is a special event. The Geography department made the decision to do the bulk of their work during an early part of the two-year course. The Head of Geography explains the advantages of this: 'I am happy to get it out of the way. . .and also the other thing is if there is some major disaster over the summer, there is always time to re-hash it'. The disadvantages are that pupils' conceptual and affective skills are less developed at an early stage of the course than they would be nearer the end.

Three important local factors have further contributed to an amelioration of the problem. The school itself follows a modified academic curriculum, in that certain subjects offered at GCSE level with large external coursework requirements are considered to be inappropriate to offer at examination level (the school, for instance, does not offer HE: Child Development or HE: Food). Furthermore, other craft subjects, such as CDT: Technology, which the school does offer at examination level, have as yet proved to be unpopular and have therefore been chosen by a small number of pupils. Further, large parts of the core curriculum are not assessed using coursework techniques (Modern Languages, Mathematics as yet). The problem is therefore minimized in this instance.

The second important local factor is that the school is both a boarding school and acts as a base for day-pupils for a considerable proportion of the day. The extent of both control over and the provision of resources for the completion of coursework assignments is therefore greatly increased. Each boarder is required to study from 7.30 to 9.00 p.m. in all the houses and then from 9.30 to 10.00 p.m. in some. Also, the tutorial system that operates allows teachers to review and monitor progress for each pupil under their care. Each pupil has an individual interview with his or her tutor every fortnight. The greater penetration of school into the lives of pupils, in particular with boarders, allows the process of coursework completion to be better structured and more extensively monitored than elsewhere. The longer school day (there are timetable lessons on Saturday morning) includes a period of activities (Games, Combined Cadet Force, etc.). Some fifth-year pupils were using the opportunities provided here to do extra work on coursework projects. If coursework is fully integrated into the academic ethos of the school in such a way as it not to seem an extra burden, then it becomes less of a problem.

The third important local factor is the extent to which class time is used for coursework purposes. A policy of using class time was given official backing by the Director of Studies: 'I think all of them should be doing what History is doing', which is using the possibilities of class time to their fullest potential. The Head of History explains how it works by using the example of his son who is a pupil at the school:

> But my son who is now in the fourth year does, you know, if he gets himself organized he can do an enormous amount of it here. Certainly, with my own subject, History, and I think with most other subjects, the smarter ones have discovered that if they use their classwork time intelligently, because my fifth years they have five lessons a week and two homeworks... and a double lesson of that on coursework. If they work hard in that double lesson, they can get all their coursework done that they need to get done, meet all the deadlines and have an evening off.

Given the existence of these local factors and policies, coursework has not proved to be as problematic as it has in other schools.

Élitist and accountability aspirations within the school empower the work and examination ethic pupils and staff subscribe to. This manifests itself in three ways, and has become part of the accepted discourse or, as Foucault (1986) argues, it operates as a 'normalizing judgement': a clear divide between 'C' and 'D' grades is perceived by both staff and pupils alike; GCSE is seen as only a stepping-stone to sixth-form study; and ability is conceived in stratified terms. The Head of the Classics department makes the point that the notion of a graded examination such as the GCSE offering equally positive results to all who enter is a misnomer:

> Yes, people talk about GCSE as being positive achievement, don't they? Now if, as people could have predicted if they had any sense, that the A, B and C is still referred to as pass grades, and the others as fail grades; and the notion of positive

achievement for someone who gets a G, seems to be rather stupid. Rather silly. I mean, it doesn't make very much sense, I mean, if you get a G employers would consider that to be hardly worth anything.

Pupils equally subscribe to such beliefs:

> D is a failure. . . . No, I think the staff think that it is not true; well, of course, they want us to get higher than a D; but they all say it's not a fail; but to get in the sixth form here you've got to get at least Cs.
> Ds are a failure. I'm looking for As in all my subjects.

Though GCSE was designed as a common examination, and though grades below a C are meant to register positive success for certain pupils, pupil perception and the perception of the teachers was that a D grade registered as a failure. The Director of Studies warned against this, though: 'It is difficult to get the school to recognize D as a success. They see very much A, B or C as a pass'. But with the pressures of accountability for teachers and with the much publicized relationship between O-level pass grades and the top-three grades in GCSE, the distinction between C and D grades is perceived as a natural cut-off point.

Though the adoption of curricular policies designed to maximize examination results would, on the surface, seem to satisfy the needs of parents for certification, the process is more complicated than this. The English department, for instance, had to make a decision when the GCSE was introduced, about which examination scheme they should follow, and though some members of the department felt that better examination results would be achieved by the adoption of 100 per cent coursework syllabuses in both English and English Literature, in the end a more cautious approach prevailed. The department has in fact chosen to do the English B Syllabus, Scheme 2 (MEG no. 1501) which is assessed 100 per cent by coursework and the English Literature, Scheme 2 (MEG no. 1502), which is assessed by 40 per cent coursework and 60 per cent end-of-course examination. The reasons given shed light on the relationship between an independent school and its parents, and the constant need to be accountable to them. Thus too radical an innovation, such as an examination without any end-of-course assessment, as mentioned by a teacher, may be misunderstood by parents:

> We didn't last time and the reason why we didn't do it to start off with was that we felt, and it has indeed proved to be so, that in a school like this, particularly I am afraid the weaker ones, the parents sort of expect you to. . . in other words, if they fail on 100 per cent coursework I think the parents vaguely think it's your fault.

On the other hand, teachers who believe that success can be measured by examination results may choose to adopt coursework procedures that extend the boundaries of what would be considered fair practice, and are thus in conflict with our previously articulated notion of professionalism. The History and Biology departments offer us two examples. Lampton School follows MEG History Syllabus no. 1613 – British and European History, 1867 to the present day – which asks each candidate to (p. 3) 'submit either one piece of work, or two shorter pieces, on a subject related to the period they have studied. Each piece of coursework may be composed of several pieces related to a common theme'. The pupils are allowed a choice from five topics, all of which they are familiar with. Out of their five lessons a week, one double during the Christmas term of their fifth year is given over to coursework and they are also allowed a homework that evening to complete it. Most do not need to, since they finish what they need to do in class. The work is divided into two sections. It is tightly structured and it does involve some library research. The Head of History describes the extent of teacher input at this stage:

> According to the regulations laid down by MEG we have to structure it much more than I would have like.... They get their pack of documents, books and told to use the library; and they've got to write on what did the suffragettes achieve. They've got four questions.... There is an enormous amount of teacher input at the very beginning. It's us telling them what the board wants.

The pupils then complete section one. They hand it in to the teacher, who reads it carefully and makes a note as to how each piece could be improved. With certain pupils the teacher may suggest that it is not worth re-writing, but the majority of pupils will be encouraged to go away and re-draft their work. The teacher meanwhile will have gone through with each candidate the piece of submitted work, pointing out its faults and showing each candidate how to improve. The Head of Department explains how the process works:

> The MEG rules are, as far as we understand them, they write section one, which is for 40 marks. Then bring it in, we mark it. You sit down and say this has got 21 out of 40. It has got 21 because of a, b, c, d, e. I will do this at the beginning of the double and I will go through each one with each candidate. We have only got 20 in the set which is possible therefore, and you then say if you want to get 40, you've got to do this, this and this, and that is it. They may come back to you in the course of the lesson.

After one re-drafting exercise it is handed in as a completed piece of work and marked formally by the teacher. The same process is gone through with the second section. Since the process is essentially a school-based one, involving controlled exercises with, in part, teacher-provided resources, the problem of unfairness caused by inequality of resources doesn't arise. On the other hand, though the strategies adopted here preclude unfair and excessive parental input, they do allow the teacher to provide an excessive amount of help and they do place in question the reliability of the assessments being made. The approach adopted is in sharp contrast to approaches adopted in History departments in other schools (Scott, 1990).

In a similar way, the Biology department uses 'enhancement' that, though it can be justified on the grounds that it encourages a learning process, is also designed to produce better or enhanced assessed performances from students. The need to find a means of assessing in a positive way the skills and aptitudes of their pupils means that teachers within the Biology department deliberately set more assessed practicals than they need to. This allows a choice to be made at the end of the course, so that 'best' performances can be submitted for examination. There is also built into such a strategy devices for improving the quality of each one of those assessments. So 'worse' performances are discarded both at the end of the two years and at the time they are done. The Biology teacher explains what happens:

> As an example I have just done one with the fifth form when they were asked if they could identify a key for twigs, you see. Now they all did it pretty satisfactorily except for these two girls who made a complete mess of it. So they came to see me and said they just didn't understand what they were doing. So we had 20 minutes in the lunch hour going over how to make a key. They happened to be boarders, and I am always in early, so as soon as they had had breakfast, I got an entirely different set of material (I think I used shells and things), and put it out for them, and they did a key. They did it very well, so that was able to go on the top of their original assessments.

Thus this re-working of the original assessment acts in a formative sense, that is the original weakness was diagnosed, remedial teaching took place and pupils were then re-assessed and shown to have acquired skills they did not have previously. The formative element in assessment is emphasized here at the expense of summative reliability.

This is in contrast to the Latin teacher in the school who will deliberately forgo formative learning opportunities so that the reliability of the assessments being made can be maintained: 'You definitely do hold back. You bear in mind you don't want to fall into the trap of giving them too much help because it would be obvious'. That is obvious to the moderator. Furthermore, the professional ethic this teacher employs means that he avoids any forms of teacher imput that could be construed as unfair: 'If you've got professional pride, you avoid it at all costs'. Thus at different points within the complex structure of decision-making within the school, different conceptualizations of the debate win out and different policies are adopted. The second case study provides us with an alternative set of experiences.

ST THOMAS' SCHOOL

The second case, which has been given the name of St Thomas', is an independent day school for girls. It covers the full age range with a nursery section, but no sixth form. At 16 some of its pupils will join LEA-maintained sixth forms; others will transfer to local independent schools. About 20 per cent each year choose to continue their education at A-level. Others will do vocational courses, such as nursery-nursing diplomas and their like, at nearby colleges. The upper school (11–16) takes in about 200 girls, 40 in each year. The school is selective in that it will not accept pupils with severe learning difficulties, though allowance is made for pupils who have come up through the preparatory department of the school. The Deputy Headmistress explains the rationale for the school's entry policy: 'I mean we do have exams, and if they really were weak, we just wouldn't take them, because we can't help them. Yes, I mean we do get some weaker ones up, but they've come through the preps, so we feel we can't turn them away really'. At the age of 11 a number of pupils will transfer to other local independent schools, which are able to offer bursaries and other such inducements, and which are also able to offer a wider curriculum. At 13 St Thomas' attracts pupils from the State-maintained sector, whose parents have been happy to see them educated in LEA middle schools, but do not feel that their local LEA upper school can give their child the sort of education they want. Numbers for each year are kept at 40 because the school would be unable to accommodate any more. Indeed, the school has no playing fields and for games lessons pitches at the local council park are used. Its small size is used to sell the school to prospective parents.

Though the school has adopted a selective entry policy, this has in effect meant that only a small number of low-ability children have been excluded. The school's intake, expressed in examination terms, is therefore loosely comprehensive. A small number of highly motivated and high-ability pupils are on roll (one girl in the first year of the GCSE achieved four As, two Bs and two Cs). A senior teacher expresses a commonly held view of the school's intake: 'We don't get very many bright children here. They tend to be very average'. Accountability, though still considered to be important, is being conceptualized in a different way from Lampton. There is an acceptance that the school will cater for a different clientele. Those pupils who are considered to need a particular learning environment – small classes, close contact between pupil and teacher, small numbers within the school, continuity between the different stages of education and single-sex provision – will, in theory, find what they need at St Thomas. In other words examination achievement is not considered to be a priority. Furthermore, gaining access to sixth forms and ultimately to institutes of higher education, though en-couraged, is not considered to be a significant criterion for judging success or failure within the school. A teacher explains:

> we have to accept that the sort of child we get here is not going to be a world beater. Some will, some will go on to university, but for most of them if we can allow them to grow up in a secure and reassuring environment then we have succeeded.

This approach has consequences for curriculum provision, in that an analysis of option choices (see Table 4.4) indicates clear evidence of dif-ferentiated routes for different types of pupils. Practical and vocational subjects (Commerce, Typing and HE: Food) are chosen in the main by pupils from the lower sets within the school. Chemistry, Physics, French and German are favoured by the high-ability sets. In a similar way the subjects on offer reflect a desire to offer a specialist curriculum to a certain type of girl. It is thus gender specific. The 'normalizing judgement' (Foucault, 1986) that empowers curriculum-making at St Thomas' incorporates a conceptualization of 'the sort of girl we have here', who is 'in the main not

Table 4.4   Choice of options by ability – fourth year at St Thomas' School, 1988–9 (%)

	Total	Higher-setted pupils	Lower-setted pupils	Higher-setted pupils	Lower-setted pupils
Geography	64.3	72.7	55.0	59.3	40.7
Art	40.5	36.4	45.0	47.1	52.9
Physics	26.2	31.8	20.0	63.6	36.4
Chemistry	38.1	50.0	25.0	68.8	31.2
Commerce	33.3	18.2	50.0	28.6	71.4
French	69.0	86.4	50.0	65.5	34.5
HE: Textiles	16.6	18.2	15.0	57.1	42.9
HE: Food	26.2	18.2	35.0	36.4	63.6
HE: Child Development	26.2	22.7	30.0	45.5	54.5
History	66.6	63.6	70.0	50.0	50.0
German	14.3	22.7	5.0	83.3	16.7
PE	11.9	13.6	10.0	60.0	40.0
Typing	59.5	40.9	80.0	36.0	64.0

Notes
1.   Sample 1 was 42 fourth-year pupils (all the fourth year); 2.   sample 2 was 22 higher-setted pupils (in more than one of the top sets for English, Mathematics and Biology); 3.   sample 3 was 20 lower-setted pupils (in less than two of the top sets for English, Mathematics and Biology); 4.   English, Mathematics and Biology are not option subjects.

very academic, hard-working, well-mannered and who has been brought up nicely' (a teacher). This acts to define both pupil needs and to influence curriculum provision within the school.

St Thomas' timetable is organized around a limited number of subjects (see Table 4.4). The curriculum has evolved historically to cater for the needs of their clientele. So CDT and Computer Studies are not offered at examination level, though all pupils do one lesson of Information Technology a week. There is no streaming or setting in the first year. The second and third years in the upper school are set for Mathematics, English and French. If a pupil is considered to be a reasonable linguist then she is encouraged to start German at the beginning of the third year. Though Mathematics and English are compulsory subjects throughout the five years of the upper school, French at GCSE level becomes optional. In the summer term of the pupils' third year, the pupils are provided with a list of possible subjects from which they have to choose six. This means that the majority of pupils will take nine GCSE examinations (English would include English and English Literature). Typing is also offered but not at GCSE level. On the other hand, pupils of lesser ability may end up taking only seven (they won't take English Literature and they will take Typing). The teacher responsible for the timetable explains how the system works:

And we send a list home of possible subjects for them to say which ones they might
be interested in and then following the response to that, we then decide what
option blocks we're going to have. And so if there's only a few who haven't chosen
it at all, we put it right across the year. With National Curriculum coming in, it
might happen with more subjects. We might, for instance, in a few years time start
Balanced Science and everybody does that science.

Thus Biology with last year's fifth year became a compulsory subject because
all the pupils opted for it with the exception of two. Though St Thomas' is a
single-sex school, gender stereotypical responses to the various sciences
remain (Kelly, 1981; Equal Opportunities Commission, 1982). Biology
always proves to be a more popular option than Physics, which attracts small
numbers of high-ability pupils. Indeed, this emphasis on pupil choice results
in considerable disparity of number between different subject groups. Last
year's fifth year opted in small numbers for Physics (9), German (6) and RE
(6). One of the English groups was as large as 25, and the Geography group
numbered 22. This principle of free choice is not absolute, but does involve
an element of guidance: 'We try to guide them into that, but it's not a free
choice really'. Last year the English, Mathematics and Biology departments
set their pupils at examination level. Other departments were not able to
because of small numbers.

The introduction of the GCSE proved problematic with a number of the
departments, despite experience of teaching at CSE level and despite the
experience of assessed project work in a number of subjects. This account of
St Thomas' History department is very different from the one given by
teachers at Lampton. The adoption of pastoralist ideologies here influence
both how old and new curricula are perceived, and determine the success or
otherwise of the introduction of a new examination technology.

History proved to be such a popular option that it is usually designated a
core subject. The department have chosen to do MEG Syllabus no. 1606 –
British Social and Economic History, 1700 to the present day. Each student
completes an extended project, which is divided into four parts. The History
teacher explains what this involves: 'Yes, we did our structured assignment,
rather like this with four parts, and we tried to meet each of the criteria that
they wanted you to meet, you know – historical recall, employment of information, empathy and analysis of evidence'. The project itself is structured
round a visit to the Black Country Museum in June of the pupils' fourth year.
Its theme is Industry, though this represents a change from the previous year
when the theme was suffragettes. The department changed in part because of
the poor way they were received by the City of London Museum the previous
year, thus emphasizing the importance of the initial museum visit. They went
in costume. The length and scope of the project with certain pupils has proved
to be a demotivating experience: 'Last year we had trouble with motivating
them. The first one was alright, but it became less of an exciting experience.
Now we want to speed it up this year'.

The History teacher at St Thomas' has had previous experience of project work as the school used to enter pupils for O-level and CSE and the latter was in part assessed by coursework project. She suggests that, because it is the school now that decides on the theme for coursework, and because the work itself has to conform more closely to the syllabus criteria, the experience of producing a long piece of work is no longer as worth while:

> They could choose, you know. They chose something they enjoyed, and it was their choice, it wasn't restricted to a syllabus, and so I had people getting high marks doing Ancient Egyptian, marvellous projects, wonderful things they would choose. Now we are restricted to a syllabus, so that restricts for a start.

The second suggestion she makes is that, because project work is more highly structured and teacher directed – a deliberate move by the syllabus writers to prevent copying and to introduce more analytical techniques in a systematic form – they do, paradoxically enough, make fewer demands on the pupils: 'but I just feel that when I look back at some of the very best of CSE projects, they were better, they represented more input from them, they were very much more interesting to read'.

The third element of her critique is that because the GCSE has moved to a greater extent towards a skills-based curriculum and away from chronological narrative, an essential part of the historical experience is lost: 'It is getting away from History as a narrative and History as a story'. She is conceptualizing the curriculum not in terms of a set of devices by which examination results are maximized, nor in terms of meeting general vocational needs; but in terms of a loosely structured narrative, in which her pupils' needs are met by reconstructing History as a chronological story. This conflicts with the new approaches implicit in GCSE History where assessment is more obviously tied to a model of differentiated achievement, where assessment is directed towards historical skills and tighter definitions of performance, and where chronological narrative structures have been weakened. She thus has problems with coming to terms with an examination in which a different ideology of assessment is in play (SEC, 1985; Broadfoot, 1986).

CONCLUDING REMARKS

Close attention to the detail of curriculum decision-making in response to a new innovation allows us to understand the diversity of approaches different schools within the independent sector take. It also allows us to conceptualize the relationship between policy formation and implementation as a contested activity with different outcomes at different places within each site (Ball and Bowe, 1989). Thus the contention that GCSE coursework processes confer educational advantages on groups and types of pupils (Scott, 1989) is only true for particular local settings, and can only be understood ultimately at the level of the classroom – the final outcome of policy. Furthermore, within sites of policy formation and implementation, which operate through hierarchies of power and influence, some of our curriculum conceptualizations are going to have greater influence and potency than others. Lampton, for instance, is an example of a school in which humanist, pastoralist and professional conceptualizations of the curriculum have tended to lose out to other forms, though there is evidence that at specific moments in the school's history each has exerted a significant influence. St Thomas', on the other hand, perceives its role essentially in pastoralist terms and operates with a different notion of accountability. Both the success of the new examination and its reliability as an assessment instrument are going to depend, therefore, on the different ways different schools in both the independent and maintained sectors formulate their organizational and curricular strategies. The two case studies that have formed the central part of this chapter, then, are testimony to the diversity of approaches that has characterized the introduction of the GCSE.

REFERENCES

Arnold, M. (1932) in W. J. Dover (ed.) *Culture and Anarchy*, Cambridge University Press.
Ball, S. (1987) *The Micro-Politics of the School, Towards a Theory of School Organization*, Methuen, London.
Ball, S. and Bowe, R. (1989) When the garment gapes: policy and ethnography as practices (unpublished conference paper, St Hilda's *Ethnography in Education Conference*), 13 September.
Bantock, G. H. (1968) *Culture, Industrialisation and Education*, Routledge & Kegan Paul, London.
Beloe Report (1960) *Secondary School Examinations other than the GCEs*, Secondary School Examinations Council, London.
Bourdieu, P. (1973) Cultural reproduction and social reproduction, in R. K. Brown (ed.) *Knowledge, Education and Cultural Change*, Tavistock, London.
Broadfoot, P. (1986) Assessment policy and inequality: the United Kingdom experience, *British Journal of Sociology of Education*, Vol. 7, no. 2, pp. 205–24.
Burgess, R. G. (1984) *In the Field: An Introduction to Field Research*, Allen & Unwin, London.
DES (1985) *General Certificate of Secondary Education: The National Criteria*, HMSO, London.
Eliot, T. S. (1948) *Notes Towards a Definition of Culture*, Faber & Faber, London.
Equal Opportunities Commission (1982) *Gender and the Secondary School Curriculum*, Manchester.
Foucault, M. (1986) *The Foucault Reader* (ed. P. Rabinow), Penguin Books, Harmondsworth.
Giroux, H. A. (1983) *Theory and Resistance in Education*, Heinemann, London.
Halsey, A. H., Heath, A. F. and Ridge, J. M. (1984) The political arithmetic of public schools in G. Walford (ed.) *British Public Schools: Policy and Practice*, Falmer Press, Lewes.
Hammersley, M. and Atkinson, P. (1983) *Ethnography: Principles in Practice*, Tavistock, London.
Kelly, A. (1981) *The Missing Half: Girls and Science Education*, Manchester University Press.
Kingdon, M. and Stobart, G. (1988) *GCSE Examined*, Falmer Press, Lewes.
Mortimore, J. and Blackstone, T. (1981) *Disadvantage and Education*, Heinemann, London.

Peters, R. S. (1965) Education as initiative, in R. D. Archambault (ed.) *Philosophical Analysis and Education*, Routledge, London.

Peters, R. S. (1966) *Ethics and Education*, Allen & Unwin, London.

Scott, D. (1989) Formative and summative tensions in the assessment of GCSE coursework – a case of educational disadvantage (unpublished conference paper, St Hilda's *Ethnography in Education Conference*), 9 September.

Scott, D. (1990) *Coursework and Coursework Assessment in the GCSE*, Centre for Educational Development Appraisal and Research, Warwick.

SEC (1985) *Working Paper Two – Coursework Assessment in the GCSE*, London.

Skilbeck, M. (1976) *Curriculum Design and Development, Unit 3, Ideologies and Values*, Open University Press, Milton Keynes.

Stenhouse, L. (1982) The conduct, analysis and reporting of case study in educational research and evaluation, in R. McCormick (ed.) *Calling Education to Account*, Heinmann, London.

Stevens, F. (1960) *The Living Tradition*, Hutchinson, London.

Torrance, H. (1987) School-based assessment in GCSE: aspirations, problems and possibilities, in C. Gipps (ed.) *The GCSE, An Uncommon Examination* (Bedford Way Papers no. 29), University of London Institute of Education.

Walford, G. (1984) Introduction: British public schools, in G. Walford (ed.) *British Public Schools: Policy and Practice*, Falmer Press, Lewes.

Walker, R. (1974) The conduct of educational case studies, in B. Dockwell and D. Hamilton (eds.) (1980) *Rethinking Educational Research*, Hodder & Stoughton, London.

Williams, R. (1961) *The Long Revolution*, Penguin Books, Harmondsworth.

Woods, P. (1986) *Inside Schools: Ethnography in Education Research*, Routledge & Kegan Paul, London.

5

HOMESICKNESS AND HEALTH AT BOARDING SCHOOLS

Shirley Fisher

INTRODUCTION

Leaving home to reside at a boarding school may be a traumatic experience for some new pupils. People in care-giving or teaching roles should take some steps to reduce the impact of loss of direct daily contact with home and to minimize the adverse effects of immediate exposure to a new school environment. Homesickness and the related distress following arrival at the institution can be a very profound experience for some pupils and can impede adaptation to social and educational aspects of school. For many pupils the experience recurs across successive school years or is so devastating that running away is seriously considered or carried out.

The vast majority of pupils who board at school are in private schools. While only about 20 per cent of private-school pupils are boarders, the private sector provides 95 per cent of all English boarding places. Excluding children in special schools, in January 1988, a total of 120,113 pupils resided at their schools, with only 6,532 in State-maintained schools (DES, 1989). Moreover, while there has been a decrease of about 10 per cent over the last decade in the total number of children who board, the decrease has been greater in the State sector than in the private sector. In 1980 there had been 100 State-maintained schools with some boarding provision, but by 1990 there were only 58, compared with about a thousand private schools. Overall, there are more boys who board than girls, with 63 per cent of boarders being boys in 1988. This is largely a reflection of the greater number of boys than girls in private education, and a decade earlier the disparity was greater. In Scotland (where most of the research reported here was conducted) only about 4 per cent of pupils are in private schools, with approximately 20 per cent of these pupils being boarders – just over 6,000 boarding pupils in all.

Some State boarding provision also exists in Scotland, mainly to serve the educational needs of those living on remote islands.

This chapter is concerned with some of the main psychosocial features associated with the homesickness distress pattern with a view to identifying vulnerable individuals and contexts, preventative measures and coping strategies. The understanding of the distress reaction depends on an appraisal of theoretical considerations concerning the impact of change in its broader perspectives. The next section is therefore focused on the issue of the possible reasons for adverse reaction to change.

THEORIES OF THE EFFECTS OF LOSS OF CONTACT WITH HOME

There are a number of different reasons for expecting that change and transition, although recurring features of life history, may not always be accomplished easily. First, change usually involves a break with the past and what is familiar and predictable. Second, change may involve loss of significant relationships with those in the 'old' environment. Third, change may create interruption of ongoing life activity creating a vacuum for a while. Fourth, when exposed to the new environment a person may experience loss of control due to new and unexpected events and circumstances. Finally, change often creates new roles and self-identity has to be evolved to match this. All these conditions will create pressure on the person both before and after the change. It is likely that these conditions create composite effects on the individual and that these reflect in distress levels.

Separation and Loss

Bowlby (1969, 1973) showed that the maintenance of a close bond between parent and child creates a sense of security, which is sought at times of stress. When this bond is threatened, the child reacts with alarm and distress. Such displays of alarm may be instrumental in restoring the presence of the parents.

Weiss (1975, 1990) has argued that similar attachments may exist in adult life. Peer and marital bonds may have many of the same principles as mother–infant bonds and disruption of these bonds may have similar implications. Loss of a bonded relationship may be distressing even between adults. The ultimate form of irreversible loss occurs when there is a bereavement, but temporary distancing because of moves can also create profound loss of contact.

Parkes (1972) recognizes the stages of response to infant–mother separation in the response to bereavement. Grief, anguish and anxious striving are generally followed by a period of depression and apathy.

Relatively little research has been conducted on the temporal response

patterns to leaving home, but the homesickness reaction generally contains
elements of grief, unhappiness, anxiety, phobic behaviour and depression.
The dominance and sequencing of these emotional components has yet to be
explored but there is some similarity between the homesick response pattern

Table 5.1   Features utilized in definitions of homesickness for homesick and non-
homesick first-year students

| Feature categories from definitions provided | Frequency of reported features and percentage of subjects reporting each feature | |
	Homesick ($n = 60$) $f(\%)$	Non-homesick ($n = 40$) $f(\%)$
'Missing home environment'; 'missing house, home, area', etc.	18 (30.0)	16 (40.0)
'Missing parents/family'; 'longing for people at home'	20 (33.3)	12 (30.0)
'Wanting to go home'; 'feeling a need to return home'	14 (23.3)	11 (27.5)
'Missing friends'; 'longing for friends'	18 (30.0)	5 (12.5)
'Feeling of loneliness'	3 (5.0)	7 (17.5)
'Feeling depressed'	3 (5.0)	3 (7.5)
'Missing someone close to talk to'	4 (6.7)	1 (2.5)
'Feeling insecure'	3 (5.0)	2 (5.0)
'Obsession with thoughts of home'; 'thoughts about home'	3 (5.0)	3 (7.5)
'Feeling unhappy'	1 (1.7)	3 (7.5)
'Feeling unloved'	2 (3.3)	1 (2.5)
'Disorientation'; 'feeling lost in new environment'	2 (3.3)	1 (2.5)
'A longing for familiar company and places'	1 (1.7)	1 (2.5)
'Thinking of the past'	1 (1.7)	2 (5.0)
'Feeling of not belonging'	1 (1.7)	1 (2.5)
'Regret that life had changed'; 'a feeling of regret'	3 (5.0)	0 (0.0)
'Feeling isolated'; 'cut off from the world'	2 (3.3)	1 (2.5)
'Feeling uneasy'	0 (0.0)	2 (5.0)
'Feeling ill'	1 (1.7)	0 (0.0)
'Dissatisfaction with present situation'	1 (1.7)	0 (0.0)
'Unable to cope'	1 (1.7)	0 (0.0)
'Unable to do anything'	1 (1.7)	0 (0.0)
'Hating the present place'	0 (0.0)	1 (2.5)

Note
The following features were endorsed by only one person in the following groups.
Homesick: 'Thinking that home was better than here'; 'feeling of making a mistake';
'sinking feeling in stomach'; 'loss of appetite'; 'feeling of desperation'; and 'crying'.
Non-homesick: 'New self-reliance'; 'feeling of desolation'; and 'feeling unsettled'.

(*Source:* Fisher, Murray and Frazer, 1985.)

and the response to bereavement. Leaving home is, however, obviously different from the total loss created by death because home remains available to be contacted and visited.

As illustrated in Table 5.1 and 5.2, research in Dundee showed that parents and family featured in definitions of 'homesickness' provided in written form by pupils at school, whereas missing routines, friends, activities and home comforts featured more in the definitions provided by university students. Clearly, the forms of the homesickness response may change with age and

Table 5.2   Features utilized in definitions of homesickness for homesick and non-homesick school pupils

Feature categories from definitions provided	Frequency of reported features and percentage of subjects reporting each feature	
	Homesick ($n = 82$) $f(\%)$	Non-homesick ($n = 33$) $f(\%)$
'Missing parent family'; 'longing for people at home'	54 (65.9)	25 (75.8)
'Missing home environment'; 'missing house, home, area', etc.	28 (34.1)	12 (36.4)
'Wanting to go home'; 'feeling a need to return home'	21 (25.6)	10 (30.3)
'Missing friends'; 'longing for friends'	12 (14.6)	1 (3.0)
'Feeling of loneliness'	10 (12.2)	1 (3.0)
'Crying'	3 (3.7)	3 (9.1)
'Unsettled'	4 (4.9)	1 (3.0)
'Hating the present place'	4 (4.9)	1 (3.0)
'Feeling unhappy'	4 (4.9)	1 (3.0)
'Not getting on with people'	3 (3.7)	0 (0.0)
'Dissatisfaction with present situation'	3 (3.7)	0 (0.0)
'Feeling depressed'	2 (2.4)	1 (3.0)
'Disorientation'; 'feeling lost in new environment'	2 (2.4)	0 (0.0)
'Regret that life had changed'; 'a feeling of regret'	2 (2.4)	0 (0.0)
'Never been away from home before'	2 (2.4)	0 (0.0)
'Feeling ill'	2 (2.4)	0 (0.0)
'Unable to do anything'	2 (2.4)	0 (0.0)
'Feeling unloved'	0 (0.0)	2 (6.1)

Note
The following features were endorsed by only one person in the following groups. *Homesick:* 'problem at school'; 'missing someone close to talk to'; 'obsession with thoughts of home'; 'looking for familiar company and faces'; 'feeling isolated'. *Non-homesick:* 'feeling uneasy'; 'unable to cope'; 'feeling full and weary'; 'thinking home is better than here'.

(*Source:* Fisher, Frazer and Murray, 1986.)

experience. This would be expected given that, with increasing age, bonds between children and parents are changed (see Weiss, 1990).

Interruption and Change of Lifestyle

Discontinuity created by change from residence at home to residence at school may be disruptive because it creates interruption of existing life routines and security is therefore threatened. The human disposition to develop routines and habits may be of evolutionary value in aiding survival by enabling the maximum development of skills and capacity. Predictable life events are more comfortable in that a person knows what to expect and has better control over the environment.

Laboratory studies in California (Mandler, 1975) have shown that when tasks are interrupted there is raised tension sometimes manifest as anxiety and that completion of the task attenuates this. Although leaving home for school is planned for, nevertheless it can involve interruption of desirable hobbies, ways of behaving, relationships and may create tension and anxiety as a result.

Pupils report that much time is spent day-dreaming about home: 'I was sitting down to drink a cup of chocolate with my father'; 'I miss taking the dog for a walk first thing'. These thoughts may act like bitter-sweet memories driving nostalgia. Interestingly, medieval medical texts on the distress of leaving home led to the introduction of the term from 'algia' (pain) and 'nosos' (past) = 'pain of the past'. Bitter-sweet memories of this sort may drive distress in the new environments by acting as reminders of the past.

Reduced Control

The new environment is likely to be an influential factor in the response to leaving home. The underlying theory for this was proposed by Fisher (1984, 1986) in terms of the level of perceived control. New and especially challenging environments present a person with a period of low environmental control: new faces, places, routines and rules have to be assimilated. There may be different geographical and cultural factors as part of the background context. These may also be initially associated with low control. In that sense joining a boarding school abroad may create extra pressures on a person.

Loss of control over the environment is increasingly recognized as a source of stress. Fisher (1986) provides a detailed review of forms and manifestations of control and argues that sometimes what seems like lack of control may actually be a powerful form of control. A sick person or an elderly relative may exert a powerful form of control over the household. Children at school may control the teacher, even incurring punishment in maintaining control. Controlling the source of punishment has been described as the 'Cool Hand Luke' syndrome (*ibid.*).

The child arriving at a new boarding school may perceive low control over aspects of the new environment. We found in studies of pupils in Scottish boarding schools, that some new pupils could not find the dining room; could not understand how to get clothes washed; lost personal possessions; did not follow the timetables easily; felt bewildered by lessons; could not remember the class teacher's name, name of house matron; etc. All these losses really represent low control over the environment because the pupil does not have a good conceptual grasp of what is going on and what is required of him or her. In turn this should raise the risk of distress and negative experience. The boarder has even more of these low-control factors to cope with because he or she has to adjust to being newly residential for the first time.

Role Change

When people move to new environments they often change to new roles and new status. Thus a person may move to take up a new job, become married, vocational training, etc. A child who leaves home for boarding school assumes the new identity of being a pupil in residence at a school and may, in the British private educational sector, have to live up to expectations created by a new role and status in society. Public schools are often associated with 'upper-class' rules and moves and even the accent and intonations adopted by pupils may be different.

It has been shown that in circumstances of role change there is focus on the self and self-image: a person is faced with the need to perform in public and is conscious of the need to provide an acceptable image. It has been found that the amount of self-focus increases with the strangeness of the new environment. It has been argued that discrepancy between achieved and desired state of self will be resolved when a person becomes familiar with the new environment and has adjusted to his or her new role (see Hormuth, 1984).

HOMESICKNESS AND DISTRESS

The term 'homesickness' is commonly used to describe the adverse reaction pattern that develops in some people after leaving home to become resident elsewhere. It is less commonly used to describe the reaction following moving home (i.e. when the whole home and family unit relocate).

Dictionary definitions of homesickness include 'pining for home' (*Chambers Dictionary*, 1972) and depressed by absence from home (*Concise Oxford Dictionary*, 1964). The issue of whether homesickness is situationally determined or is dependent on personal traits or home background is very much an issue yet to be resolved.

Written personal definitions obtained across a number of studies using questionnaires and diary studies (see Fisher, 1989) showed that the main forms of the homesick response concern missing, grieving for and wanting to go home. There is much in common with bereavement. Symptoms include dizziness, depression, sadness, absent mindedness, disorientation, sleeping and eating abnormalities, feeling lost, loneliness, crying, anxiety and agitation. It is thus a complex motivational–emotional state dominated by preoccupation with home. It has much in common with bereavement.

About 18–20 per cent of school pupils newly boarding at school spontaneously use the term to describe their experience in the first few weeks, but 60–70 per cent will endorse positively a scale indicating that they experience homesickness in the first weeks of the first term. This suggests that providing the label catalyzes the recognition of the experience. This is not unusual in research on the experience of emotional and clinical states: people often do not categorize easily the complex of emotional or distress experiences and diagnosis in clinical conditions of distress is normally made by psychiatrists and psychologists.

For the majority of those who report homesickness, the experience is short lived, although it may recur across successive terms of following years. For about 10–15 per cent, however, the experience can be profound and intensely distressing, even to the point where a child is at risk of deviant behaviour or suicide. In intense cases, homesickness appears to be very like clinical depression.

Table 5.3 illustrates that whether by cause or consequence homesickness is associated with the occurrence of physical ailments. As the table shows, homesick pupils report more days off school and seeing a doctor more often. The causal direction needs researching: perhaps feeling unwell is associated

Table 5.3　Variables associated with homesickness reports for boarding school pupils

Variable	Homesick (n = 83)		Non-homesick (n = 34)	
	$\bar{X}$	SD	$\bar{X}$	SD
Non-traumatic ailments	2.95	1.62	2.38[a]	1.28
Day affected	27.28	45.72	14.53[a]	12.71
Activities affected	3.94	11.59	6.09(NS)	10.16
Number of times doctor seen	1.88	1.49	1.32[a]	1.17
Traumatic ailments	0.06	0.24	0.09(NS)	0.29
Days affected	1.95	10.99	1.53(NS)	5.23
Activities affected	1.95	11.11	0.73(NS)	3.68
Number of times doctor seen	0.06	0.24	0.09(NS)	0.29

Note
[a]$p < 0.05$. Larger means indicated higher scores on the attributes listed; NS = not significant.

(*Source:* Fisher, Frazer and Murray, 1986.)

with the need for the home and comforts of home. There is, however, sufficient evidence from other sources on stress and ill-health to suggest that distress following being home might have a causal role in ill-health (see Fisher, 1988).

Of the majority group of mild reporters, diary studies have shown that homesickness occurs in episodes – a little like attacks of grief or panic. These episodes are more likely to occur in the early morning or late at night. For the 10–15 per cent of intensely homesick pupils, the experience is non-episodic and total and occupies the thoughts of the victim nearly all the time. Pupils report themselves as obsessed with the need to go home and feeling totally grief stricken all day (see Fisher, Frazer and Murray, 1984, 1986). For example, one boy aged 13 wrote: 'Please researchers come and take me home. My mother and father would want you to. I am so homesick I can't stop crying. It will never be different'.

There is little evidence of a sex difference across the populations studies. The exception was a finding by Fisher and Elder (1990) of a preponderance of females reporting homesickness in a school in the Australian Bush. On this occasion, conditions were rather special in that the school places heavy emphasis on physical work and trekking in the mountains in adverse conditions. This probably proved more demanding for girls than boys and may account for the increased feeling of homesickness.

ENVIRONMENTAL FACTORS IN HOMESICKNESS REPORTING

In general our parallel studies on homesickness among university students have shown that the greater the geographical distance between home and the residential location, the greater the risk of homesickness. However, this effect is not found for boarding-school populations – only for university students (Fisher, Murray and Frazer, 1985; Fisher, Frazer and Murray, 1986). This may suggest that the restrictions on home visits operated by most schools prevent geographical distance from being an important variable, whereas for a student at university, time and cost are factors that prevent visits home and that might make a person feel isolated.

The perceived unpleasantness of the new environment may be a major factor in homesickness. Those who report homesickness generally view the new environment in negative ways. In particular it seems that friendships and aspects of the academic and institutional environment do not come up to expectations. Of course, this might be consequence and not cause, but there is the hint as with females at the Australian school that uncongenial environments promote the experience of homesickness. Therefore creating pleasant environments in schools and reducing the harshness of daily life may be important in the long term.

PERSONAL DETERMINANTS OF
HOMESICKNESS EXPERIENCE

Very little evidence has indicated that there might be personality factors in homesickness reporting, the exception being in the findings by Fisher, Frazer and Murray (1986) that extroverts are less likely to report homesickness than introverts. However, there is some important evidence obtained in the context of a longitudinal study of university students (Fisher and Hood, 1988), which showed that students most likely to be homesick in the first six weeks in residence at a university were distinguished two months prior to leaving home by raised levels of mild depression relative to their non-homesick counterparts.

Depression, even in mild form, is associated with passivity and self-denigration and a tendency to self-blame for negative outcomes. Passivity is a particular feature of depression, which might be of importance because the act of striving to adapt to the new environment is likely to act to attenuate the experience of homesickness. Fisher, Frazer and Murray (1986) reported from diary studies of boarding-school pupils that the day's events have the capacity to keep homesickness at bay. Thus, being busy, active and taking part in life in a new environment can be vital. Those who remain passive and withdrawn are less able to benefit by having alternative information to focus their thoughts on.

Figure 5.1 illustrates two possible conceptualizations of the impact of leaving home on a person. The first conceptualization (demand-strength model) assures that the impact of separation is different for different people and that the degree to which our limited-capacity mental resource is dominated by home thoughts directly reflects the impact of separation. Thus for episodic reporters the impact of separation is assumed to be fairly low and there are only some periods when home materials dominate thinking. For other people, the experience of preoccupation with home is total because the impact of separation is profound. These non-episodic reporters are swamped mentally with thoughts of home so that the limited-capacity mental resource is unable to process environmental information.

The lower part of Figure 5.1 illustrates an alternative conceptualization. The new environment presents a person with challenge and with sources of new environmental information. The homesick thoughts can thus be kept at bay if a person actively samples the environment. The episodic reporter is assumed to attenuate periods of homesickness because environmental input competes effectively for the mental resource. By contrast, the non-episodic reporter is unable to become committed to the new environment in this way and is swamped instead by unmitigated thoughts of home.

Thus one model assumes that the severity of the state of preoccupation is determined directly by the impact of separation. The second model assumes that the new environment has a moderating role to play because information from the new environment is able to dominate mental resources and thus

1. DEMAND STRENGTH MODEL

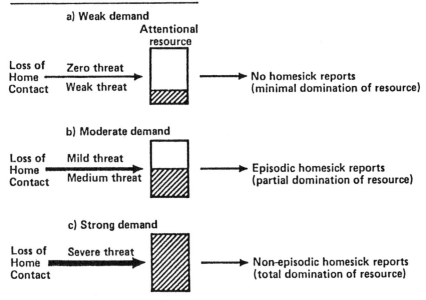

a) Weak demand

Loss of Home Contact

Zero threat
Weak threat

Attentional resource

No homesick reports
(minimal domination of resource)

b) Moderate demand

Loss of Home Contact

Mild threat
Medium threat

Episodic homesick reports
(partial domination of resource)

c) Strong demand

Loss of Home Contact

Severe threat

Non-episodic homesick reports
(total domination of resource)

2. COMPETING DEMANDS MODEL

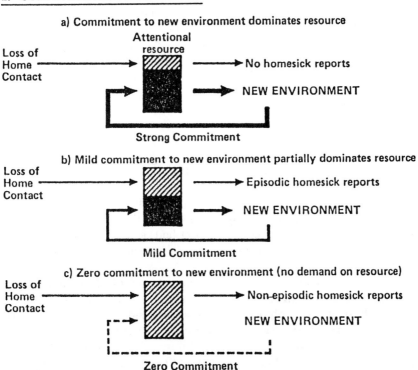

a) Commitment to new environment dominates resource

Loss of Home Contact

Attentional resource

No homesick reports

NEW ENVIRONMENT

Strong Commitment

b) Mild commitment to new environment partially dominates resource

Loss of Home Contact

Episodic homesick reports

NEW ENVIRONMENT

Mild Commitment

c) Zero commitment to new environment (no demand on resource)

Loss of Home Contact

Non-episodic homesick reports

NEW ENVIRONMENT

Zero Commitment

Figure 5.1 Attentional-demand models of homesickness reporting (Source: Fisher, 1989).

reduce the processing of thoughts about home. In effect the new environment can act as a distraction. For those who are mildly depressed and who tend to react passively this benefit is reduced.

EXPERIENCE AND HOMESICKNESS

A finding from research on the incidence of homesickness (Fisher, Frazer and Murray, 1986; Fisher and Hood, 1988) was that moves away from home to reside at a previous institution reduce the risk of homesickness for a current move. Moves away because of holidays, staying with relatives, etc., are not beneficial in the same way. Therefore there is some selective immunization against reporting homesickness, which arises because of previous selected experiences. Clearly being away from home *per se* is not as important as being away but coping with the experience of the new institution. Perhaps the control model (described previously) is an important predictor of home-sickness. Those who have left home to reside in institutions previously have learnt about how institutions work, how to be self-sufficient, etc., and this protects against adverse effects for subsequent moves.

Work reported by Fisher, Elder and Peacock (1989) indicated that those who moved to a school located in the Australian Bush, having boarded or having been day-school pupils at the parent school (200 miles away), were less homesick than those completely new to the school. Thus the total con-text of the move cannot be neglected. However, the difference between pre-vious day-pupils and previous boarders was not significant. This might suggest that familiarity with residential procedures, etc., is less important as a factor ameliorating homesickness than social support created by familiar peer-group contexts.

JOB STRAIN AND HOMESICKNESS

An observation arising from research with university students was that about 35 per cent of those reporting homesickness in the sixth week of the first (new) term had not arrived homesick, but had developed the experience as time progressed. In other words, the new environment was to some extent creating the conditions for homesickness.

This finding is against the separation model (described previously) where the loss of contact with home is instrumental in creating distress because about a third of those reporting homesickness simply do not recall being homesick on arrival. We have found for university students that exposure to the new university environment is stressful for all who undergo it, including those who remain living at home (Fisher and Hood, 1988). Therefore, clearly a new university environment is a source of strain for all students. Perhaps school environments have similar properties.

Table 5.4 Cognitive failure, mental health and adjustment profiles before and after the transition in homesick and non-homesick residents*

	Not homesick (n = 42)		Homesick (n = 22)	
	$\bar{X}$	SD	$\bar{X}$	SD
At home				
MHQ1	22.81	(8.60)	29.20‡	(12.5)
Obsessional (personality)	2.61	(2.20)	3.72†	(2.7)
Somatic	3.21	(2.50)	4.54†	(2.7)
Depression	1.89	(1.60)	3.82‡	(2.8)
CFQ1	32.64	(10.66)	36.90(NS)	(12.3)
Sixth week at university				
MHQ2	23.00	(11.54)	33.04‡	(14.1)
Anxiety	3.78	(3.10)	6.48‡	(3.7)
Somatic	2.63	(2.10)	5.17§	(2.9)
Depression	2.56	(2.30)	4.48‡	(3.2)
Obsession (symptoms)	2.54	(1.60)	3.35†	(2.1)
CFQ2	38.21	(11.88)	42.78(NS)	(13.5)
CAQ	100.69	(17.70)	84.31§	(18.2)
DRI	4.00	(3.20)	8.50§	(4.2)

Notes
* As designed by 'not homesick' versus three other categories of 'homesick' on self-rating scale (from Fisher and Hood, 1988); †$p < 0.05$; ‡$p < 0.01$; §$p < 0.001$.

Table 5.4 illustrates that there is a rise in psychoneurotic scores for residential students. This substantial stress effect is particularly manifest in terms of obsessionality and depression and is worse for those who subsequently report homesickness. The increase in depression and obsessionality, however, is also true for non-residential or 'home-based' students, which indicates that the experience of the new environment is important.

These findings raise the possibility that the experience of strain is a major ingredient in homesickness. In other words, being removed from a protective, familiar environment to one of challenge but novelty and lack of protection might create a longing for home. This gives a new role to the school or home environment than we envisaged earlier in the chapter. Perhaps the new environment has the potential not just for moderating homesickness by providing distraction but also by actively creating conditions for distress. This is then manifest in terms of homesickness.

When university students who reported homesick were asked to rate the amount of academic demand made on them and the degree of control over that demand the results showed that relative to their non-homesick counterparts they perceived more 'demand' and less 'control'. They appear overwhelmed. This has not been tested in a school context, but it does at least hint at the important role of the new environment as a determinant of homesickness. What, of course, remains unknown is whether the effect is cause or consequence. Perhaps, as we argued previously, the potentially homesick are more passive and withdrawn and more likely to fail to become committed. The new environment thus continues to overwhelm them and day-dreaming about home becomes a form of escapism, which has negative emotional outcomes.

REDUCING HOMESICKNESS

Clearly some people will experience homesickness in new environments and effort must be directed at reducing the length, frequency and direction of bouts. Pre-experience of the school and its rules, meeting potential classmates and house members will be important. Personalizing the institutional environment, especially sleeping accommodation, will be important. Many people find sharing a room stressful – lack of privacy can be threatening.

More user-friendly school environments can be created if seniors are trained to be caring and helpful, rather than authoritarian and distant. Success at games, house or school activities will encourage commitment and reduce the tendency to withdraw. Therefore, situations where a person can easily succeed or which are matched with known success will be helpful. Initially, keeping pupils happily busy is the best technique.

For those who are homesick, visits home may merely exacerbate the problem. However, letting a pupil know that he or she would not, in the end, be kept at school against his or her will is important. Counselling of the distressed is important because the emotional problems can be dealt with. The expression of stressful experiences and worrying thoughts has been found to be a major factor in reducing overall impact (see Pennebaker, 1988).

REFERENCES

Bowlby, J. (1969) *Attachment and Loss. Vol. 1. Attachment*, Basic Books, New York, NY.

Bowlby, J. (1973) *Attachment and Loss. Vol. 2. Separation, Anxiety and Anger*, Basic Books, New York, NY.
DES (1989) *Statistics of Education 1988*, London.
Fisher, S. (1984) *Stress and the Perception of Control*, Lawrence Erbaum Associates, London.
Fisher, S. (1986) *Stress and Strategy*, Lawrence Erlbaum Associates, London.
Fisher, S. (1988) Life stress, control strategies and the risk of disease: a psychobiological model, in S. Fisher and J. Reason (eds.) *Handbook of Life Stress, Cognition and Health*, Wiley, Chichester.
Fisher, S. (1989) *Homesickness, Cognition and Health*, Lawrence Erlbaum Associates, London.
Fisher, S. and Elder, L. (1990) unpublished paper
Fisher, S., Elder, L. and Peacock, G. (1989) Circumstantial determinants of homesickness incidence, *Children's Environment Quarterly* (in press).
Fisher, S., Frazer, N. and Murray, K. (1984) The transition from home to boarding

school: a diary-style analysis of the problems and worries of boarding school pupils, *Journal of Environmental Psychology*, Vol. 4, pp. 211–21.

Fisher, S., Frazer, N. and Murray, K. (1986) Homesickness and health in boarding school children, *Journal of Environmental Psychology*, Vol. 6, pp. 35–47.

Fisher, S. and Hood, B. (1988) Vulnerability factors in the transition to university: self-reported mobility history and sex differences as factors in psychological disturbance, *British Journal of Psychology*, Vol. 79, pp. 1–13.

Fisher, S., Murray, K. and Frazer, N. (1985) Homesickness, health and efficiency in first year students, *Journal of Environmental Psychology*, Vol. 5, pp. 181–95.

Hormuth, S. (1984) Transitions in commitments to roles and self-concept change: relocation as a paradigm, in V. L. Allen and E. van de Vlert (eds.) *Role Transitions: Explorations and Explanations*, Plenum Press, New York, NY.

Mandler, G. (1975) *Mind and Emotion*, Wiley, New York, NY.

Parkes, C. M. (1972) *Bereavement*, International University Press, New York, NY.

Pennebaker, J. W. (1988) Confiding traumatic experiences and health, in S. Fisher and J. Reason (eds.) *Handbook of Life Stress, Cognition and Health*, Wiley, New York, NY.

Weiss, R. (1975) *Marital Separation*, Basic Books, New York, NY.

Weiss, R. (1990) Loss and recovery, in S. Fisher and C. Cooper (eds.) *On the Move: The Psychology of Change and Transition*, Wiley, Chichester.

6
SMALL PRIVATE SCHOOLS IN SOUTH WALES

Janis Griffiths

INTRODUCTION

The study on which this chapter is based was stimulated by the lack of detailed educational research on the lower end of the private sector, as opposed
to the upper end – the Headmasters' Conference (HMC) or similar schools.
Increasing academic interest in the sector as a whole, rather than simply in
the up-market HMC and equivalent schools, is marked by publications such
as those by Griggs (1985) and Salter and Tapper (1985). This chapter, which
focuses on private schooling in South Wales and is based on research undertaken chiefly between 1984 and 1986, is thus a contribution to a discussion
that should serve to reduce confusion – academic, political and lay – as to the
diverse character of the private sector and the nature of the establishments
within it.

Since the mid-1980s circumstances have changed and many of the smaller
schools have altered their provision. Some have closed; others have opened;
yet others have expanded to capture new markets. Some single-sex schools
have become co-educational, while some of those that catered for secondary-
age children have opened primary departments or even added nurseries. It is
a characteristic of private education in the area of study – South Wales – that
the sector is fluid. Personal observation, however, suggests that the broad
conclusions reached at the time of the study remain valid and of continuing
interest.

The schools studied were located in the hinterland of a major port. Social
geography alone makes this an interesting area for research. The region is
dominated by one wealthy city – Cardiff – and its dormitory towns. The area
to the west of Cardiff is mainly given over to farming and to suburban communities with a substantial middle-class population. North of Cardiff and

the rural west lie the largely working-class towns of the Valleys, settlements whose origins lie in the industralization of South Wales in the late eighteenth and nineteenth centuries.

The area is characterized by a lack of former direct-grant schools. The one institution of genuine ancient foundation – a school in a rural market town – evolved naturally into a State grammar and subsequently comprehensive co-educational school. Only one school within the hinterland of Cardiff would probably qualify for 'public-school' status and this school declined partici-pation in the study. Parents who wish to send their children to high-status HMC and comparable schools therefore have to look outside the region. However, South Wales abounds in small private schools of a type sadly under-represented in the literature on independent schooling. These are run as businesses or as small charitable religious trusts.

The lack of expensive fee-paying schools makes South Wales atypical. However, it enables the focus to be thrown very sharply on establishments that appear to offer very little in the way of status or the building of old-boy networks. They represent none the less an alternative to the local State com-prehensive or primary schools. Most of their pupils attend on a day basis; there are very few boarders in the region studied.

This sector justifies study, not least because of the large number of pupils catered for. It would account, for example, for the larger part of the 11,500 children being educated in private schools in Wales alone in 1983 (Welsh Office, 1984). While, for example, Kalton (1966, p. 13) focuses on 166 HMC schools, one third of which were former direct-grant institutions, and the Labour Party identified 259 'public schools' (Labour Party, 1980, p. 5) in a discussion document of 1980, there is a vast range of smaller schools that deserve attention. The Independent Schools Information Service (ISIS) lists literally hundreds of schools in each of its regions and it is the many smaller private schools that are most accessible in terms of location and cost to parents dissatisfied or disillusioned with the local maintained sector.

In 1983 the Welsh Office listed some twenty non-maintained schools in the study region (Welsh Office, 1984). Some schools in this list proved impossible to contact. Conversely, Welsh Office information did not include the sec-ondary section recently developed as an adjunct to an existing tutorial col-lege. The fact is that there are few lists of independent schools and the Welsh Office's was not comprehensive. HMI are currently (1990) in the process of inspecting all of the independent schools in Wales; their records will pre-sumably be definitive. It should be noted that not all of the schools in the area belonged to ISIS, the umbrella organization for independent schools, or had their names lodged in the *Parents' Guide to Independent Schools*, a large volume published by SFIA Educational Trust. Twenty schools were eventually contacted but only twelve participated in the study. Two schools bluntly re-fused any contact and six schools ignored repeated requests for information beyond that provided by their prospectuses. These refusals to participate may have had as much to do with demands on heads' time as an inherent distrust of the survey. Those headteachers who participated were often extremely generous with information and time.

Ten schools were visited during the course of the survey. In these cases taped interviews were conducted with headteachers on the basis of previously prepared questionnaires. Two other schools completed questionnaires submitted to them. The anonymity of the respondent schools is protected throughout this chapter.

The headteachers who allowed themselves to be interviewed seemed, in general, sympathetic to the aims of this study, although uneasy sometimes about the taping of our conversation. One headmistress, who was otherwise very helpful and informative, was unwilling to be taped. Other heads were ready to answer in confidence as long as certain comments were made and information given with the tape-recorder switched off. In the light of the content of other interviews these precautions seemed unnecessary as the off-the-record comments often proved innocuous.

There is a clear disadvantage to this method of survey in that one may gain the impression of a school a headteacher intends, and little more. In fact, interviews varied considerably in the degree to which detailed information was given. One head read the contents of his punishment book for the term, while another was succinct in the extreme, answering only those questions that appeared on the questionnaire and discouraging discussion of specific points. Most responses fell between these two extremes.

Additional information was acquired by conducting a qualitative survey based on a snowball sample where ex-pupils, staff and some present-day pupils at small schools were contacted. The survey could not be a based on a precise sampling technique simply because there is little information as to the market for the services of private schools. It was not even possible to discover a gender breakdown though, as was discovered during the course of the study, there appears to be a discrepancy between what parents are prepared to pay for their sons and their daughters, with a corresponding effect on numbers of each gender at private schools.

GENERAL CHARACTERISTICS OF THE SCHOOLS

Obviously, the number of children attending any independent school will vary from year to year and even from term to term. Private schools in the study area, however, tended to accommodate far fewer pupils than the local maintained schools. The largest, a high-status secondary institution, had 400 girls in 1982, but generally respondent schools catered for between 120 and 270 pupils.

The Chairman of the Executive Council of the Independent Schools' Association in the region, interviewed in May 1985, noted that both boarding and day fees in Wales tend to be lower than in any other region of Britain

(*Western Mail*, 10 May 1985). In the schools studied, a sliding scale of fees was common, based on the age of pupils and their relative demands on the school's facilities. Fees were revised frequently, if not annually. In 1984 a parent of a senior-age day-pupil could expect to be paying between £1,000 and £1,500 per annum in fees. In addition there could have been extra charges for music tuition, for example, or examination fees. If outlay on the often rather elaborate school uniforms is taken into account, then it becomes obvious that for many parents entry into the lower end of the independent sector was not a cheap proposition, especially if more than one child was to be provided for.

The Assisted Places Scheme is not significant among the private schools of South and Mid-Glamorgan, although local parents may benefit from the scheme by sending their children to other schools in South Wales. A small primary school claimed to have received fees from the Social Services for an especially troubled child who could not tolerate the large numbers of children in a maintained school and who needed a watchful atmosphere.

A few of the schools offered scholarships or bursaries including the one school that supplied the choir for Llandaff Cathedral and that offered places on the basis of musicality as well as ability. In general, the opinion of the headteachers was sharply divided; one said, 'I do not need to give away what others are willing to pay for', whilst another suggested that scholarship children set the pace for children of lesser ability. Three schools said that they were flexible in respect of fees paid in cases of sudden hardship such as death or bankruptcy, but this could depend upon the child concerned. Headteachers were generally restrained in their comments upon matters of finance but at least one alluded to bad payments and litigation for unpaid fees.

Most of the schools visited boasted some degree of social mix and were at pains to avoid claims of exclusivity to the researcher. However, for the majority of working-class parents, these schools would be out of the question on financial grounds alone. Social variety for one head consisted of parents from 'trade, management and the professions' and for another it was that the sons of publicans mixed with the sons of 'old money'. Another, off the record, asserted that a certain school was for the children for 'Indian doctors and Pakistani grocers'. A fruitful area of study might be the extent to which schools of the kind being considered are valued by aspirant ethnic minority groups who mistrust State provision. This might be especially true where they are located within inner-city areas as the middle-class suburbs generally possess the better-regarded maintained schools.

Most co-educational schools reported that they had a significantly higher number of boys than girls. One school reported double the number of males. A deeper investigation would probably reveal interesting parental attitudes about willingness to pay for the education of girls and boys. Speculatively, it may be that the education of boys is more likely to be seen as problematical in some way, thus prompting parents to switch to independent education as part of a pragmatic solution to a specific problem. Older schools tended to be single sex and newer schools were co-educational. One headteacher expressed reservations that, by remaining single sex, half of the potential market for his school was excluded. This school has since become co-educational.

Pupil–teacher ratios lay between 1:13.4 and 1:9, averaging out at 1:11.75. These figures do not take into account the one privately run school that catered for children with special needs, which was intensively staffed. In maintained schools for the same period in Wales, pupil–teacher ratios were above 1:18. Of the classrooms visited in the private sector, many were very small and the advantage of low numbers may be counterbalanced by the fact that, in many schools, there did not appear to be more space per individual pupil. This may be of particular significance when dealing with primary-age children who are often less firmly fixed in their desks than are secondary-age pupils.

ADAPTATION TO CHANGE

It was noteworthy at the time of the study that, although the Conservative government ostensibly favoured independent schools, some of the schools may have been under considerable threat from economic recession and demographic trends. Attempts to widen the net of prospective consumers by expanding to co-education or nursery schools seem to be the survival techniques of the threatened, rather than evidence of a secure and confident future. If all were well, why would schools need to adapt? Projections drawn from Welsh Office statistics of 1983 and 1984 show a shortfall of some 500 pupils between the expected and the actual number attending private schools. Given the predicted decline in Welsh birth rates, this shortfall may be of considerable medium- and long-term significance. Some headteachers commented that the downturn in the economy since the late 1970s had had an influence on school numbers: 'We are not doing badly now, but were positively over-crowded in the late 70s/early 80s. Everyone wanted us then' (member of staff, sample school). 'One or two parents have given economic hardship as the reason for leaving... what with business not doing so well... even went bankrupt... but not many' (headteacher, sample school, taped interview). Here we had the clear paradox that a Conservative government with the pro-claimed aim of shedding dead weight in the economy may have done more to make life hard for the smaller and less exclusive schools by cutting away at business incomes than the previous Labour government, which had overseen an inflationary economy at a time when demographic trends increased the school-age population of Wales. Higher-status schools are unlikely to have suffered in the same way, as there will probably always be a market for the prestigious internationally or nationally known institution. Claims of ex-pansion further down the scale, perhaps, need to be treated with a modicum of caution.

IMAGE-MAKING AND THE PRIVATE SCHOOLS

In this context it is interesting to examine the manner in which the schools studied present themselves to potential customers and the methods they use to attract pupils.

Attitudes towards advertisement of services varied widely from school to school in the Cardiff area. One or two schools were very good customers of the local Press and had large boxed adverts in a variety of journals and free sheets. Others did not advertise at all. One headteacher remarked that it 'smacked of touting of custom, it makes for a bad image'. None advertised in the national Press where a wide variety of schools in the south of England frequently offer their services. Rather, the public image-making is maintained by rather more subtle means among the small schools of the Cardiff region.

Certainly local schools drew strength from the extent to which the national image of independent schools would seem to have been and remain good. Magazines often offer special supplements aimed at parents. A typical example appeared in the *Telegraph Sunday Magazine* for 18 November 1989 and contained the following: 'Private education has never been more popular or more expensive. . . . [A] widespread anxiety over aspects of the state system, in particular large classes, unruly behaviour, teaching which provides an insufficient challenge and unimpressive exam results. The Government's new reforms – a compulsory national curriculum. . .will lead to improvements in time'. As has been noted, it is of course true that the reforms the government is imposing on the maintained sector will not apply to private schools.

In 1983 and 1984, whole pages were taken by ISIS in the local Press of South Wales. Editorial articles written by the then chairman of South Wales ISIS would appear. These had the tone of friendly advice-giving and such was their frequency that one was entitled 'What! More about schools' but although they were careful not to mention political parties and organizations of any kind, political polemic would creep in. The following paragraph appeared in an article from the *South Wales Echo*, 31 March 1984:

> Were, by some sensational stroke, maintained sector schools able to emulate the flexibility; individuality; adaptability to special styles, needs and considerations; versatility in building, syllabuses and the mobile approach of their teachers, of independent schools such that the latter were to be driven out of business, then a government of any colour could move in and take over, imposing uniformity first and then a stereotyped education wide open to indoctrination.

Indeed, in the public presentation of the application of market values to education, and in the identification of the private sector with 'traditional standards', ISIS has been very influential, both as an organization uniting all sections of the independent sector, and as a propaganda body stating the public case for private schools and providing defenders of fee-paying with ammunition to combat Labour policy.

Documents such as *Independent Schools – the Facts* (ISIS, 1982b), *Independent Schools – The Right to Survive* (ISIS, 1981) and *Freedom Under Fire* (ISIS, 1982a) spearheaded the defence of private schools in the run-up to the 1983 General Election. ISIS publications were often made use of in Press advertising on behalf of schools in the study region, for example in the *South Wales Echo*.

Freedom Under Fire, for instance, presents a State monopoly on education as a step along the road to totalitarianism: 'people who want to abolish independent schools also shout loudly against Fascism and Racialism in other countries; talk about apartheid and they deplore it'. Opponents of the private sector are associated with the 'insensitive planners who approved the tower blocks and built the over large comprehensive schools, both of which are recognised as disasters' (*ibid*.) A mixed economy in education is seen as an essential element in British society and of 'the British genius in government' (*ibid*.). The stress is placed on parental choice and the freedom to pay as basic human rights. The belief of many parents that their children should be educated in a school 'which has a Christian foundation and where Christian values are stressed' (*ibid*.) is emphasized.

If ISIS publications and schools' advertising in the local Press were calculated to appeal to parents dissatisfied with the maintained sector and hankering after 'traditional standards', prospectuses present the image of individual schools to prospective purchasers in the educational market.

Descriptions in advertisements of the independent schools in Mid- and South Glamorgan tended to be fairly factual, detailing such items as small classes or the age-range of the children who would be considered for a place at the school. This means that, until more HMI reports are published, parents will have to base their choice of schools on largely impressionistic grounds. Their first source of information must be the prospectus. These productions varied enormously among the schools contacted – from cyclostyled sheets to glossy colour productions. Despite the potential impact of a well-produced prospectus, glossy productions were in the minority. It is the content that has, therefore, to bear scrutiny and whose approach is relevant to this study.

Two of the prospectuses carried handwritten invitations from the headteacher to the prospective parent to visit the school. The schools that were too well known locally to require aggrandizement through the prospectus were the ones that tended to offer the most basic of material, but others contained considerable detail including an analysis of GCE results over a period of time.

Many of the texts were illustrated with elegant line drawings of the school badge or symbol. They attempted to establish a sense of tradition. One school had the prospectus printed in a particular lurid purple; this represented the uniform shade and also the colour of the entrance hall of the building! Many offered a potted history of the school and made play of the date of establishment, in one case, 1870. Even the headmaster of the latter school was willing to admit that it had changed a great deal in character since its foundation. In even the most perfunctory prospectus, certain key words and expressions recur:

> imitation of the good Grammar Schools of yesteryear
> offering a traditional academic education
> The School provides traditional and academic tuition
> the school is in historic setting
> distinguished record, offering an education that is both traditional in its approach and [. . .]

The economic basis for these small and, in the frequently repeated words of the ex-pupils, 'tatty' little schools, seems to be that they cater not only for those who would automatically send their children to private schools but also for those who mistrust or misunderstand recent educational innovation. This view was supported by the number of schools that had their junior-school desks arranged in neat rows rather than in the more usual groups or tables of the State-maintained primary school.

School uniforms played an important part on the image-making of the private schools. Delamont (1980, p. 51) has already raised the class implications of uniform. The very ornateness of uniform seems to preclude its being bought at a chain store and the colour schemes were frequently very striking. Hues were unusual, even violent, for quite young children – purples, browns, maroons and royal blues, rather than the easy-buy and easy-launder greys and blacks of the local State-school children. Hats and caps were still worn in some of the schools. Headteachers were conscious of the advertising potential of the uniform: 'For a big school like A, the uniforms are seen all about the city whereas we are a bit out of the way here' (headteacher, sample school). 'Our girls were known as the "purple pleases"' (headteacher, sample school). It takes little effort of the imagination to see how schools can capitalize on the association in the mind of the purchasing parent with the high-status grammar schools of their youth and, of course, with the elaborate and archaic clothing that was once demanded by very high-status public schools. Parents certainly respond to this; one of my sample said: 'They pour out of B (State comprehensive) looking like nothing on earth. . . but X (child on same estate) looked really nice. . . I saw him waiting for the school bus. . . like a little man'. Another said: 'I couldn't wait to see him in it, he *did* look smart. . . I could have eaten him up, he was gorgeous'. Ex-pupils of these small private schools were ambivalent in their attitude to uniform. Some had enjoyed feelings of exclusivity and parental admiration but others felt frankly exposed in a hostile neighbourhood. One interviewee reported that he had waited for the school bus to go around the corner at night and, even in winter, had stripped himself of all distinguishing marks including blazer, scarf and cap before sprinting home to change. Once in play clothes he was perfectly acceptable to his friends but in the school uniform he was prey to taunting and the threat of physical abuse.

Once parents have been attracted to a school by such things as reputation or prospectus, it is likely that an invitation to visit the head will follow. The headteachers' offices themselves are very comfortable, almost reminiscent of the film set view of a school. Cups, trophies, books and tea on china cups in front of a coal fire were the norm. Gowns were hung casually behind doors, suggesting that academic robes are actually worn in the schools. These rooms are obviously of significance because they are important in creating impressions for the visitor. Staffrooms, where visited, were frequently much shabbier and the headteacher's office was often much larger than many of the actual teaching rooms of the school.

LOCATION AND ACCOMMODATION

When the study was undertaken, it was expected that there would be geographical links between areas of affluence and the physical location of independent schools. This simple relationship did not appear. As schools were visited, it seemed that this link was of less significance than the availability of suitable accommodation. Private schools in the Cardiff region are an inner-city and an Edwardian suburban phenomenon, contrary to claims made in the Labour Party document (Labour Party, 1980, pp. 43–7). Areas that have become densely populated with houses that could be described as 'executive-style' homes on large estates or that have grown up since World War Two have no private schools. The large town of Barry has few suitable large Victorian buildings and those that could house a school have no land available, so there are no schools. The much smaller genteel residential district of Penarth had four private schools, one of which closed in 1985. Another school became co-educational during the same period, but housed its girls in a separate building bought for that purpose. It seems that parents who are prepared to pay for an education are also prepared to pay the cost of transporting their children and most of the schools claimed very large catchment areas. Given this, an inner-city location makes good commercial sense providing a central and easily accessible service for a large number of parents employed in the business district of the city.

While HMC schools are often located in the homes of the former country gentry and aristocracy, smaller independent schools are just as firmly located in the domestic buildings of the former middle classes. Two of the sample schools occupied large rectory buildings that had been replaced by smaller and more comfortable modern buildings. Others were villas of Edwardian or 'stockbroker Tudor' style and one newly opened school was housed in the abandoned head office of a public utility. The size of class possible in rooms designed for household purposes is one severe limitation upon the size of the schools. Many had extended into small terrapin extensions. Play areas were occasionally very small but this was not universally the case. Some schools had to rely on outside agencies to provide sports facilities. Local-authority leisure centres were used for this purpose and one school rented facilities from a nearby charitable institution. The two boarding schools visited did have large areas of land adjoining. In these cases, the land was not allocated to any particular purpose but was under grass or playing fields. One school owned up to nine acres of adjacent fields, much of it, one might guess, of high value as prime development land.

Facilities to which particular attention was paid in the prospectuses of the South Wales schools often proved to be less exciting when viewed in reality. The language laboratory of one school was housed in what may have been the dressing room of the original occupant and could have housed three pupils beside the teacher at most. The researcher is in no position to judge laboratory equipment when seen, but the libraries were frequently shabby and, more telling, seemed to be dusty and ill-used. In contrast all the schools appeared well equipped with computers. This seems to be one way in which the schools benefit from the extreme goodwill of parents. One of the head-teachers pointed out that he had received a great deal of superseded business hardware and software as a donation.

In the main, however, the impression schools offered was of something familiar and well known. Desks in primary classes unfashionably tended to be in rows rather than blocks – a limitation often of the accommodation of schools in premises built as private houses. Blackboards and a strong smell of chalk were pervasive, although schools did have whiteboards and OHP equipment. There may well be an element of financial stringency about these arrangements but they are also directly reminiscent of the schools parents themselves remember. In one school the sound of children chanting tables was heard. In another, the multiplication tables appeared as a poster.

Very significantly in terms of the politics of education in Wales, none of the schools visited offered the Welsh language as a subject at the time of the study, although many of the primary schools offered conversational French.

Some schools that were geographically close to each other shared facilities. A single-sex girls' and a single-sex boys' school opened their A-level classes to members of each other's sixth form. In this case the co-operation appeared to work well because there was no overlap of market for pupils.

THE PERCEIVED ADVANTAGE OF
THE PRIVATE SECTOR

If fee-charging schools are not able to offer significantly improved facilities, what do they offer beyond the possible kudos of being known to pay for your children's schooling? Indeed, ex-pupils themselves were often extremely aware of what they had missed by attending a school that necessarily had to offer a grammar-school curriculum because there were very few facilities for practical, art and craft subjects or too few pupils to make up a worthwhile club or rugby team: 'I would have enjoyed Drama, but not enough other people were interested to make up the number for a club so I had to join an adult group' (male, 24 years, sample school). Ex-pupils claimed to have gained precisely the benefit that Fox (1985) says that parents who have been mobile into the service class are looking for, although it should be noted that Fox only studied HMC parents: 'Some parents believe that in addition to the possession of the necessary qualities and skills to compete in the market place it is important to believe in oneself and to have that ability to convince others of one's worth' (*ibid*. p. 59). It is interesting to speculate how precisely this long-term change in outlook was achieved. Ex-pupils attributed their change in outlook to a number of things, such as small classes and the feeling of being known to the whole school: 'It may be as a result of being aware of privilege, as you say, but I think too that I felt sheltered from the worst of it outside' (female, 24 years, sample school).

Sociologists are familiar with the 'A stream mentality' from the work of Lacey (1970). In a school where there is only one entry class per year, it might be that pupils are freed from the burden of being in the 'thick class'. This may be of special significance if, as is likely, many of the children are of average or lower-than-average ability.

Parents and ex-pupils report that the decision to send a particular child to a private school is often made for pragmatic reasons. Many of the ex-pupils had received a portion of their education within the State-maintained sector or had siblings who were being or were educated in LEA schools. Among older ex-pupils the decision to 'go private' was often as a simple response to 11+ failure: 'I failed the 11+ but my mother believed me to be bright; I suppose I am. The whole family believed in a good education and so the decision was made and I went to X [a sample school] a grammar [*sic*] school'. Constantly recurring phrases were used in their discussion, many of which could have come from the advertising literature of the schools: better discipline, smaller classes, better atmosphere. Some of these are assumptions but they do not lack value for that – parents and pupils appear to fear the large scale and anonymity of maintained schools, being prepared to accept the often poorer facilities for a sense of belonging.

Another consistent theme, particularly among younger age groups, is bullying, which was both actual and potential. Many local comprehensives have fearsome reputations for bullying and for initiation rites, which take place outside the school grounds and which are therefore not the province of the school to control:

> They've got this tree outside Middle School and the third years catch all the second years and throw them in it and the boy I know nearly lost his eye because it's got these really big thorns and everybody gets thrown in and the teachers don't do anything as it's outside school.
>
> (Male, 11 years, sample school)

Measor and Woods (1984, pp. 16ff.) cover this ground very thoroughly and emphasize the mythical nature of some of the tales told. Certainly, it is difficult to tell to what extent the respondents actually were bullied as incidents described were few, and unspecific in content. 'They called me names because

I'm foreign', came from a 25-year-old of southern European origin. The intensity of name calling is hard to judge, but the effect appears to have been traumatic. If one accepts that bullying may be as much a factor of personality as much as social class or school locale, then the much smaller scale of the independent school alone seems to offer some measure of protection or guarantee that the culprits will be caught. The small school can live up to its own reputation even though most schools must have suffered incidents of petty theft and violence. Some of the ex-pupils noted that the schools could also tolerate mildly deviant behaviour: 'The main disadvantage was that the school was very tolerant of eccentric, undisciplined or anti-social behaviour. Everyone developed a strong, very distinct character, which may not always have been an advantage later. You could say that we did not get the corners knocked off us' (female, 27 years, sample school). This point is echoed by Punch (1977, p. 58) in his study of Dartington Hall School, which was renowned for its toleration (even celebration) of eccentricity.

The schools were beneficiaries of some very generous gifts from parents and fund raising for charity was also important. HMI found that one very small school had raised over £1,000 for charity through fêtes and sponsored activities (Welsh Office/HMI, 1985 p. 22). A subsidiary benefit of this fund-raising activity is that the schools often found themselves in the local papers as a result of it! Parents who were questioned on the voluntary donations made to the school did not perceive their contributions as tips or gratuities:

> if you are paying for young children, then you are willing to pay and pay and go on paying. It's the only thing to do if you want the best. What can you do? It goes on Christmas rubbish, it goes on the school; which do you think is best?

Such evidence might tend to support the Labour Party assertion (1980) that the existence of private schools deprives the State sector of some very committed parents.

There is, too, an informal influence that parents feel they have over the education they pay for, as opposed to that provided 'freely' by the State:

> I had some rows with the headmaster [of a State primary] over [a particular educational approach] and eventually he refused to see me except at the PTA which he chaired. Here [the independent school] at least he'll see me. I don't know what good it does, but he is polite.
>
> (Parent, sample school)

The headteachers of the schools visited expressed quite polarized views when questioned on the influence of parents. These responses could be categorized in two ways and are exemplified by the quotations that follow. Only further and more detailed research would show how far these responses were for the benefit of a visitor or if they actually expressed the relationship between fee-paying parent and headteacher:

1. *The 'fall over backwards' response:* 'We have a reputation for adaptability here. . .pace-setters. . .consumer orientated.'

2. *The 'you get what you pay' for response:* 'Parents know what we offer. If they like it they pay. We have a reputation.'

This would suggest that one of the attractions of the independent sector for some parents is the fact that they can express interest in their child through the medium of being a paying customer. Parents would seem to prefer this means of expression rather than through formal membership of committees, such as governing bodies. Further research would have to be done to test this assertion properly.

It was during the interviews with the headteachers that the influence of parental attitudes to the school came to the fore. It became apparent, for example, when questioning turned to matters of discipline. When head-teachers were asked to comment on extreme cases of indiscipline, their remarks would often be prefaced with 'parents were beginning to comment'. It was clear that in any case where expulsion or suspension had been con-sidered necessary, a deciding factor had been how parents would respond when the story got home. Independent headteachers may have to be respon-sive to parents in a way that State-sector headteachers do not. It would have been too much to expect any of the headteachers to admit to unwarranted parental interference and so the question was not asked at the time, though perhaps with recent changes in school structure in the maintained sector, it might have more validity today.

CONCLUSIONS

Since the study was originally undertaken, there have been many ways in which legislation has introduced change into the structure, management and curriculum of maintained schools. However, issues that were of interest in the mid-1980s remain crucial. It is possible that a combination of recent government initiatives and public anxiety about provision in the State sector will drive parents to seek alternatives to LEA schools including schools that have opted out. But in any case, the work done by Fox (1985) needs to be extended if we are to understand the aspirations of parents who are going to have a far greater say in the running of maintained-sector schools in the future.

Independent schools at the lower end of the market-place, particularly those run as a business, rather than enjoying the high financial benefits of being educational trusts, operate within a market and are vulnerable to its fluctuations. For smaller schools, existence is precarious and this would be true whatever the political or moral climate. When rolls fall or costs increase, the small size of the schools does not give them much of a safety net. There are obvious grounds for anxiety about a situation where educational decisions are quite so vulnerable to financial considerations.

Some recent research, such as the essays in Walford (1984) and the work of Tapper and Salter (1984), Fox (1985) and Johnson (1987) looks in a new way at the independent sector, at parental concerns, and at the relationship between the private sector and the State. This chapter has tried to lift the veil a little on the type of private school that excites little comment but may be more representative of the sector and thus of the parents within it than larger and more famous institutions. There is room for a far more detailed and larger survey of such schools. In particular, this might yield a more objective understanding of what they offer and the values they transmit through their clientele to society at large.

REFERENCES

Bamford, T. W. (1967) *Rise of the Public Schools*, Nelson, London.
Delamont, S. (1980) *Sex Roles and the School*, Methuen, London.
Fox, I. (1985) *Private Schools and Public Issues*, Macmillan, London.
Griggs, C. (1985) *Private Education in Britain*, Falmer Press, Lewes.
ISIS (1981) *Independent Schools – The Right to Survive*, London.
ISIS (1982a) *Freedom Under Fire*, London.
ISIS (1982b) *Independent Schools – The Facts*, London.
Johnson, D. (1987) *Private Schools and State Schools*, Open University Press, Milton Keyner.
Kalton, G. (1966) *The Public School: A Factual Survey*, Longman, London.
Labour Party (1980) *Private Schools – A Discussion Document*, London.
Lacey, C. (1970) *Hightown Grammar*, Manchester University Press.
Measor, L. and Woods, P. (1984) *Changing Schools: Pupil Perspectives on Transfer to a Comprehensive*, Open University Press, Milton Keynes.
Punch, M. (1977) *Progressive Retreat*, Cambridge University press.
Salter, B. and Tapper, T. (1985) *Power and Policy in Education*, Falmer Press, Lewes.
SFIA Educational Trust (1984) *The Parents' Guide to Independent Schools*, Maidenhead.
Tapper, T. and Salter, B. (1984) Images of independent schooling: exploring the perceptions of parents and politicians, in G. Walford (ed.) (1984), op. cit.
Walford, G. (ed.) (1984) *British Public Schools: Policy and Practice*, Falmer Press, Lewes.
Welsh Office (1984) *Statistics of Education in Wales*, Vol. 8, Government Statistical Service, Cardiff.
Welsh Office/HMI (1985) *Report by HM Inspectors on Clive Hall School, Cardiff, South Glamorgan*, Welsh Office, Cardiff.

7

MUSLIM PRIVATE SCHOOLS

Pauline Dooley

MUSLIMS IN BRITAIN

Muslims form the largest religious 'minority' in Britain. One estimate of their numbers claims there are two million (Ashraf, 1987). Most are immigrants or descended from immigrants who came to Britain in the 1950s and 1960s from troubled situations in Cyprus, Malaysia, the Middle East, Africa, Bangladesh and India. They came in search of security and jobs, the majority settling in the five main conurbations of Greater London, the West Midlands, West Yorkshire, South Lancashire and Central Clydeside, often employed in manufacturing industries. Many members of that first generation may have had a relative lack of fluency in English and have become conscious of a loss of community identity in Britain – their experience of British education policies eroded, rather than developed, a Muslim community identity.

The Islamic religion is described by its adherents as a 'full way of life'. Religious beliefs permeate everyday aspects of living: dress, food, cleanliness as well as prayer, its forms and times. Thus some accommodation is required by schools in Britain. Fundamentalist Muslims believe that this has not been understood by non-Muslim parents and teachers. They want a modern, quality education that also conforms to the Sharia (Islamic Law), laid down in the tenth century and little changed since (Hiskett, 1989). However, aspects of Western society conflict with these Muslim beliefs, making it difficult for them to live in a non-Muslim country. Particular difficulties arise over the materialistic basis of Western culture, individual- and competition-based learning methods, co-education and the way religion is taught.

These are made more difficult by the complexity of British attitudes to Muslims, and images of Islam in the media have doubtless contributed to ignorance and prejudice. The rise of Islamic fundamentalism in Muslim states must affect those in Muslim minority groups (Halstead, 1986) as well as non-Muslims who read about it.

Of particular importance has been the recent Salman Rushdie affair, which has increased British fear of Muslims. The author questioned the Muslim faith in his novel *Satanic Verses* and, in response, the late Ayatollah Khomeini issued a death sentence for apostasy and urged British Muslims to carry this out. Since, that time Rushdie has been in hiding, and a formerly peaceful protest by Muslims has developed into anti-Rushdie marches, and calls for book-banning and book-burning ceremonies. In Bradford, which has a history of good race relations, temperatures have run high with 'racial violence' by groups of white youths (*Guardian*, 18 July 1989).

The speed of events, the confusion of Middle East politics with the Muslim faith and the lack of understanding regarding Muslims and free speech apparently create fear in a nominally Christian population and a willingness to accept 'fundamentalists' as the Muslim norm. This creates suspicion, a lack of sympathy and even hostility towards Muslim requirements of education.

In Britain there is no specific education policy for Muslims because they are categorized as an 'ethnic minority'. Ashraf (1987, p. 84) sums up the education policies for minority groups as follows:

> In the typical pragmatic British way, the policies have been changing towards 'immigrants' and now the 'ethnic minorities'. Government at first took a laissez-faire attitude (Rose, 1969). The newcomers, including the Muslims, were expected to be absorbed into the majority society. As attention was drawn to the educational disadvantage of the people a new policy of integration started emerging. At first, the policy was categorically assimilationist. By 1965 when it was realized that the chances of assimilation were remote, the authorities started talking of a multi-cultural society. By 1977 the concept of a multi-cultural curriculum emerged in a Green Paper entitled 'Education in Schools: A Consultative Document'. It is 'unity in diversity' that Swann Committee stated in 'Education for All' (DES, 1985). The idea is the reorientation of our education system to serve a multi-racial society (HMSO, 1978).

MUSLIM EXPECTATIONS OF EDUCATION

By developing their own private schools, some Muslims have made it clear that 'assimilation', 'integration' and even 'multiculturalism' have been unsatisfactory. These policies have developed unevenly across local authorities and in some cases remained rhetorical gestures. Even where multiculturalism is practical some Muslims would claim that Islam is not adequately taught.

The Swann Report, *Education for All* (DES, 1985), a government inquiry 'into the Education of Children from Ethnic minority groups', stressed the need for a pluralistic perspective to permeate a school, with education for cultural diversity. The majority report comes out against the 'isolationist' policy of 'separate schools', although a minority report supports them until current schooling is fair to all children.

A document evaluating Swann (Islamic Academy/Islamic Cultural Centre, 1985) from a Muslim point of view was promptly published by the Islamic Academy, Cambridge ('an Islamic study centre of recognised excellence') and the Islamic Cultural Centre, London ('a widely respected Islamic cultural institution') (Hiskett, 1989, p. 24). These institutions claim to speak for the Muslim community but, in practice, may not represent the majority of Muslims in Britain: 'there is much written and anecdotal evidence to show that the first generation "Muslim in the street" is somewhat more eclectic in his attitudes than the rhetoric of the "Ulama" [religious leader] suggests' (Hiskett, 1989, p. 9).

The joint Islamic Academy/Islamic Cultural Centre document supports the desire to allow communities to remain distinct and to combat racism, yet cannot accept their means of doing so. It condemns the Swann Report as being based on secularist philosophy, which can never cater 'for the growth of man in all his aspects: spiritual, intellectual, imaginative, physical, scientific, linguistic. . . and motivate all these aspects towards goodness and the attainment of perfection. The ultimate aim of Muslim education lies in the realization of complete submission to God' (*ibid.* para. 3.2).

The document is critical of Swann's stance on cultural pluralism, which is based on 'rationally justifiable shared values' (*ibid.* para. 3.3(b)) because the judgement of what is 'rational' and 'shared' will be made by one group. As Jones (1986, pp. 108–9) suggests:

> rationality itself is problematic in a pluralistic context. We are probably safe in assuming that validity would not be an issue in which cultures are likely to clash.
> But rationality involves more than agreement on the valid forms of argument. It also involves agreement on basic prejudgements which are problematic in that they are assumptions basic to various culturally 'vouched' for ways of looking/modes of reasoning, but are themselves intractable to any known verification procedure. . . .
> In an important sense, foundational prejudgements are 'articles of faith'.

He compares the Western cosmology of physics and the Islamic theistic cosmology and criticizes Swann for failing to recognize that the 'rational' views of two groups in British society contradict each other.

On 'shared values' the Islamic Academy holds the view that what the majority secular group judge as shared will certainly be anti-Muslim: 'The multicultural curriculum. . .will reflect the cultural heritage of the selector, and lead to cultural domination in disguise by the selector's group' (Islamic Academy/Islamic Cultural Centre, 1985, para. 3.3(c)). The 'national values' Swann wants schools to transmit 'are devised basically from pseudo Judaeo-Christian and mainly secularist stances, which do not take account of values upheld by the Muslim, Hindu, Sikhs, Buddhist and other faith communities' (*ibid.* para. 4.1).

This secularist stance on religion, reinforced in school life, is considered particularly objectionable as it does not imbue pupils with any feeling for spirituality. The teaching of the school conflicts with any religious teaching at home and some young Muslims find themselves in home and school lives 'between two cultures' (Anwar, 1981). In consequence, some Muslim parents prefer to send their children to Church of England, rather than county schools, as these at least support a 'confessionalist' approach to religion (See, for example, *The Listener*, 1 February 1990).

Swann's particular values of autonomy and a critical approach to one's faith and culture are not those of Islam. Muslim pupils, the Islamic Academy/ Islamic Cultural Centre (1985, para. 3.3 (c)) argue, may be taught to be critical 'only after their spiritual and intellectual powers have been properly disciplined'. Halstead (1986, p. 36) argues that there are different forms of autonomy: 'In strong autonomy the principal of rational deliberation is developed into the belief that all assumptions should be challenged and that all beliefs must be held open to a vigorous criticism based on rationality'. This is the position supported by Swann. However, the Muslim position is not incompatible with 'weak autonomy' in which a person has internalized the process of deliberation and is not unreflective or uncritical of authority.

Another Muslim value is that of the importance of group (Badawi, 1979). Individual excellence is balanced with that of the group: issues involving the survival of the community have a high priority. This is not only incompatible with Western individualism and competitiveness, but almost incompatible with the multicultural school. The Islamic Academy/Islamic Cultural Centre reject Swann's case for a 'pluralistic perspective' on all these grounds.

Although Western and Islamic education seem incompatible in several respects, this criticism represents the most extreme Muslim views. Many needs of the Muslim community, as some schools have demonstrated, can be met by compromise within the State school system.

One request of the Muslim community, according to the Muslim Educational Trust (Sarwar, 1983) is that of mother-tongue education. They wish minority community languages to be maintained in schools or the teaching of them to be carried out as part of the modern-languages curriculum. Swann acknowledged this but saw it as 'best achieved within the minority communities themselves, rather than within mainstream schools' (DES, 1985, para. 31.5). Only some LEAs therefore make provision for this teaching. All Muslims need Arabic, to study the Qur'ān and Hadith (traditions and sayings of Mohammed) but, although there are syllabuses and examinations for GCSE and A-level standards, it is not often available as a language option in schools. Another adaptation to the curriculum suggested by Sarwar (1983) is that Muslims should not attend lessons in music, dance, art and sex education.

The Sharia (Islamic Law) includes prescriptions on food, dress and prayer (*ibid*. 1983). Most food is permissible except meat which is not halal (lawful), i.e. slain in the name of Allah. Dress for women includes a *shalwar-qamis* (trousers and pinafore) and a *chador* (headscarf) for secondary pupils.

Muslims need to attend daily ablutions and obligatory prayers, which mostly fall in school hours and require a room being available.

In particular, prayer-rooms may be difficult to provide in some crowded schools, though in Birmingham, where there is a high proportion of Muslims, many schools do. However, the headteacher of a Sparkbrook school, a practising Christian, refused to make such provision and sent Muslim children home when she found them praying in the school car park. Muslim leaders asked for her resignation and dismissal (*Times*, 26 May 1988).

None of these requirements is totally incompatible with Western schooling and, particularly where there are large numbers of Muslims, could be acceptable. Bradford LEA, for example, has provided halal meat to Muslim children since 1983 (Sarwar, 1983); the *shalwar-qamis* is acceptable school dress in many inner-city schools. Yet repeatedly there are incidents showing that schools are unable to compromise on these issues.

At Altrincham Girls' Grammar School, where Muslims wear *shalwar-qamis* and have a prayer-room, two girls asked to wear their *chadors* and were forbidden to do so by the headteacher who considered scarves a safety hazard in PE and science lessons. The governors banned them but after two years of disagreement, in 1990, the girls took a stand and started wearing their scarves to school. Following coverage in the national Press, the school governors amended their rule allowing scarves to be worn in the school colours (*Guardian*, 26 January 1990). According to one of the girls, 'We are not fanatics or fundamentalists. We just want the right to continue our education and practice our faith' (*Guardian*, 19 January 1990). It is interesting to note here that an otherwise accommodating school allowed this issue over uniforms to prevent girls receiving their education, and that the girls themselves, denying outside pressure, chose to make a stand. The school had received no complaints regarding the curriculum.

MUSLIM PRIVATE SCHOOLS

Whilst some Muslims are content to attend LEA schools with their varying degrees of adaptation, other Muslims have felt the need to establish their own private schools to provide a satisfactory education.

There are about fifteen private Muslim day schools in Britain, sponsored by the Muslim community and fee-paying pupils. They are a relatively recent phenomenon; the first was founded in 1979 but they have developed from supplementary schools, which have existed as long as Muslims have been here. Along with the churches and the synagogues, the mosques have always made their own supplementary position to the education system.

Sparkbrook, Birmingham, for example (Homan, 1985), has an evening school run five days per week by volunteers, all Muslims, who teach the Qur'ān, Islamic Studies and Arabic (the language of the Qur'ān) in single-sex classes. Similar arrangements can be found in most of Britain's 350 Mosques.

Day schools are a natural development of such classes. All of the Muslim schools in Britain are private schools that, unlike many Church of England and Roman Catholic schools, do not obtain any government aid. Many readers of this chapter will be unaware of the nature of Muslim schools, so there follows descriptions of the schools visited.

Islamic College, London, was founded in 1985 and has seventy pupils with a waiting-list of thirty. The twelve staff are all Muslim and all have qualified teacher status; moreover, they are paid on the same salary scale as teachers in any State school. In this one-form entry school, most classes have between twelve and fourteen pupils in a wide mixed-ability group. Fees in 1990 were £300 per year and the ability of parents to pay is sufficient qualification for a boy to enter the school. Additional expenses are met by donations. According to the school prospectus (1989), 'The curriculum reflects the unique orientations of the school combining together aspects of temporal and moral education. . . so that the pupil can successfully face the realities of life, with the combined force of secular qualifications and sound moral values'. The curriculum comprises English, Mathematics, Biology, Chemistry, PE, Physics, Geography, Craft, Design and Technology (CDT), History (Islamic and General), Fiqh (Islamic jurisprudence), Tajweed (Science of Qur'ānic recitation), Aqaid (Beliefs), Arabic, Bengali and Urdu. Most of these are compulsory and English is the medium of instruction.

The school is housed in a tall terraced house. Narrow stairways make the simultaneous passage of boys up and down the stairs difficult, and classrooms are small with few noticeboards. The small classes fit in adequately, though in one room, where a snooker table is set up, space is tight. The tiny staffroom is also used for computer teaching; PE takes place in a hired hall and CDT involves work on a boat on the river. Scientific equipment is minimal, so the teacher relies greatly on demonstration rather than experiments by the pupils; there is no microscope, so projector slides are shown. GCSE examinations in eight subjects including English, Maths and Science, were taken by the pupils in 1990. Islamic studies was added in 1991.

The school would like to increase its roll but would certainly need larger premises. An HMI report in 1990 expressed itself as satisfied with progress but commented on the need for better accommodation. However, an application by the school to purchase the buildings of a recently closed school in the same road has been turned down by the LEA.

Islamic College maintains a close relationship with the local Muslim community and parents are encouraged to visit; there is a steady stream of visitors for the headteacher throughout the day. Homework diaries are completed daily and signed by parents.

School discipline, according to the prospectus (1989), includes 'observance of Islamic etiquettes [*sic*] and culture' and a merit system provides awards for behaviour, punctuality, etc.: 'to stimulate healthy competition'. The school Registrar, in an interview, explained that such a social curriculum could only be provided by a Muslim head and Muslim teachers: 'We give them a way of life'.

Discussions were held with four of the five classes centring on how their school differed from other, non-Muslim schools. The subject of racism from teachers and fighting among pupils was frequently raised: 'Here we're all brothers'. One felt that their teachers cared about them more, and understood their parents more than teachers in other schools. Some pupils complained about the lack of facilities in the school for practical lessons in languages and science: 'It is not a real school', said one who was about to leave.

On the need for Muslim schools, these pupils' opinions were very mixed: some spoke of the need for 'Islamic ethos' whilst others felt they would be happy in any school where they were understood. The career plans of the fourth form included becoming 'an *imam*' (prayer leader), 'an engineer', 'a politican for the Muslim party' and 'a footballer or a football teacher'.

Muslim Girls' High School, Leicester, has 109 pupils and a waiting-list. There are five full-time teachers, three part time and a headteacher receiving five hours per week remission for her role. The teachers of Maths and Urdu are Muslim; the rest, including the head, are not. The headteacher stresses that the teachers are chosen for their quality – degrees and qualifications count for much more than being Muslim. As the school does not teach Islamic Studies the small number of Muslim staff is not seen as a problem. The school is in buildings attached to and owned by the mosque, and the girls attend supplementary classes at the mosque every school night and Saturday morning.

This close relationship with the mosque enables the school to exist with a staffing policy that allows non-Muslim staff, yet it also makes some restrictions. For example, the school day has to be timed to allow pupils to attend mosque classes. While some forms of art are highly valued, representations of humans and animals are criticized and such artwork on the walls has, in the past, been taken down by mosque members. The reputation of the mosque is 'fundamentalist' so it is assumed, incorrectly, that the school is also. The headteacher would prefer separate premises.

Rows of shoes line the corridor from which lead the eight schoolrooms including a staffroom. Over coffee and biscuits (for those not fasting during Ramadan), staff discuss the morning's sports lesson in a nearby hall during which some girls complained of lethargy due to their fasting. It seemed that some took advantage during this period, using weakness as an excuse for homework not done and uniforms not washed or ready for school. In the corridor they sounded lively enough. The staff themselves enjoy the school because it is a small, close, single-sex community: none complained about receiving less than the standard scale of pay.

The girls, according to the headmistress, enjoy it for similar reasons: they do not feel harassed by other pupils or discriminated against by staff. She tells how teachers in other schools sometimes under-estimate the girls, particularly if they are Asian – for example, encouraging one girl to become a nurse when she was more interested in, and capable of, becoming a doctor. Most importantly, the school is trusted by the parents, which means high attendance and a good relationship – which the headteacher builds up by house visiting. Only because of this, she feels, can the girls have access to education and careers. She argues that some parents will keep their daughters at home rather than send them to a mixed or non-Muslim school. At this school they have access to a curriculum that includes GCSEs in nine subjects (e.g. Chemistry, History and Childcare, despite limited facilities). Having spent their adolescence in the safety of the school and the foundations of their faith well-formed, girls may find that their parents allow them to attend mixed further and higher education colleges in their more settled post-school years.

An interview with five of the girls suggested that they particularly enjoyed the school for its freedom from harassment and its friendly atmosphere. 'We're all friends, it's a community, it's why I like to come here.' 'I can get on with my studies here, I don't have to justify myself.' 'In the other school we were teased about taking our shoes off.' Each girl had some idea about her future: 'We aren't going to get married straight away, there's no need now. I'm going to study Law or Medicine'. Another planned to go into further education but wasn't sure whether her parents would allow her to; yet another was anxious about her future mother-in-law.

King Fahad Academy, London, is unique in Britain in being a financially well-endowed Muslim school. Funded by Saudia Arabia, it was founded to cater for the children of Saudi diplomats who wanted an education similar to that at home; it also takes in children from across London in response to Muslim demand. New buildings were added to a clossed-down school and the college opened in 1985.

The school entrance is staffed by a security guard and opens into a large light entrance hall; a model of the school is centrally placed in a glass case, and pictures of Saudi leaders adorn the walls.

The Registrar in his open-plan office is used to welcoming visitors. At the time of the visit, the school secretary was sitting at the next desk mailing letters to those who had taken the college entrance examination in March. Of the 680 who applied (fees are 'less than £2,000'), only 130 will be accepted – those who do best in the examination, with preference shown to diplomats' children. There are 1,000 pupils altogether, including some Christians, who can withdraw from prayers. A site seven miles away houses the girls' secondary school, whilst on the main site is a mixed kindergarten, boys' and girls' lower schools, and a boys' secondary, each with their own facilities. A tour of the boys' school showed a well-stocked library, staffed by a librarian and becoming computerized. The beautiful mosque is exclusively for school use.

Seventy-five per cent of the teachers at the academy are not Muslims. The Registrar is not concerned about this, wanting the best teachers, well qualified and experienced: 'If we have two applicants equally excellent, we would be tempted to take the Muslim. But they are not appointed purely for that'.

Pupils are offered a wide range of subjects including Arabic and Islamic Studies, sports and gymnastics. The teaching is in English and students take GCSE and A-level examinations. According to the Registrar, boys and girls have equal access to the curriculum. 'Until now girls have shown no interest in CDT, although they do Computer Science. We will do any subject if there are the numbers. Girls do have Home Economics and we are considering it for boys'.

He feels that a Muslim School is necessary:

> Parents want an excellent education but not at the expense of their culture or belief. In some schools they can forget about that. In this atmosphere they [the pupils] are confident, not seen as outsiders. That's a terrible feeling: it stops your mind all the time, apart from all the other pressures.
>
> Instructions from home will not be contradicted here, there is stability. You can get on with work.

As these examples show, Muslim private schools are not homogeneous but vary in resources, selection procedures, curriculum, staff qualifications and beliefs – and especially in their accommodations to Western values. Even within this group of schools there is considerable variety as to the degree of 'separateness' deemed appropriate.

THE CASE FOR STATE-SUPPORTED MUSLIM SCHOOLS

Parental rights to express school preferences were given high profile in the Education Act 1980 and following that, Muslims spoke out more for State aid in the education of Muslim children. They claimed, reasonably, that they paid taxes like everybody else and, therefore, they are entitled to the same facilities enjoyed by other denominations.

The Educational Reform Act of 1988 created the way for even greater demand for separate Muslim schools (Arkwright, 1990). First, by not mentioning ethnicity or multicultural education it showed lack of concern for the educational problems and demands of minority groups. Second, it had more sections on RE than any previous education Act and emphasized that the subject and school worship should be of a 'wholly or broadly Christian character' (HMSO, 1988, section 7 (i)), doubtless the usual practice in most schools. A zealous group of Christian peers pressed for this as the school population became increasingly multifaith.

Third, section 52 of the Act provided the basis for a new category of schools financed directly by central government – grant-maintained schools. 'Opting out', as it was called by the media, required application to be made to the Secretary of State following a vote of the parents. A parallel concept, 'opting in', developed in this ethos of free choice, which involved the idea that private schools should be able to choose to be funded by the State either in the form of Muslim voluntary schools or as grant-maintained Muslim schools.

The Education Act 1944, in an attempt to keep Synagogue and Church leaders content, did provide for this by granting some religious schools a special status. Thus, as well as 'county' schools set up and paid for by local authorities, we have 'voluntary' schools that have links with religious bodies. For Muslim schools the voluntary-aided category seems an ideal one in which to locate, having State links and being appropriately funded.

Nationally, approximately one third of primary and one fifth of secondary schools are voluntary aided. Most are Church of England schools, the rest Catholic, with some Methodist and twenty Jewish schools: none are Muslim, Sikh or Hindu and the history of applications so far makes their situation unpromising.

The procedure for obtaining voluntary status is that of consultation with the LEA, followed by application to the Secretary of State for approval. It has proved impossible so far for Muslim schools to gain voluntary-aided status; planning regulations have proved insurmountable and LEA backing has been difficult to obtain for small schools. A few Muslim schools have so far attempted to gain voluntary-aided status and others are waiting to apply.

Islamia Primary School in London's Brent authority was the first to apply. This popular school has a waiting-list of 600 pupils and the application has received considerable media coverage. In 1986 the 'hung' local council voted to support the school's application to the Secretary of State but the DES warned that school premises would first need enlarging. A planning application to bring this about was turned down by Brent Council in 1987. The following year a Tory motion asked that the school be allowed to buy or lease one site of a local high school likely to be closed due to falling rolls; this was defeated by Labour councillors but it was agreed that discussions should continue (*The Times Educational Supplement*, 17 June 1988). The secretary to the trustees is quoted as saying 'Considering that for the past five years the council has been telling us to find more suitable premises the decision is disgusting'.

Only weeks earlier, Brent Muslims had submitted proposals to the council for two Muslim secondary schools. The application was lodged with the Secretary of State in 1988 and, in May 1990, by which time Brent Council had withdrawn its opposition, his decision was announced: 'The neighbourhood has spare places already so there's no case for establishing a new school to be maintained out of public funds' (*ibid*). It is noticeable that this logic has not been applied to the setting up of city technology colleges (CTCs), which have been supported with public funds even in areas where there is a surplus of school places. Shropshire's Chief Education Officer has opposed the setting up of a CTC in Telford on these grounds (*Education*, 29 June 1990).

The Secretary of State's refusal does not augur well for Zakaria Girls' School in Batley, Yorkshire, which has been hoping to become the first voluntary-aided Muslim secondary school. In 1987 it applied to its local authority, Kirklees, for planning permission for further building but was refused. In 1988 the education committee of that authority decided against recommending to the full council its application for voluntary-aided status. As a result, Muslim community leaders threatened a protest of over 1,000 people outside the meeting of Kirklees Council and Muslim parents threatened to withdraw their daughters from school. Despite the protests, Kirklees authority upheld the education committee decision. The Zakaria trustees want ahead with their submission anyway, directly to the Secretary of State. At the time of writing a decision is still awaited, but is unlikely to be favourable.

The issue of Muslim schools and voluntary-aided status has also caused confusion within party politics and we find Rhodes Boyson, former Conservative spokesperson for education, and Jack Straw, Labour education spokesperson, in agreement on Muslim rights. In 1989 the Labour Party proposed in its policy review that Muslim schools be granted voluntary-aided status on the grounds that private schools are a barrier to fully comprehensive schooling. Jack Straw (1989) proposed it as a way of 'preparing pathways' for Muslim schools to enter the State system.

Baroness Cox, right-wing peer and chair of the Parental Alliance for Choice in Education (PACE), claimed that her organization supported Zakaria's application: 'We stand for parents' rights to secure for their children an education which is in accordance with their deepest beliefs' (*Guardian*, 4 January 1989). PACE had previously supported white parents in Dewsbury who withdrew their children from a local-authority school, objecting to the large number of Asian pupils on the roll. A spokesperson for the Zakaria parents explained their union with PACE: 'What is at stake is not race but culture and religion. We have different religions but both are preferable to some kind of secularistic mishmash' (*ibid*). Roy Hattersley, Shadow Home Secretary, and Rhodes Boyson have also reaffirmed 'Muslim rights' (*Guardian*, 17 July 1989; *The Times Educational Supplement*, 21 July 1989).

There have been some doubts on all sides including resistance from some Muslims and divisions inside the Labour Party. The Conservative backbencher, MP Rowe, commented: 'The existence of schools which present doctrinal material was probably a mistake. I now think we are paying a heavy price' (*The Times Educational Supplement*, 25 February 1989). Interestingly, no party has suggested dismantling the voluntary-aided system (*Guardian*, 28 July 1989).

GIRLS AND MUSLIM EDUCATION

One major issue dividing those who do and do not support Muslim schools is the education of girls. Some Muslim organizations insist on separate schooling for boys and girls, particularly in the years immediately after puberty, and this may be interpreted as a sexist practice.

Walkling and Brannigan (1986) claim that the existence of Muslim schools presents an anti-sexist, anti-racist dilemma. An education based on preparing women for home and children is in need of review. They argue that if we try to respond to the wishes of all the community, by providing separate Muslim schools, we cannot also support the Equal Opportunities Act against sex discrimination. They express the view that education should be transforming, willing to go against the background of the pupils, including their parents' wishes for conformity. Pupils, they stress, not parents, are the clients, and should be given the opportunity to question beliefs, whether or not minorities wish to preserve them.

These views have been heavily criticized by Troyna and Carrington (1987) and Arkwright (1990), who claim Walkling and Brannigan make unfounded assumptions. First, they assume that Western education is 'transforming' but, although school policies may be anti-racist and anti-sexist in the 'weak' sense (Arnot, 1985), they are not in the 'strong' sense because they do not 'challenge existing structures' (Troyna and Carrington, 1987, p. 62). They therefore legitimate the practices that maintain the inequalities. Furthermore, there is tremendous discrepancy between written policies and what happens in schools. Arkwright (1990) points out that the Christian churches' voluntary-aided schools are certainly not transforming, are sexist and, in their selection policies, probably racist. Halstead (1986, p. 28) explains that a strictly Qur'ānic Muslim view is of women and men as 'spiritual equals', 'complementing not competing'. However, other writers (Union of Muslim Organizations of UK and Eire, 1975; al-Faruqi, 1988) stress the need for differences in education because men and women have different rights and responsibilities. The Qur'ān emphasizes roles of wife and mother: 'It is a full-time job and no mean feat, managing with responsibility, a home and family, (Union of Muslim Organizations of UK and Eire, 1975, p. 12). Mohammed Siddiqui interprets the Qur'ān as follows: 'men and women will have different rights and responsibilities and neither sex should feel jealous of the other if this involves lesser rights for one sex against the other' (*ibid*. p. 12).

Al-Faruqi (1988) gives a more liberal interpretation. She explains how, in the history of Islam, during the 'centuries of decline' (1250–1900), women's role began to deteriorate leaving a tremendous lag in the education of girls. She claims that many Muslims would admit that their societies do not fulfil the Islamic ideas of the Qur'ān. The Qur'ān, she says, 'does at least imply the pursuit of knowledge by all Muslims regardless of their sex' (*ibid*. p. 37). She stresses that there are differences between 'equality' and 'identity' and that differentiations between sex roles is a natural and desirable state.

Khan (1985) fails to understand why this is an issue at all, as single-sex schools are a part of Western culture and many grammar and public schools are single sex. Jack Straw (1989) suggests that the 'women issue' is nothing to do with Islam, but pupils would be more confident in Islamic schools. He claims that the role of women in Islam is misunderstood by non-Muslims and that Muslims' concern about their daughters' education is shared by non-Muslims. Certainly there is research to suggest that girls perform better academically in single-sex, rather than mixed, schools, especially in tradition-ally male subjects (see, for example, Spender, 1982; Weiner, 1985).

A number of researchers have also criticized those those who have con-demned Muslim beliefs as inherently sexist. Parmar (1981) expresses the view that it is typical of the media and researchers to treat Asians, in particular young women, as pathological, and the view that they have fixed values can lead to low expectations and achievement in school. Research suggests that Asian girls are considered 'passive' and 'docile' by their teachers and this is reflected in the experiences they are given and the careers counselling they receive (Brah and Minhas, 1985). Wilce (1984, p. 8) quotes a Manchester community-worker who believes that the limited knowledge of teachers focuses on extremes and leads to racism: 'They go to the mosques and so on, and those people often take a fundamentalist line. . . . Teachers end up saying "You are not allowed to do this. It is not in your culture"'. Whilst some girls do have to balance carefully home and school lives (Wilce, 1984), Parmar (1981) suggests that race awareness-training for teachers is really required so they can be critical of the focus on black youth, as in permanent identity crisis.

She, and Brah and Minhas (1985), note growing resistance and militancy against the stereotyped view that there is always tension between home and school and suggest that there is tremendous support for girls to go into higher and further education: National Union of Students' statistics focus only on those who oppose it (*ibid.*). The work of Afshar (1989), with three genera-tions of Muslim women in Yorkshire, shows their tremendously high expec-tations of education for younger generations. It may be racism on the part of the white teachers that leads to the stereotyping of Asian and Muslim girls. Although the relationship between race and gender issues is complex, teachers cannot tackle one without addressing both (Brah and Minhas, 1985). These authors also criticize Walkling and Brannigan (1986) for stereotyping Muslims and treating them as an homogeneous group demanding Muslim schools. The spokespersons for Muslim groups, highly articulate and highly organized, do not necessarily, as Arkwright (1990) points out, represent the totality of Muslim opinion despite Swann's (DES, 1985) belief otherwise. Some Muslims, for example, have spoken out publicly against Muslim schools (*The Times Educational Supplement*, 21 July 1989).

Taylor and Hegarty (1985) explained that some Muslim parents have requested the setting up of single-sex schools, whilst other groups had re-quested special arrangements for sex education, sports and dress to be made within the existing schools.

A survey of fifty Pakistani girls in a Manchester school, and their parents (Shaikh and Kelly, 1989), suggests that although they see important cultural reasons for a Muslim education, the majority prefer the adaptation of State schools to separate schools.

The majority of these parents supported post-school education for their daughters; three quarters were willing to consider mixed establishments. The girls who opposed separate schools did not want the isolation they might bring; those who supported them wanted to avoid the teasing they suffered in State schools.

Like other Western groups, Muslim women are having to deal with sexism from other Muslims. Taylor (1983) argues that women must be allowed to speak for themselves and we should not rely on 'the pronouncements of male "community leaders" whatever the race' (Shaikh and Kelly, 1989). For example, in a letter to the *Guardian* (22 July 1989) a representative for 'Southall Black Sisters/Brent Asian Women's Refuge' responds to Jack Straw's (1989) comments in support of Muslim schools: 'This view assumes that those communities are unified wholes with no internal divisions, and that women have no independent voice. . . . We oppose separate schools of any denomination on the grounds that they foster an atmosphere of bigotry and apartheid. More centrally they seek to control the lives of women'. Thus we find that there is debate on sexism within the Muslim community itself.

MUSLIM PRIVATE SCHOOLS AND THE FUTURE

While there is little or no change in British schooling to accommodate Islam, some Muslims will see private schools as the only alternative for their community, though it is likely that pressure for State funding, in various forms, will increase. For example, in London schools that have majorities of Bangladeshi children, Muslim leaders are encouraging parents to take over the schools (*Education*, 16 March 1990) and 'opt out'. They are to develop 'Islamic Model Schools' in which there are Islamic values, no sex education, no Christian teachers and no National Curriculum.

A further consequence of failure to change might be the development of racially segregated schools, instigated by white parents. One result of increased parental choice has been some pressure for majority white schools for white pupils. In the Dewsbury affair white parents succeeded in withdrawing their children from a school with a majority of pupils of Asian descent and, since the Education Reform Act, there have been an increased number of such incidents. For example, parents who complained that their daughter's primary school held 'multifaith' rather than 'Christian' assemblies were not heeded by the local council so, supported by PACE, they asked the Secretary of State for a ruling (*The Times Educational Supplement*, 4 May 1990). At the time of writing the girl is being taught at home and hopes to attend a local over-subscribed school with few Asian pupils.

Of even greater concern is the case of Cleveland, where the education authority allowed a white parent to transfer her daughter because she claimed the child was 'learning Pakistani' (*The Times Educational Supplement*, 27 April 1990). The Secretary of State supported the claim that a parent's right to choose could over-ride the Race Relations Act 1976. The Equal Opportunities Commission in Manchester deals with similar cases at least once a month, which suggests some considerable pressure for all-white schools. If all-black schools develop as a result of this, they are unlikely to be of long-term benefit to their pupils.

The demand for voluntary-aided status will have to receive an official response, which is seen to be fair: currently the Secretary of State is seen to be playing for time. To say 'no' to Muslim, Hindu and Sikh schools whilst allowing Christian schools to expand will be seen as unjust and inflammatory as well as increasing the number of private schools and possibly increasing fundamentalism. A private-members' bill introduced into the House of Lords, in early 1991, aims to make it easier for schools established in accordance with religious faiths to receive public funding: through voluntary-aided status or opting in to grant-maintained status (*The Times Educational Supplement*, 6 July 1990).

An alternative is to dismantle the voluntary-school system. Britain would then have a wholly secular system like that of the USA or much of Western Europe. This is an unlikely choice and has not been proposed by any major political party. It might be considered preferable to allow any school that wished to become voluntary aided: although this would lead to religious and racial segregation, it might be no greater than that already being brought about by the decisions of white parents. Hiskett (1989), in a paper published by the Social Affairs Unit, considers this the best option for all. The present policy of the Commission for Racial Equality is that, if there are aided denominational schools, all religious groups should have parity (*Independent*, 26 April 1990) though an elaboration of this view is anticipated.

A further possibility is to create a system that is run by, but not for, the Church, leading to multifaith voluntary-aided schools (Jeffcoate, 1984), though this also seems unlikely in the present political climate. These would be ways to 'prepare pathways' for Muslim schools following a National Curriculum to enter the State system as suggested by Straw (1989, p. 9).

Another way forward is to improve supplementary schooling as recommended by Swann (DES, 1985). Rex (1986) suggests that such schools are given financial support to encourage biculturalism and language development, while Homan (1985) proposes education vouchers, allowing parental choice, to fund them. It is doubtful whether this would satisfy all Muslims as there has been growing dissatisfaction with the schools (*ibid*.), yet it would ensure the teaching of Islam by those who embrace the faith, and are qualified to teach it by having sufficient knowledge of the texts.

As has been shown, Muslim parents are as varied in their views and as pragmatic as any others. There are areas on which many would compromise so there needs to be improvement in the State system that takes more account of parental opinion. Joly (1989) describes negotiations between Muslims and Birmingham schools in which issues relating to assemblies, dress and separate-sex swimming lessons were discussed and settled; they were able to incorporate some aspects of Muslim cultural practice in the school and provide Urdu and Bengali language teaching. Food requirements and curriculum adaptation proved much more difficult to agree upon but guidelines for schools were developed.

Rex (1986) suggests that only deliberate institutionalization of multiculturalism would bring real change, through the reform of books, syllabuses and examination schemes. Added to this might be the recruitment and training of more Muslim teachers (Sarwar, 1983), experimentation in teaching, such as girls-only classes in some subjects (Arkwright, 1990) and implementation of anti-racist approaches.

So far, many minority groups, including Muslims, have not been granted any institutional or political power enabling them to bring about change. So long as the DES is inactive in this, its ideological position must be assumed 'assimilationist' (Troyna, 1982) and, for some Muslims who wish to have their beliefs taught in an ethos free from prejudiced harassment, private schools will be seen as the only alternative.

REFERENCES

Afshar, H. (1989) Education: hopes, expectations and achievements of Muslim women in West Yorkshire, *Gender and Education*, Vol. 1, no. 3, pp. 261–72.

Al-Faruqi, L. L. (1988) *Women, Muslim Society and Islam*, American Trust Publications, Indianapolis, Ind.

Anwar, M. (1981) *Between Two Cultures*, Council for Race Relations, London.

Arnot, M. (ed.) (1985) *Race and Gender: Equal Opportunities Policies in education*, Pergamon, Oxford.

Ashraf, A. (1987) Education of the Muslim community in Great Britain, *Muslim Education Quarterly*, Vol. 5, no. 1, pp. 82–6.

Arkwright, J. (1990) Anti-racist and anti-sexist education policy: where do Muslims fit in?, *Multicultural Teaching*, Vol. 8, no. 2, pp. 28–33.

Badawi, Z. (1979) Traditional Islamic education – its aims and purposes in the present day, in S. N. Al-Attas (ed.) *Aims and Objectives of Islamic Education*, King Abdulaziz University, Jeddah.

Brah, A. and Minhas, R. (1985) Structural racism or cultural difference: schooling for Asian girls, in G. Weiner (ed.), op. cit.

DES (1977) *Education in Schools: A Consultative Document*, HMSO, London.

DES (1985) *Education for All* (the Swann Report), HMSO, London.

Education (1990a) Islam's star rises in London's East End, Vol. 175, no. 11, p. 261.

Education (1990b) Canny Cates points to Islamic failure, Vol. 175, no. 26, p. 622.

Halstead, J. M. (1986) *The Case for Muslim Voluntary-Aided Schools*, Islamic Academy, Cambridge.

Hiskett, M. (1989) *Schooling for British Muslims: Integrated, Opted-Out or Denominational?*, Social Affairs Unit, London.

HMSO (1978) *The West Indian Community. Observations on the Report of the Select Committee on Race Relations and Immigration*, London.

HMSO (1988) *Education Reform Act*, London.

Homan, R. (1985) The supplementary school in S. Mogdil, G. Verma, K. Mallick and C. Mogdil (eds.) (1985) *Multicultural Education: The Interminable Debate*, Falmer, Lewes.

Islamic Academy/Islamic Cultural Centre (1985) *Swann Committee Report: An Evaluation from the Muslim Point of View*, Islamic Academy, Cambridge.

Islamic College (undated) *Islamic College, London. A Brief Introduction*, London.

Jeffcoate, R. (1984) *Ethnic Minorities and Education*, Paul Chapman, London.

Joly, D. (1989) Ethnic minorities and Education in Britain. Interaction between the Muslim Community and Birmingham schools, (Research Paper No. 41), Centre for the Study of Islam and Christian-Muslim Relations, Birmingham.

Jones, M. (1986) The Swann Report on 'Education for All': a critique, *Journal of Philosophy of Education*, Vol. 20, no. 1, pp. 107–12.

Khan, S. (1985) The education of Muslim girls, *Multicultural Teaching*, Vol. III, no. 2, pp. 33–4.

Parmar, P. (1981) Young Asian women: a critique of the pathological approach, *Multiracial Education*, Vol. 9, no. 5, pp. 19–29.

Rex, J. (1986) Equality of opportunity and the ethnic minority child in British schools, in S. Modgil, G. Verma, K. Mallick and C. Modgil (eds.) *Multicultural Education: The Interminable Debate*, Falmer Press, Lewes.

Rogers, R. (1981) Denominational schooling, *Multiracial Education*, Vol. 10, no. 1, pp. 27–33.

Rose, E. J. B. *et al.* (1969) *Colour and Citizenship*, Oxford University Press, Oxford.

Sarwar, G. (1983) *Muslims and Education in the UK*. Muslim Educational Trust, London.

Shaikh, S. and Kelly, A. (1989) To mix or not to mix: Pakistani girls in British Schools, *Educational Research*, Vol. 31, no. 1, pp. 10–19.

Sonyel, S. R. (1987) The underachievement of Turkish Muslim children in British Schools, *Muslim Education Quarterly*, Vol. 4, no. 3, pp. 75–87.

Spender, D. (1982) *Invisible Women: The Schooling Scandal*, Women's Press, London.

Straw, J. (1989) Islam, women and Muslim schools, *Muslim Education Quarterly*, Vol. 6, no. 4, pp. 7–9.

Taylor, H. (1983) Sexism and racism: partners in oppression? *CASSOE Newsletter*, June.

Taylor, M. J. and Hegarty, S. (1985) *The Best of Both Worlds?*, NFER-Nelson, Windsor.

Troyna, B. (1982) The ideological and policy response to Black pupils in British in A. Hartnet (ed.) *The Social Sciences in Education*, Heinemann, London.

Troyna, B. and Carrington, B. (1987) Anti-sexist/anti-racist education – a false dilemma: a reply to Walkling and Brannigan, *Journal of Moral Education*, Vol. 16, no. 1, pp. 60–5.

Union of Muslim Organizations of UK and Eire (1975) *Islamic Education and Single-Sex Schools*, London.

Walkling, P. and Brannigan, C. (1986) Anti-Sexist/anti-racist education: a possible dilemma, *Journal of Moral Education*, Vol. 15, no. 1, pp. 16–25.

Weiner, G. (ed.) (1985) *Just a Bunch of Girls*, Open University Press, Milton Keynes.

Wilce, H. (1984) Walking the tight rope between two cultures, *The Times Educational Supplement*, 10 February.

8

THE RELUCTANT PRIVATE SECTOR: OF SMALL SCHOOLS, PEOPLE AND POLITICS

Geoffrey Walford

INTRODUCTION

This chapter describes part of a loose grouping of more than a hundred private schools that have several common features. First, they are all small schools, usually smaller that most LEAs believe to be financially viable or desirable in terms of curriculum coverage. Second, there is close contact between parents and the school, with parents often playing a major part in the organization and running of the school. Third, and most importantly, these schools are officially private schools but, unlike most other private schools, they are not ideologically committed to the idea of private provision, but are private simply because they believe that State provision is inadequate or unsuitable. Ideally, these schools would wish to obtain funding from the State, possibly through becoming voluntary-aided or grant-maintained schools. This range of many small private schools is actively seeking a way out of the private sector and into the State-maintained sector, and might thus be regarded as 'reluctant private schools'.

It is worth remembering that there is already some diversity of ownership within the State-maintained sector. After the Education Act 1944, the majority of Church of England and Roman Catholic schools became part of the State-maintained sector with voluntary-aided or voluntary-controlled status. While these schools still remain the property of the Church, and the Church has some degree of control over them, the State pays all of the re-current costs and the bulk of new capital expenditure. By the mid-1980s, at primary level, some 17 per cent of children in England were in Church of England schools, and 10 per cent in Roman Catholic, while at secondary level the figures were 11 per cent and 9 per cent respectively. There were also a few Methodist and Jewish voluntary schools (O'Keeffe, 1986). Many other religious groups, in particular Muslims, believe that natural justice demands that there now should be other forms of voluntary schools and that they are being discriminated against in their applications to establish their own voluntary schools. But, while the Muslims' case has had wide prominence and discussion in the media, the very similar cases for State funding that are being put by various other diverse groups have had less attention. These very different groups and types of school they represent have recently come together to campaign on the one major issue they hold in common – the wish not to remain as private schools but to 'opt in' to the State-maintained sector. This chapter explores the nature of these various small schools and describes and analyses the political campaign they have mounted to fight for the common goal of State funding. The schools will be discussed within several broad groupings, and it will be shown that the educational ideologies supported by these groupings have many aspects in conflict. The present movement is a good example of a single-issue political campaign where major differences are submerged in order to fight to obtain a single objective.

THE CAMPAIGN FOR STATE-SUPPORTED ALTERNATIVE SCHOOLS

In Britain there have been very many attempts to obtain State funding for private schools. Indeed, it might be argued that any history of a campaign for State support for alternative schools must date back to before 1833, for this was the first year during which the British government was persuaded to give financial support to a private Church organization to support 'the erection of school houses' (Walford, 1990b). In one way or another, successive governments have continued to give support to various non-government-controlled schools since that time (Walford, 1987). However, the Campaign for State Supported Alternative Schools (CSSAS), which is of interest here, was started in December 1979 during an Advisory Centre for Education (ACE) conference. Its aim, according to Laura Diamond (1989), co-founder of CSSAS, was to encourage the establishment of small, democratically organized, alternative schools funded by the State.

One of the key political figures involved in the campaign was Michael Young, now Lord Young of Dartington. Educated at the progressive Dartington Hall School (of which he was written a biography of the founders – Young, 1983), Young became an eminent sociologist (see, for example, Young, 1958; Young and Wilmott, 1957, 1973; Young and Schuller, 1988) and an outstanding political campaigner on education and consumer issues. Among many other prominent positions, he is President of the Consumers' Association, the National Extension College and (the organization of most interest in this chapter) ACE. A long-time advocate of increased choice in education, Young spoke at an ACE conference in December 1978 about what he saw as the increasing uniformity of education provision within the comprehensive system, and of his fear that parents might feel forced to use the private sector to obtain the diversity of provision they wished for. As a result of this meeting, a small group of parents, teachers and ACE workers developed a document, *A Case for Alternative Schools within the Maintained Sector* (ACE, 1979), which was later adopted as the policy document for the CSSAS.

It is important to note that CSSAS was a narrowly based campaign. It brought together only those people interested in a particular type of alternative school, rather than supporting all of the demands for State funding for private education. In the policy document (*ibid.*) it was made clear that CSSAS supported non-fee-paying schools, which were to be non-selective on grounds of ability or aptitude and which would not discriminate on grounds of race, sex or religion. It was accepted that it would be necessary to demonstrate sufficient demand for a particular school before State funding was forthcoming, and that HMIs and health and safety inspectors should play a part in ensuring appropriate standards. Whilst admitting that several models were possible, the one advocated was that of a democratic, open, non-hierarchical, non-coercive and non-violent school. In short, the vision of schooling to be supported was that of the progressive free school that had become popular in the 1960s and early 1970s, and that drew upon the child-centred and libertarian education ideas of educationists such as A. S. Neill, Homer Lane, Dora Russell, John Holt, Neil Postman and others. These ideas had spawned some 20 or 30 small, private, free schools during that period, organized by parents and teachers anxious to rid themselves of the hierarchical oppressiveness of many State-maintained schools (Wright, 1989). These 'new romantics', as Hargreaves (1974) has designated them, had an influence on educational thinking far out of proportion to their numerical strength, but attempts to translate their thinking into the State sector were few and short lived. Michael Duane's Risinghill (Berg, 1968), R. F. Mackenzie's (1970) Braehead and John Watts' (1980) Countesthorpe College (Gordon, 1986) all came to tragic ends. The private free schools also had limited lifetimes, and by the time of the launch of CSSAS in 1979 only two of the newer free schools survived – Kirkdale School and White Lion Free School. In practice, the campaign had been launched because the free schools were finding it increasingly difficult to support themselves from their own resources, but it had been started too late and the external environment changed too quickly for the campaign to be successful. After some initial success in terms of membership and publicity, by 1982 only a handful of dedicated workers remained, and the last newsletter was published in 1984.

Diamond (1989) analyses the failure of CSSAS in terms of mistakes made within the organization, the difficulty of the task and the changing external environment. She argues that the attack on progressive education led by the Black Papers was an important part of this changed environment (Cox and Dyson, 1971). These right-wing writers had reviled progressive education as lowering educational standards and diverting the schools from their task of training young people for work. At the time of publication, the Black Papers had been largely ignored by most of those involved in education, but by the 1980s the vision of schooling presented by them had become the accepted wisdom of government. Rhodes Boyson (1974), one of the original Black Paper writers and co-editor of the 4th Paper (Cox and Boyson, 1975), was for a time a Minister for Education within the Conservative government. Under such new circumstances, calls for the State to help prop up ailing free schools sounded somewhat ridiculous.

Diamond (1989, p. 79) also argues that the campaign would have been more likely to have been politically successful if it had included other sorts of alternative schools that did not necessarily fit within the restricted free-school model, for example, the Steiner Schools and the Small School at Hartland. Although not fully following the 'new romantic' model, these schools have many features in common with the model, and might be seen as a more acceptable 1980s version of the original.

THE HUMAN-SCALE MOVEMENT

The Small School at Hartland in Devon is a unique secondary school founded and organized by a small group of educational activists who still retained some of the idealism of the 1960s. The school's founder, Satish Kumar, is Chairman of the Schumacher Society and editor of *Resurgence*, a magazine with a concentration on environmental issues. The school was started in 1982 simply because Kumar had recently moved to Hartland and there was no local secondary school for his children (Winsor, 1987), but it has since become the centre of a wider movement for State-supported small schools. In 1989 the school had 2 full-time teachers on low salaries, 13 part-time staff and 31 pupils (Blackburne, 1989). The head, Colin Hodgetts, trained as a clergyman, and he is former director of Christian Action and co-ordinator of a programme to resettle Vietnamese refugees in Britain, and sees the school as a continuation of his campaigning career. Together, Kumar and Hodgetts managed to convince charitable foundations such as the Calouste Gulbenkian Foundation and the Sainsbury Family Charitable Trust that the school was worth supporting on an experimental basis, and that it could serve as a basis for future small secondary schools funded by the State. With this in mind, a team of researchers from Exeter University was asked to evaluate the school over a three-year period. Their report, published in 1989, argued that the school was providing a full curriculum, that mixed-age teaching was successful, but that the school did have the special benefits of an influx of skilled people who could teach part time, and that the school had yet to capitalize on all the educational advantages of small schools (Golby, Treharne and Taylor, 1989).

Meanwhile, the Schumacher Society, under the chairmanship of Satish Kumar, had decided to develop a movement to spread the small-school model. Philip Toogood, previously a controversial head of Madeley Court Comprehensive School in Telford, was invited to Hartland to teach and co-ordinate a conference to launch the Human Scale Education Movement. At Telford, Toogood (1989) had established semi-autonomous minischools, each with about 100 pupils, within the first to third years of his large comprehensive school. Timetables were blocked into half days, pupils given a territory of their own and parental involvement encouraged. After seven years, however, he retired early after conflict with the LEA over how the school was to be run.

These activities led to his appointment at Hartland where Toogood taught and co-ordinated the first conference of the Human Scale Education Movement. The movement has three main initiatives for action and support: minischools, small schools and flexischooling. Minischooling is simply the restructuring of large schools into smaller ones as had been done at Madeley Court. Small schools are to be encouraged especially where the intention is that they should be free and have open access. Flexischooling is a way of encouraging schools to combine school-based learning with home-based or community-based education, which developed out of Education Otherwise activities (Meighan, 1988).

In 1987 Toogood moved to become head of the private Dame Catherine's School in Ticknall, Derbyshire, which has about 35 children aged 4–16, with three qualified teachers and many local 'teacher aides'. Thanks to an eighteenth-century trust, it occupies the village's former primary school, and is able to offer free education to the local community's children, supported by the voluntary fund-raising activities of local parents and villagers. The mixed-age learning environment means that teaching is again individualized, but here the emphasis is on developing a high degree of self-reliance and resourcefulness, and on the children learning for themselves 'so that they really own the knowledge that they acquire' (Toogood, 1988). It follows the ideas of flexischooling (Meighan, 1988) where flexibility and diversity in teaching approaches is championed and where the classroom is seen as just one possible location for learning. Some of the children spend only part of the week at the school and are taught by their parents at home for the remainder. The school sees itself as an open-learning centre for the children and adults of the local community. Dame Catherine's has also become the base for a new bimonthly journal, *Education Now*, and for a publishing co-operative that links university and polytechnic academics with practising teachers and campaigners.

THE EDUCATION REFORM ACT 1988

State-maintained small schools have fared badly during the tenure of successive Conservative governments. Very few small secondary schools now exist and many small primary schools have been closed as a result of falling school rolls and economic constraints on LEAs. While parental support for small schools has generally been high, local and central government have seen them as uneconomic and unable to offer the quality and diversity of educational experience obtainable in larger schools. On the other hand, and in some conflict, the Conservative government has gradually increased its interest in the idea of extending choice in education, first through the Assisted Places Scheme and later through open enrollment, opting out and the development of private city technology colleges (CTCs). CTCs gave new impetus to those fighting to obtain State funding for existing alternative private schools. They argued that, if the State could support parents' choice for technological education, why could it also not support parents' choice for a variety of other forms of private education?

It was almost inevitable that attempts to persuade the government to extend the CTC model to include other types of alternative private schools would be made in Parliament as the Education Reform Bill was passing its way through both Houses. As with many of the successful amendments, the action took place in the Lords rather than the Commons, with somewhat similar amendments being proposed by Lord Young of Dartington and the right-wing Black-Paper contributor, Baroness Cox. On 16 May 1988, at the committee stage (Hansard, 497, 38–41), Lord Young moved his amendment 230 entitled 'New foundation schools. Extension of parental choice'. The vision of educational choice presented here was far wider than that of CSSAS of a decade earlier. State funding was sought for schools that would vary in respect of educational principle, size of school, curricula emphasis, method of teaching and particular faith or philosophy espoused. The free school was now just one of a variety of models to be supported, but some of the former idealism was still to be detected in the demands that the schools should be academically comprehensive, open without discrimination to all children in their catchment areas, and that the schools should admit children on the basis of criteria compatible with the practice of their local authority if they could not accept all applicants. A further restriction was that they were not 'to propagate doctrines tending to foment racial, religious or other forms of intolerance' (*ibid.*), but Young made it clear in his speech that his amendment included the possibility of Hindu, Moslem and Buddhist schools to supplement existing denominational schools. He elaborated the example of Denmark, where he claimed that there are no fee-paying schools, as all types of school are State supported. In fact, about 8 per cent of pupils in Denmark attend private schools and, as government support is up to a maximum of 85 per cent of the school's expenditure, most of these pupils do pay fees (Doyle, 1989). While these fees are generally small some are substantial (Mason, 1989), which means that, even though some free places are available to children from low-income families, there remains a barrier between the State and private sectors in Denmark.

Of particular interest with regard to the pedigree of Lord Young's ammendment was that is was grouped with a related one from Baroness

Cox and they had agreed to support one another's amendments. Baroness Cox suggested that the route to greater diversity and choice in schooling was to make it easier for private schools to attain voluntary-aided status. She was particularly concerned about the number of small schools that had tried unsuccessfully to obtain such status over several years. In her supporting speech she explicitly mentioned the Yesodey Hatorah Jewish School, the John Loughborough Seventh Day Adventist School in Tottenham and the 'many other Christian and Muslim schools which are mushrooming in various parts of the country' (Hansard, 497, 43). She argued that all of these schools were supported by parents, often at great personal cost and sacrifice, because they were dissatisfied with local-authority schools, and that the Secretary of State for Education and Science should be given extra powers to grant voluntary-aided status against the advice of LEAs.

There were clear differences in emphasis between Lord Young and Baroness Cox in their presentations as well as in their favoured solution to the problem of increasing State support for a variety of schools. This was noticed by Lord Peston, who claimed that the two amendments were fundamentally different – one being about openness and the common school working on comprehensive principles, which he could support, and the other about narrow doctrinaire schools, which he could not. In reply, however, both Lord Young and Baroness Cox glossed over these differences, with Young making it clear that his amendment would include religious schools of various denominations.

Baroness Hooper, on behalf of the government, argued that the new schools proposed by Lord Young were unlikely to be able to provide a broad and balanced curriculum, and explained that it was open to such schools that could do so to apply for voluntary-aided status. She stated that the amendment would not be timely for inclusion within the 1988 Act, but added that this did not mean that 'the idea will be lost for all time' (*ibid.*). Lord Young's amendment was withdrawn, Baroness Cox's not moved and the campaigners re-grouped for a new onslaught at a later date.

THE RADICAL RIGHT'S CAMPAIGN

The differences in approach correctly identified by Lord Peston in the debate reflect the very different origins of the two amendments. While that of Lord Young can be seen as being linked to the 'new romantics' of the 1960s, that of Baroness Cox derives from the new right in education, which had explicitly attacked progressive teaching and the ideas of the free-schoolers. Caroline Cox is one of a small group of right-wing educationists whose ideas on education have gradually become government orthodoxy. She originally trained and practised as a nurse, then read Sociology, and eventually became Head of the Sociology Department at the Polytechnic of North London. There she rose to prominence after publication of *The Rape of Reason* (Cox, Jacka and

Marks, 1975), which discussed student action within the Polytechnic of North London. From 1977 to 1984 she became Director of the Nursing Education Research Unit at Chelsea College, she was made Baroness in 1982 and, from 1983 to 1985, was Director of the Centre for Policy Studies. She is a key member of several small but influential right-wing educational groups including the Academic Council for Peace and Freedom, the Educational Research Trust, the Hillgate Group, the National Council for Academic Standards (NCAS) and the Parental Alliance for Choice in Education (PACE) (Griggs, 1989). She was a contributor to one of the early Black Papers (Cox, Jacka and Marks, 1977) and to the Hillgate Group's two influential pamphlets, *Whose Schools?* (1986) and *The Reform of British Education* (1987). Unlike Lord Young, she is firmly in favour of selective schooling. For example, with John Marks and M Pomian-Srzednicki, she examined the 1982 examination performance for over 2,000 schools in 61 LEAs, and claimed that the results showed a clear superiority for schools within a selective system over comprehensive schools (Marks, Cox and Pomian-Srzednicki, 1983). This research was the centre of a long dispute with the DES and with other researchers who claimed that the findings were erroneous (see, for example, Steedman, 1987; Cox and Marks, 1988; Preece, 1989). A later study by Marks and Pomian-Srzednicki (1985) found an advantage to the selective system in terms of average numbers of O-levels and CSE grade 1 passes per pupil, but found no difference between the two systems when the full ability range was taken into consideration (Gray and Jesson, 1989). This last finding is rarely discussed by Cox. A balanced analysis of the several studies on this issue would indicate that, while the direction of difference is uncertain, the magnitude of differences is small. Nevertheless, *Whose School?* (Hillgate Group, 1986) ignores a vast range of research literature and presents a picture of decline in standards due to comprehensivization.

The main thrust of the two Hillgate pamphlets is a strident attack on LEAs, some of which are seen as being responsible for 'corrupting the minds and souls of the young' through anti-sexist, anti-racist and anti-heterosexist initiatives (Hillgate Group 1986, 1988). A strong 'back to basics' movement is encouraged in terms of curriculum, selective admissions policies advocated for popular schools and a greater diversity of schools receiving funding directly from central government is proposed. The second pamphlet makes it clear that the long-term aim is that of a privatized education system with a 'pupil entitlement' or voucher from the government, which would be encashable at fee-paying as well as non-fee-paying schools.

In order to attain this long-term aim, Caroline Cox and others on the political right with similar aims (for example, Sir Rhodes Boyson and Stuart Sexton) have actively supported a variety of new small schools in the name of parental choice, and have claimed that the existence of these schools is an indicator of growing dissatisfaction with LEA provision. Diversity is encouraged, and opting out of LEA schools into schools that cater for idiosyncratic parental demands is presented as a positive response to the perceived short-comings of the State system. This means that some of the schools that have received active support from the educational new right have had some features with which they might reasonably disagree. For example, the standard of physical facilities available has sometimes been low, and styles and standards of teaching have varied widely. This contradiction can be illustrated through a consideration of the new fundamentalist Christian schools Baroness Cox specifically supported in the Lords' debate.

EVANGELICAL CHRISTIAN SCHOOLS

One of the most interesting groups of private schools seeking funding from the State is the new Christian schools. These schools share an ideology of Biblically based evangelical Christianity, which seeks to relate the message of the Bible to all aspects of present-day life whether personal, spiritual or educational. A growing dissatisfaction with what is seen as the increased secularism of the great majority of schools has led small groups of parents (usually members of a local Independent Evangelical Alliance Church) to open their own schools for their children, which aim to provide a distinctive Christian approach to every part of school life and the curriculum.

A good example of such a school is Oak Hill School. Since it was first opened in September 1984 with 24 children, Oak Hill School has expanded to cater for about 130 children aged between 5 and 16. Its 100 primary-age pupils are housed in a redundant 1950s' church, situated in a council housing estate on the outskirts of Bristol. The buildings have been adapted and renovated to provide classrooms, offices, hall, staffroom and so on, and now look very similar to many State-maintained primary schools. This school, however, is run by the Bristol Christian Fellowship, which is a group of four Biblically based evangelical Christian local fellowships, and provides an education that centres around the desire to teach children to grow in a personal relationship with God. Although the school eventually intends to offer courses leading to standard GCSEs, its curriculum is integrated and topic based rather than subject based. Within the overall topic of Justice and Righteousness, for example, the top juniors might study the stewardship of Creation, including polution of the environment, destruction of rain forests and similar issues. The focus is on the child knowing God, knowing His created world and knowing other people. The school has six full-time staff, about six others sharing classes on a morning or afternoon basis and about 20 more part-time staff. The general expectation is that parents with children at the school will pay 10 per cent of their income, but this does not allow teachers to be paid full salaries. Payment to teaching staff is thus made according to need.

It is striking that the new Christian schools are the result of a grass-roots movements in education that stems from the belief that education is the responsibility of the parent rather than the State. The school is seen as an extension of the values and beliefs taught within the home and church. Deakin (1989b), who is Head of Oak Hill School, argues that the human-centred philosophy that dominates the majority of schools in this country is evident throughout the entire curriculum of those schools, and that it shapes the value systems and philosophical frameworks within which all the disciplines are taught. Further: 'our schools tend to reflect our society, where there is increasing secularisation, a rising materialism and excessive individualism. Alongside this there is unremitting evidence of a profound lack of respect for authority, and chaos in the area of personal values and morality' (Deakin, 1989b). Religious education itself is often of particular concern to the parents involved in these schools. It is argued that the secularization of most schools has led to a commitment to a multifaith approach to religious education, where religions are examined through their observable characteristics rather than in terms of faith, belief and commitment. This approach is seen to encourage a secular and aridly sceptical view of life and to devalue all faiths other than that of secular humanism. Deakin (1989b) argues that a multicultural society should make room for all faiths, provided they are expressed in a spirit of mutual tolerance, and that government should fund a range of schools to allow parents to educate their children in their own faith.

As there is no national organization overseeing these schools, it is difficult to trace their emergence, but it would appear that the first school of this type to open in Britain was in Rochester in 1969 – a time when some other parent groups throughout the country were opening libertarian free schools for their children. A few more new Christian schools followed in the early 1970s, but it was not until the early 1980s that substantial growth occurred. In 1980 there were about ten such schools, but by 1988 there were at least 53. Thirteen of these schools were in or very near to London, and the south of England in general dominated the geographical distribution. Five were in Manchester, and only the two in Scotland were further north than York. The growth in popularity of these schools is shown in the increase in the number of pupils in each school as well as the total number of schools. The Christian Fellowship School, Liverpool, for example, has increased from 30 pupils in 1981 to 185 in 1989 (*ibid.*). The main constraint on further expansion for many of these schools is usually a limitation in the physical space available in the existing premises rather than any lack of potential pupils. The demand for places must be understood in the light of evangelical Christianity at present being one of the fastest-growing religious groups in Britain and, unlike many traditional Christian denominations, it has a membership age-profile that is biased towards the young and middle aged, for whom the responsibilities of educating their children are current concerns.

One of the early campaigning organizations on behalf of some of these schools was the Christian Parent-Teacher League (CPTL) founded in 1986, but which only became specifically interested in the formation of new Christian schools in the late 1970s. By the mid-1980s, Youth With A Mission was involved with running schools, and Christians In Education, which had been formed in 1986, acted to bring together the Heads of the schools. In 1988 it was decided to establish the separate Christian Schools' Trust (CST) 'to promote and assist in the founding of further schools' (CST, 1988). It also provides assistance with the development of curriculum materials, helps co-ordinate the dissemination of such materials, provides in-service training for teachers and organizes conferences. Being a charity, the trust is not permitted to engage in political activity, so the separate Christian Schools Campaigns (CSC) was established with the long-term goal of obtaining public funding for the schools (CSC, 1989). Amongst the nine patrons of this separate campaigning organization are Lord Young of Dartington, Baroness Cox, Viscount Tonypandy, Anthony Coombs, MP, Michael Alison, MP and Prof. David Regan. In 1989 an umbrella organization, the Christian Schools Association, was formed, which incorporates the work of the trust and campaigns. At that point 47 schools were involved, at least 13 of which had made initial applications to their LEAs for voluntary-aided status.

It is fascinating that such educational 'heavyweights' should be prepared to become patrons of CSC. Several are known to support evangelical Christianity, and were active in amending the Education Reform Act 1988 to give a greater emphasis to Christianity in RE and regular assemblies, but the recent history of some of these evangelical schools has been fraught with controversy and questions over their educational standards. In particular, some of these schools suffered badly in the Press following poor reports from HM Inspectors during 1985 when at least four evangelical Christian schools were served with notices of complaint (DES, 1985a–d). Areas of concern within these reports included inadequate and unsafe accommodation, lack of resources, unstimulating environments and inadequate curriculum. The HMI report on New Court Christian School, Finsbury Park, for example, stated that 'In general the school is very poorly resourced in every area; there is an urgent need for planned resourcing related to the curriculum at every level' (DES, 1985d). At the time of inspection, with 71 pupils on roll, only one member of staff had a recognized teaching qualification. The report ended with the paragraph: 'The school undoubtedly has the best interests of its pupils at heart and wishes to provide for them as well as possible within the framework of its strongly held religious convictions, but the present provision is still far from achieving acceptable standards'.

In all of these four reports (DES, 1985a–d), however, the Accelerated Christian Education (ACE) teaching programme used by the schools was a common area of concern. Although now far less used than in the mid-1980s, ACE teaching materials and methods were an important part of the growth of these new Christian schools, for the existence of ACE enabled small groups of Christian parents to contemplate providing all-age Christian schooling for their children at low cost and with little or no teaching experience required by those adults in charge. ACE is a highly standardized system of individualized instruction, where all of the information, materials and equipment necessary to set up and run a school are provided at reasonably low cost. The whole programme was developed in the USA, where fundamentalist Christian schools are again the fastest-growing group of private schools (Peshkin, 1986; Cookson, 1989), supported by a profit-making corporation that started in 1970. Based in Louisville, Kentucky, ACE provides directions for establishing the school, training for staff and materials for pupils aged 5–16. According to Rose (1988), by about 1987 ACE was used in 5,000 schools in the USA and a further 600 schools in 86 other countries. Rose (*ibid.* p. 117) describes ACE as 'having taken the scientific management of schools to the extreme. Their model more closely approximates to that of the factory or office: there are "supervisors" and "monitors" rather than "teachers"; student "offices" rather than desks; and "testing stations" that create "quality control"'. Pupils work on their individual Packs of Accelerated Christian Education (PACEs) in separate cubicles, which are designed to limit student interaction by having vertical screens between pupils. Students are able to gain the attention of their supervisor or monitor by raising one of two or three small flags that are provided for each pupil.

> In each subject the programme consists of some 140 to 150 numbered workbooks (PACEs), and the pupils proceed from one to the next in order. Pupils are said to complete on average a total of 20 pages per day, but this will vary considerably from pupil to pupil.
> 23. In general PACEs consist of a series of information passages each followed by exercises based on it. In mathematics these exercises consist of formal computations, sometimes expressed as 'problems'; in other subjects they take the form of questions requiring brief answers, lists to be matched or sentences in which missing words have to be supplied or certain words have to be underlined or similarly annotated...
> 24. Each workbook contains one or more intermediate 'check-up tests' and a concluding 'PACE test'. The exercises and check-up tests are completed in pencil and scored by the pupils themselves from answer books kept at the central 'scoring station'. Errors are erased and new answers written in until all are correct.
>
> (DES, 1985a)

Largely similar descriptions of the ACE learning environment, process and curriculum are given in all four DES reports of the ACE schools inspected during January and February 1985, and are echoed by Skinner (1981) in his description of Emmanuel Christian School, Fleetwood, which he visited in 1981. More strikingly, a very similar description is given by Rose (1988) in her study of an American ACE school she calls 'The Academy'.

ACE seems to have had two pathways into Britain. The first was through a group of Americans linked to the Brentwaters American Air Force Base in Suffolk who first formed Faith Christian Church and in September 1980 opened Faith Christian Academy (DES, 1985a), which, at the time of inspection, made almost exclusive use of ACE and served only American children. ACE's second pathway into Britain was through Fleetwood Full Gospel Church, which opened Emmanuel Christian School in 1979. The church had been considering establishing a day school for some years, and the discovery of ACE materials and methods allowed them to proceed. By 1981 there were about 70 pupils (Skinner, 1981). The Principal of the school, Dr Michael Smith, who was also British co-ordinator of ACE, viewed Emmanuel as a 'pilot school' and, through conferences and visits, actively encouraged other reformed Church groups to establish their own schools using ACE. He met with considerable success, with six churches taking his advice by early 1981 (CPTL, 1981).

Deakin (1989b) is circumspect in her discussion of the use of ACE materials. She claims (*ibid.*) that 'used wisely, they can provide a beneficial means of achieving certain goals. However, they are only useful in so far as they serve the stated aims of the schools and do not impede the process of curriculum development'. In practice, only about ten of the schools now still use ACE materials and many of the newer ones have never done so. Schools are now involved in developing their own materials and, even where used, ACE methods no longer dominate the learning process as they once did. The CST is now involved in developing its own Christian curriculum materials and in running in-service courses for teachers, which encourage far greater critical thought than do ACE materials.

However, the ACE system was an important part of the development of these schools for it allowed them to come into being. While various commentators have quite correctly seen the implementation of packaged learning materials as part of the proletarianization and deskilling process of the majority of qualified teachers (Apple, 1981, 1982, 1987; Buswell, 1980), they have not discussed its role in enabling unqualified personnel to establish their own schools. Whether it is desirable or not is a separate issue, but such systems can actually up-skill or re-skill parents by giving them confidence in their own abilities such that the system is eventually overthrown. The problem comes when those adults within the schools remain dependent upon packaged materials, and retain a limited curriculum that stifles creativity and undervalues oral skills.

THE CURRENT CAMPAIGN

Lord Young and Baroness Cox's attempts to introduce 'opted in' private schools into the Education Act 1988 was unsuccessful, but it had achieved considerable media coverage and had made the possibility of such a development in the future more conceivable. The momentum has been maintained through a series of meetings. One of the first of these consisted of little more than a media event staged for the slack news period following the New Year. On 8 January, a total of about 30 people gathered in John Loughborough School, Tottenham, to hear Sir Rhodes Boyson and a variety of other speakers representing a diverse range of schools and educational organizations. The

meeting was organized by Gerald Smith who is head of St Peter's Independent School, Northampton, but it was actually a mouthpiece for Sir Rhodes
Boyson, who argued for support for private schools as a step towards 'full-
blooded privatisation of our schools'. At this meeting partial support from
government for fee-paying schools was considered as well as full support for
non fee-paying schools. Speakers included Philip Toogood, who was representing the Campaign for Educational Choice, K. Davidson, Headmaster
of the Seventh Day Adventist John Loughborough School, and Nazar
Mustafa, Chairman of the Muslim Education Coordinating Council. For such
a small meeting it received remarkable media attention with articles in *The
Times Educational Supplement* and many national newspapers.

Many of these same speakers, including Baroness Cox, Sir Rhodes Boyson, Nazar Mustafa, Gerald Smith and Ruth Deakin, were also speakers in
favour of State support for private schools at a further meeting in mid-April.
This April meeting was arranged by the Centre for Educational Choice, a
new body established by Lord Young, with the aim to 'explore ways in which
a range of non fee-paying schools can be included in the maintained sector'.
Partial support by government for fee-paying schools was thus excluded from
consideration, and the main emphasis of the discussion was on trying to
clarify and ease procedures for new schools to become voluntary-aided
schools. The public meeting was put forward as a time for discussion prior to
a delegation going to the DES to put its case later in the afternoon. This
delegation consisted of Sahib Bleher (Muslim Education Services), Ruth
Deakin (CSC), Colin Hodgetts (Human Scale Education Movement), Prof.
Sig Prais (Jewish Educationist), Baroness Cox and Lord Young, all of whom
had earlier addressed the meeting at Westminster Hall. The meeting was
given further academic legitimacy through two other speakers – Roland
Meighan from the University of Birmingham (heavily involved in Education
Otherwise) and Les Bell from the Open University who talked on Danish
schooling, but these, and some other speakers, did not go on the DES.

The delegation was treated with considerable respect, for it was met by
Kenneth Baker (then Secretary of State for Education and Science), Angela
Rumbold (Minister of State), Robert Jackson (Parliamentary Under-Secretary of State) and nine senior DES officials. It is doubtful if they were told
that the whole meeting at Westminster Hall had numbered only about 150,
including a contingent of children from Dame Catherine's School! However,
raw numbers of supporters are clearly less important than the media attention
that can be generated, and small articles subsequently appeared in many of
the national papers.

A subsequent report on the meeting at the DES stated that Kenneth Baker
had told the delegation that there was no animus in the department towards
new applications for voluntary-aided status. It was stated that nothing is taken
into account except the educational merits or demerits of the case put forward. In practice, however, the attainment of voluntary-aided status is unlikely without the support of the relevant LEA, and only about a month earlier

the Association of Metropolitan Councils had unanimously passed a resolution against the establishment of any further voluntary-aided schools. This path to public support for small private schools is not as open as it might be.

CONCLUSION

The growth of new 'reluctant' private schools shows few signs of abating. The very success of existing evangelical Christian schools leads other evangelical churches to consider the possibility for their own children. The growing wealth and security and many Muslim families, coupled with a rise in some areas of Muslim fundamentalism, encourages the growth of further Muslim schools. It is only within the group of progressive small schools where expansion is not imminent. As the number of schools grows, so does their power to press for changes in the law to give them State funding.

Since the failed attempt to ammend the Education Reform Act 1988, there have been numerous public and private meetings designed to push for future changes. At present, the most important aspect of this political activity is that the CSC and the Centre for Educational Choice are working towards the introduction of a Private Members Bill into the House of Lords in November 1990. The draft bill, written for CSC by Stuart Sexton, seeks to amend the 1988 ACT such that certain categories of independent schools should be eligible to apply for grant-maintained status. It also aims to amend the 1980 Act to make it easier for independent schools to obtain voluntary-aided status against the wishes of the relevant LEA.

The campaign for State funding of a variety of different schools according to parents' wishes has a powerful simplicity, which has welded together a remarkable range of people and organizations from the political right and left. Freedom of choice has become a powerful ideological force, which has been partly used to conceal the right's political objective of a more inegalitarian educational system. At an individual level, it is perfectly right and proper that parents should wish to make choices on behalf of their children for their perceived benefit. A good parent will wish his or her own children to receive the best education available. But what is good for the individual is not always good for society as a whole or for certain less privileged groups or individuals within that society. Individual choices, and the sum effect of individual choices, may have benefits for those making choices, but may also harm others who are less able or willing to participate in the choice-making process (Walford, 1990a). The presence of private schools, for example, may harm State schools by taking out from the State sector those parents who are most likely to ensure that high standards of provision and teaching are maintained. The education provided in State schools may thus deteriorate with the exit of those parents with the greatest concern or financial resources. It is the duty of the State to ensure that the less privileged and less powerful are not harmed by the actions of the more privileged and more powerful – a duty that may mean that individual freedoms are constrained for the benefit of society as a whole. In practice, however, much of the present government's educational policy is designed to increase injustice and inequality of provision, and to develop a hierarchy of schools that will provide very different educational experiences for children of different abilities, social classes and ethnic groups. Whether all of the participants recognize it or not, the campaign for State funding for a variety of small private schools is part of this wider political programme.

The solution is not straightforward. The religious groups campaigning for State funding for their own schools have good grounds for their arguments, as some 20 per cent of children in State-maintained schools are already in religious denominational schools. The weight of history has meant that practically all of these religious schools supported by the State are controlled either by the Church of England or the Roman Catholic Church. There is considerable power in the argument that, if this State support for denominational schools is to continue, it should be extended to the adherents of other faiths, philosophies and particular forms of Christianity. Britain is a far more culturally diverse society in 1990 than it was in 1944, and the privileged position of certain religious organizations will eventually have to be dealt with. However, extending support to new schools, rather than removing support for existing religious schools, would bring an inegalitarian and differentiated education system one step nearer. A few individuals might benefit, but the cost to society as a whole would be great.

ACKNOWLEDGEMENTS

I am most grateful to those who provided information for this chapter and, in particular, to Ruth Deakin, who answered many of my questions and kindly gave me access to several meetings. The research was funded by the Social Innovation Research Group at Aston Business School. The responsibility for the content of this chapter is mine alone.

REFERENCES

ACE (1979) *A Case for Alternative Schools within the Maintained Sector*, London.
Apple, M. W. (1981) Curricular form and the logic of technical control, in L. Barton, R. Meighan and S. Walker (eds.) *Schooling, Ideology and the Curriculum*, Falmer Press, Lewes.
Apple, M. W. (1982) *Education and Power*, Routledge & Kegan Paul, London.
Apple, M. W. (1987) *Teachers and Texts*, Routledge & Kegan Paul, London.
Berg, L. (1968) *Risinghill: Death of a Comprehensive School*, Penguin Books, Harmondsworth.
Blackburne, L. (1989) Thirty-one cooks plus a seasoned campaigner, *The Times Educational Supplement*, 10 March.

Boyson, R. (1974) *Oversubscribed. The Story of Highbury Grove School*, Ward Lock, London.

Buswell, C. (1980) Pedagogic change and social change, *British Journal of Sociology of Education*, Vol. 1, no. 3, pp. 293–306.

Christian Parent-Teacher League (1981) Newsletter, March.

Christian Schools Campaigns (1989) Information sheet, April.

Christian Schools Trust (1988) Information sheet.

Cookson, P. W. Jr (1989) United States of America: contours of continuity and controversy in private schools, in G. Walford (ed.) *Private Schools in Ten Countries: Policy and Practice*, Routledge, London.

Cox, C. B. and Boyson, R. (1975) *The Fight for Education. Black Paper 1975*, Dent, London.

Cox, C. B. and Dyson, A. (1971) *The Black Papers on Education 1 – 3*, Davis-Poynter, London.

Cox, C., Jacka, K. and Marks, J. (1975) *The Rape of Reason*, Churchill Press, London.

Cox, C., Jacka, K. and Marks, J. (1977) Marxism, knowledge and the academies, in C. B. Cox and R. Boyson (eds.) *Black Paper 1977*, Temple Smith, London.

Cox, C. and Marks, J. (1988) *The Insolence of Office*, Claridge Press, London.

Cummings, D. B. (1979) *The Purpose of Christ-Centred Education*, Presbyterian and Reformed Publishing, Phillipsburg, NJ.

Deakin, R. (1989a) *New Christian Schools: The Case for Public Funding*, Regius Press, Bristol.

Deakin, R. (1989b) *The New Christian Schools*, Regius Press, Bristol.

DES (1985a) *Report by HM Inspectors on Faith Christian Academy, Brommeswell, Suffolk, 119/85*, London.

DES (1985b) *Report by HM Inspectors on Shekinah Christian School, Tower Hamlets, London, 155/85*, London.

DES (1985c) *Report by HM Inspectors on Life Christian School, Battersea, London, 162/85*, London.

DES (1985d) *Report by HM Inspectors on New Court Christian School, Finsbury Park, London, 176/85*, London.

Diamond, L. (1989) Building on the failure of CCAS, in C. Harber and R. Meighan (eds.) *The Democratic School*, Education Now, Ticknall.

Doyle, D. P. (1989) Family choice in education: the case of Denmark, Holland and Australia, in W. L. Boyd and J. G. Cibulka (eds.) *Private Schools and Public Policy*, Falmer Press, Lewes.

Golby, M., Treharne, D. and Taylor, W. (1989) *The Small School at Hartland: An Evaluation*, Fair Way Publications, Tiverton.

Gordon, T. (1986) *Democracy in One School?*, Falmer Press, Lewes.

Gray, J. and Jesson, D. (1989) The impact of comprehensive reforms, in R. Lowe (ed.) *The Changing Secondary School*, Falmer Press, Lewes.

Griggs, C. (1989) The new right and English secondary education, in R. Lowe (ed.) *The Changing Secondary School*, Falmer Press, Lewes.

Hargreaves, D. (1974) Deschoolers and the new romantics, in M. Flude and J. Ahier (eds.) *Educability, Schools and Ideology*, Croom Helm, Beckenham.

Hillgate Group (1986) *Whose Schools?*, London.

Hillgate Group (1987) *The Reform of British Education*, Claridge Press, London.

Hugill, B. (1989) Cross purpose, *The Times Educational Supplement*, 24 March.

Mackenzie, R. F. (1970) *State School*, Penguin Books, Harmondsworth.

Marks, J., Cox, C. and Pomian-Srzednicki, M. (1983) *Standards in English Schools*, National Council for Educational Standards, London.

Marks, J. and Pomian-Srzednicki, M. (1985) *Standards in English Schools: Second Report*, Sherwood Press, London.

Mason, P. (1989) Elitism and patterns of independent education, in W. L. Boyd and J. G. Cibulka (eds.) *Private Schools and Public Policy*, Falmer Press, Lewes.

Meighan, R. (1988) *Flexi-Schooling*, Education Now, Ticknall.

O'Keeffe, B. (1986) *Faith, Culture and the Dual System*, Falmer Press, Lewes.

Peshkin, A. (1986) *God's Choice. The Total World of a Fundamentalist Christian School*, University of Chicago Press, Chicago, Ill.

Preece, P. (1989) Pitfalls in research on school and teacher effectiveness, *Research Papers in Education*, Vol. 4, no. 3, pp. 47–69.

Rose, S. D. (1988) *Keeping them out of the Hands of Satan. Evangelical Schooling in America*, Routledge & Kegan Paul, London.

Skinner, G. B. (1981) Faith and education: some alternative models (unpublished DASE dissertation), University of Manchester.

Steedman, J. (1987) Longitudinal survey results into progress in secondary schools, based on the National Child Development Study, in G. Walford (ed.) *Doing Sociology of Education*, Falmer Press, Lewes.

Toogood, P. (1988) Painting a cage with the cage door open, *Education Now*, no. 1, pp. 16–17.

Toogood, P. (1989) Learning to own knowledge: minischools as democratic practice, in C. Harber and R. Meighan (eds.) *The Democratic School*, Education Now, Ticknall.

Walford, G. (1987) How dependent is the independent sector?, *Oxford Review of Education*, Vol. 13, no. 3, pp. 275–96.

Walford, G. (1990a) Developing choice in British education, *Compare*, Vol. 20, no. 1, pp. 67–81.

Walford, G. (1990b) *Privatization and Privilege in Education*, Routledge, London.

Watts, J. (1980) *Towards and Open school*, Longman, London.

Winsor, D. (1987) Small is educational, *The Sunday Times Colour Supplement*, 4 October.

Wright, N. (1989) *Assessing Radical Education*, Open University Press, Milton Keynes.

Young, M. (1958) *The Rise of the Meritocracy*, Penguin Books, Harmondsworth.

Young, M. (1983) *The Elmhursts of Dartington*, Routledge and Kegan Paul, London.

Young, M. and Schuller, T. (eds.) (1988) *Rhythms of Society*, Routledge, London.

Young, M. and Willmott P. (1957) *Family and Kinship in East London*, Penguin Books, Harmondsworth.

Young, M. and Willmott P. (1973) *The Symmetrical Family*, Routledge & Kegan Paul, London.

9

BLACK VOLUNTARY SCHOOLS: THE 'INVISIBLE' PRIVATE SECTOR

Máirtín Mac an Ghaill

INTRODUCTION

For twenty years teachers and policy-makers have claimed to be concerned about black under-achievement in schools. If that is true, why have they never used voluntary schools, where young black people are academically successful, as a model of good practice?

(Lavern, voluntary school-teacher)

If they swapped the voluntary schools for the ordinary schools, black kids would get all the good exams. But they wouldn't let that happen, would they? Because too many blacks would succeed and then all the whites would be asking for their schools.

(Cheryl, voluntary school-teacher)

With only a few exceptions, such as William Tyndale School, the names of English private schools tend to be better known than those of the State sector (Dale, 1989). This juxtaposition of the private and the public is central to the history of English schooling, creating a landscape of a schooling hierarchy in which the private sector is unequivocally associated with privilege and élitism. In contrast, black schools tend not to reflect this apparent natural division. The few successful full-time black private schools, such as John Loughborough School in Tottenham, and the inner-city voluntary schools described in this chapter, are much more closely linked to the State-maintained sector and do not have the élitist functions associated with most other private schools. They constitute a response of the black community to their experience of racism in English schooling (see Mac an Ghaill, 1988). Historically, white private schooling has tended to serve and to reproduce socioeconomic and educational divisions. In contrast, for the black community educational initiatives outside the State sector serve different functions. They are a central aspect of their resistance to racist practices, providing a bridge that enables black students to participate more fully in the wider society (Jones, 1985).

Dhondy (1978) has described the growth of black student and parent movements who organized around various educational issues, such as banding, bussing and educational subnormal schools. He argues (p. 81) that 'there was a black movement in education in this country from the time that our children began to be schooled here. Its spokesmen were the parents of young blacks who were born here or brought here from the West Indies, Pakistan and Bangladesh and Africa, as dependants'. It is important to emphasize that black women were at the forefront of the implementation of these strategies of resistance (see Sivanandan, 1983; Bryan, Dadzie and Scafe, 1985).

One of the most effective forms of this community response has been the establishment of black voluntary schools, which have been described (Reynolds, 1987, p. 20) as 'a movement that is rapidly emerging as a third force, next to the conventional private and state sectors in the British education system'. As Tomlinson (1985, pp. 69–70) points out, it is very difficult to be precise about the number of establishments involved, as some schools are funded by LEAs or Community Relations Councils, while others are self-supporting with volunteer teachers. Many of these schools are located in London, with schools operating in Birmingham and Liverpool since the mid-1970s and, more recently, in Wolverhampton, Manchester and Nottingham. There have been a number of studies of the development of black voluntary schools, including Chevannes (1979), Wellum (1981), Cronin (1984), McLean (1985) and Chevannes and Reeves (1987). This work has taken place against a background of increasing evidence of racist inequality in the State system, with disproportionate numbers of black students being failed (see the Rampton Report, 1981, and Reeves and Chevannes, 1981, for a critique of report). Nuttall's recent ILEA's research findings reinforce this picture of the continuing subordination of black students (Weston, 1990). Many black parents see mainstream schools as having failed to meet their children's needs (see Coard, 1971; Carby, 1982; Hilton, 1989). Black voluntary schools, which take place at the weekends, in the evenings and during the vacations, have developed as a response to this perceived failure.

The focus of this chapter is twofold: first, to describe the experiences and aspirations of those involved in this 'invisible' private sector; and, second, to use these insights to suggest how maintained schools might incorporate more positive responses to the black community. Such responses include developing teacher–parent relations, eliminating racist practices, promoting academic achievement and reaffirming cultural values. The particular focus of this chapter is an ethnographic study of a voluntary school, situated in the Midlands, named after the black nationalist leader, Marcus Garvey. (The name of the school and the names of the participants in the study have been changed to maintain anonymity.) The school, which was self-supporting, was established in 1979. Teachers are unpaid and no school fees are charged. Classes were held in a local community centre, on Saturdays and during the vacations. Twelve teachers were involved, seven of whom were formally qualified. The students ranged from 8–15 years of age, with equal numbers of males and females. Attendance among the hundred students involved varied a great deal throughout the research period. All the students and the teachers were black. Further comparative material was collected from three Asian, two Afro-Caribbean and two Irish voluntary schools. This is part of ongoing research in the local area. These data are not fully reported here but they informed the carrying out of this study.

Ethnographic accounts, such as Willis (1977) and Corrigan (1979), of white working-class males' experience of schooling have provided vital insights into the mechanisms through which inequality is transmitted. I found that the approach of inferring meanings by understanding the context, through participation in the black schools, was very productive. Ethnography provides an ideal method for capturing the subjective meanings and values of a social group, who have little personal or collective access to the power relations operating upon and within mainstream State schools. Furthermore, black students have tended to be absent from sociological studies of school youth. Important exceptions include Wright's (1985) ethnographic work and Griffin's (1985) study of black and white females' transition from school to work.

SCHOOL ETHOS

Many of the students at Marcus Garvey School were attending State schools with a majority black student population. However, they felt that these schools were essentially white institutions. Most immediately this was expressed in terms of the polarization of the predominantly white staff, who did not live in the local area, and the black student body. In contrast, Marcus Garvey School was seen as black, with black parents and community workers, who lived in the area. Similar responses were recorded in the other black voluntary schools. Equally important to the students' perception of the school as being theirs was the involvement of their parents, who were encouraged to take an active role in the organization and running of the school (Stone, 1981, p. 188). Students and parents frequently returned to the theme of the need of State schools to be accountable to their local communities.

Beverley (teacher): We started this school, a group of women who knew each other, because the schools round here are failing our children. We're not welcome at them. The teachers see you as a trouble-maker if you ask questions.
James (parent): We are accepted here [at Marcus Garvey School] and we can learn ourselves what's going on in education. It was very different in Jamaica. We learn and then we can help the younger ones.
M. M.: What's different about this school?
Deborah (student): Just about everything.
M. M.: Like what? What's most different?
Sonia (student): Like at our school, teachers hardly ever talk to you outside of lessons. Its just a job to them, en it?
Richard (student): Yeah, when I was at junior school, I asked my teacher one day, what do you do at the weekend? I thought it was completely different to us. I still don't know about them but here, they're your own people. You know the teachers.

Their kids are your mates an' all. Most importantly I would say, they know what it's like around here. You don't have to be black to sus it out, like you.

Joy (student): That is true. You feel what is different about here in the whole place, don't you? You see black people don't own anything in this society. They don't belong anywhere. You just feel better when its your own place, like our church. You feel proud. You can be yourself, the pressure is off, you can learn.

M. M.: What is this pressure that you don't get here?

Joy: To be like them; to be white!

CURRICULUM ORGANIZATION

One of the main aims of Marcus Garvey School was to supplement the mono-culturalist State schools' curriculum, with its ethnocentric teaching materials and classroom knowledge. The Marcus Garvey teachers challenged the attempt, albeit unintentional, to incorporate black youth into white cultural identities. They stressed the need for a balanced curriculum that did not serve to marginalize black people culturally. In turn, the students responded positively to the opportunity to read black literature and to attend History and Geography lessons that adopted a black perspective.

> *Ludlow (teacher)*: It's very important for all young people to feel secure and have positive images of themselves. We live in a society that denies the existance of black people. This of course is reflected in the curriculum and conflicts with the positive images that the children receive in their own families. My own children [at a local primary school] look at their readers and ask me, why are there no black people, like us? Here, we try to counter the negative feedback that they get in the rest of society.
>
> *M. M.*: What do you like about the lessons?
>
> *Cheryl (student)*: I have always been proud to be black but here you become more aware of the great things that black people have done in history. Not just men, women as well. We are given the opportunity to discover our past that has been hidden from us. I hope we're going to have lots of women writers in this society like in Africa.
>
> *Vernon (student)*: It makes you feel good and it makes you enjoy History and Geography more. Its more real, not just lessons but about you, your history, where you come from.
>
> *Deborah (student)*: In a way then you don't mind so much learning all the white history, because you know about them and your own.
>
> *Richard (student)*: I think white kids need to know as well, then they won't think we're stupid. I bet they think we only have Martin Luther King and Ghandi. They need to know about imperialism and how they have lived off black people.
>
> *Joy (student)*: They still do. The stuff here brings you closer to your parents, when you see what they have suffered for you.

LANGUAGE

One of the major curricular concerns in the schooling of black youth has been the question of language. Hall *et al.* (1978, p. 341) maintain that 'Language is the principal bearer of cultural capital and thus the key medium of cultural reproduction'. The Marcus Garvey School teachers spoke of the ambivalence of the local State schools' response to Creole, with many white teachers seeing it as a form of substandard speech. The students discussed enthusiastically how their linguistic skills, both oral and written, were developed within an environment that acknowledged the strengths of bilinguists. Below, Sharon contrasts this approach with that of her secondary school, where she and her friend were ridiculed for using their first language, which their teachers claimed would be an impediment to their academic success. Michael points out that it was white teachers' perception of Creole as linguistically deficient that contributed to black youths' academic under-performance.

> *Helen (teacher)*: The whole area of language development should be a priority for State schools. They could learn a lot from us. We work from the premises that the children's language is adequate and that you begin by supporting their language. And then proceed to ask, what form is appropriate for what occasion?
> *Lavern (teacher)*: Black pupils are linguistically sophisticated. They come from a rich oral tradition. They need to be encouraged to draw on these resources, which can then be used in a written form and so develop standard English as a necessary second language.
> *Sharon (student)*: It's different here. At school me and my friend were talking together and this teacher comes up and says, what are you two babbling about?
> *M. M.*: What did you say?
> *Sharon*: You get a lot of this. You see they feel threatened somehow, when they don't understand. And she says, 'I don't expect bright pupils to be talking like this'.
> *Michael (student)*: That's the main thing. Teachers, white teachers think that we don't do well because we don't talk like them. But really it's their own attitude. They try to divide you up from your mates if they think you're clever. But here, well they know, don't they? Because it's their language as well. They've succeeded and kept their language.
> *M. M.*: So what would you say to white teachers?
> *Michael*: Look, there's nothing bad or inferior about our language and they can't wipe it out, can they? So, they should change their attitude and look for the good things in our writing.
> *Gilroy (student)*: That's what they do here. I've learnt to write much better since I started. It's more interesting and I have more confidence and the teachers praise you more. They sort of respect your work. You would never think of ordinary teachers like that. I now write poems and short stories, using different language.

HIDDEN CURRICULUM

The Marcus Garvey School teachers were equally critical of the State schools' hidden curriculum, that is the transmission of social values, attitudes and dispositions that reflect the dominant white culture. This can be illustrated with reference to the differing material base and organization of the maintained and voluntary schools. For example, the metaphorical ladder of individual social mobility has been a central theme in the literature on educational equality (Centre for Contemporary Cultural Studies (Education Group), 1981). Many teachers working from within a social-democratic educational ideology see schooling as a meritocratic mechanism for the achievement of equality of opportunity. Voluntary schools serve to highlight that different class and cultural groups have access to different experiences and values (see Gilroy, 1981, p. 212). These schools are community based and concretely demonstrate values of collective self-help, in contrast to the mainstream schools' dominant value of competitive individualism that many teachers believe is intrinsically worthwhile. At all the voluntary schools I visited, there was no talk of professionals and clients but rather integrated social groups working together. Consequently, students did not think in terms of 'us and them' and were supportive of their peers.

> *Beverley (teacher)*: Perhaps what's most important about voluntary schools is that they show the young people that there are ways of behaving, values and beliefs that belong to our culture. These values have sustained us in hostile societies.
> *M. M.*: What are these ideas?
> *Leroy (teacher)*: Basically, these are ideas concerned with collectivism. If you look, especially, at the history of black women, they have survived by sticking together. The State schools emphasize too much making it on your own.
> *Beverley*: This idea of the individual is not natural. A lot of civilizations think in terms of the social group as a whole. Anyway, making it on your own is not an option for black people in this country.
> *M. M.*: Have you changed much since you came here?
> *Sonia (student)*: Really and truely my parents pushed me and I thought, I will learn a lot and get better than the other girls. But now I would say that I have learnt that black people must help each other and other people. That's what they do here. No one is getting paid. They work for us, for the community.
> *Michael (student)*: Yes, and another thing is at school, nearly all the teachers are white, so if you work hard, your friends say that you are trying to be like them. But here you've got black teachers in charge, who are successful and everyone is working together, not against each other. You don't wont to let them down. If you had more black teachers in schools, they could tell you these things.

RACISM AND 'UNDER-ACHIEVEMENT'

The conventional and sociological concepts that have been in use throughout the 1970s and 1980s to explain the 'educational failure' of black students were developed at an earlier period in response to the schooling of white working-class youth. The establishment of the 'problem' in terms of under-achievement, the dominant explanation in terms of cultural disadvantages and the proposed solution, in terms of the adoption of a multicultural curriculum, reflects the educability studies of the 1960s. These studies focused on the socioeconomic deprivations of white working-class students and the implementation of compensatory education, in order to attain equality of opportunity (see Carby, 1980; Centre for Contemporary Cultural Studies (Education Group), 1981).

More recent studies have been critical of the above approach and have shifted their analysis, focusing on how racist practices systematically operate against black youth (Eggleston, Dunn and Anjali, 1985; Wright, 1985; Mac an Ghaill, 1989). Of particular significance has been the process of racist stereotyping, in which youth of Afro-Caribbean origin tend to be perceived in negative terms, as social deviants. The conventional explanation of their poor academic success is underpinned by ideas concerning the assumed pathological structure of their family and kinship organization. Lawrence (1982, p. 111) examines critically the degree of consensus to be found among sociologists concerning the conception of black culture as 'weak'. It may be added that this view is common among policy-makers and teachers. Lawrence (*ibid.*) challenges this caricature, pointing out that 'Afro-Caribbean cultures cannot be described simply as deviations of European cultures but on the contrary, have been actively constructed by Caribbean people. Using memories, knowledge and the "symbol" of Africa together with their historical experiences, they have managed to subvert and in a sense overthrow European cultural dominance'. Voluntary schools provide evidence to support the black community's argument that the major problem in the schooling of their children is not that of culture but of racism. Within the supportive environment of voluntary schools, black students respond positively to the high expectations their teachers have of them. Students who have been labelled as 'failures' are given the opportunity to experience academic success, which enables them to renegotiate their State-school teachers' perception of them. Their teachers confirmed that they had re-evaluated the students, who were now seen as possessing greater academic potential and a more positive attitude to classwork. The parents and the teachers at the three Afro-Caribbean voluntary schools I visited stressed the need for local schools to give higher priority to literacy and numeracy and for them to permit more black youth to follow high-status academic courses.

M. M.: How can more kids get through the system?
Maxine (parent): Every child that comes here has her or his story to tell about racism in school.
Beverley (teacher): It's no good starting anti-racist programmes in the secondary schools. It must start in the primary school. At this stage you see teachers dividing out the black children as trouble-makers.
Maxine: Then you get all this stuff about our deprived families and all the rest of it.
Vernon (student): Like I remember in my junior school, the Afro-Caribbean kids were pushed into sport and music but they were brainy as well but the teachers did nothing on the academic side.
M. M.: Do a lot of black young people experience this?
Helen (teacher): It's a trap that's there for all of us.
Vernon: Then they blame us for being stupid.
Bernie (parent): In the schools around here our kids are mis-educated, you know what I mean? In the primary schools they don't do enough on the basics, so they slowly fall behind. Then in the secondary schools they are pushed into low exam classes.
Lavern (teacher): We set out to make demands on the pupils, high academic demands. This should be the main task of a teacher in my view, to help that child to attain his or her full academic potential.
Beverley: That's what teachers, white teachers want for their own children.
Leroy (teacher): You can see how highly motivated they [the students] are here.

We work with them, thinking out all the ways we can use to develop their knowledge and skills.

Deborah (student): At my school work is easy but here they push you really hard. They want us to succeed. At school my teachers think that I am clever now and they thought I was dumb once.

Beverley: Racism is everywhere. But you get good schools and bad schools, good teachers and bad teachers. The local schools could do much more for our kids. At one level, the whole school system needs to be changed for the sake of all working-class kids. But at the same time, in the short term, teachers should examine how they themselves contribute to the failure of so many black kids in their schools. This is part of the longer process of change.

Lavern: I think that whatever benefits the black kids in inner-city schools, this will improve the situation for whites as well. This is happening in London, after an initial backlash against anti-racism, white parents are seeing their local schools improving. We should work together more.

Beverley: Getting back to individual schools and individual teachers, I think that voluntary schools show that we can reform little bits of the system. They are a form of social engineering and the most successful response to inequality that our kids experience. What goes on here should be part of maintained schools.

Like Cronin (1984, p. 265), this study suggests that 'It is vital. . . that the relationship between teachers and pupils, rather than outcomes in terms of measured achievement, should become a central focus of research concerned with the causes of underachievement among black pupils'. Without underestimating the influence of wider class, 'race' and gender determinants of black youths' life chances, the above serves to suggest the autonomy, albeit limited, individual State schools possess to effect change. For example, in relation to teacher–student interaction, schools have the power to monitor any racist mechanisms, such as racial stereotyping, that may be in operation. This is a vital area of concern, for as Wright (1985, p. 341) points out, racist stereotyping informs such processes as '"gateways", streaming, banding, setting, suspensions and remedial units', that disproportionately operate against male and female black students' academic aspirations.

CONCLUSION

Historically, English State schooling has tended to have low status. In the last ten years, the educational move to the right has served to further undermine an under-resourced, undervalued and over-stressed public sector (Hall and Jacques, 1983). The rapid increase in curricular changes, including the introduction of the Education Reform Act 1988, has increased the disillusionment about and within State schools. In contrast, traditionally for black and white working-class immigrants, education is highly valued as a means of improving opportunities for their children, most of whom are English born. However, the schooling system has played a central part in the continuing subordination of the black community (Mac an Ghaill, 1988). Recently it has been reported that 'Some black parents. . . are so unhappy with racism and standards in schools, they are sending their children to be educated in the West Indies' (Hilton, 1989, p. 2).

This chapter opened with the question, why haven't voluntary schools being used as models of good practice? Their value has been officially acknowledged in the Rampton Report (1981). It stated (p. 45) that 'Supplementary [voluntary] schools are fulfilling an important role and can have much to offer mainstream schools in terms of advice on teaching methods and materials appropriate to the needs of West Indian pupils and of ways of building up trust and understanding'. The Marcus Garvey voluntary-school teachers and students suggest a number of initiatives that might be incorporated into State schools from this 'invisible' private sector. Such initiatives may serve to develop parent–teacher relations, eliminate racist practices, counter 'under-achievement', reaffirm cultural values and help to revitalize inner-city communities. In so doing, LEAs will begin to take responsibility to ensure that all children 'are being properly taught in safe, stimulating and supportive learning environments, and encourage them to have high expectations of themselves and exploit to the full the learning opportunities provided by the environment' (John, 1989, p. 10).

ACKNOWLEDGEMENTS

Many thanks are due to the students and teachers of Marcus Garvey School for their co-operation in this study, and to Chris Griffin, Henry Miller and Geoffrey Walford for their helpful comments on earlier versions of this chapter.

REFERENCES

Bryan, B., Dadzie, S. and Scafe, S. (1985) *The Heart of the Race: Black Women's Lives in Britain*, Virago Press, London.

Carby, H. V. (1980) Multicultural fictions (occasional stencilled paper, race series, SP no. 58), Centre for Contemporary Cultural Studies, University of Birmingham.

Carby, H. V. (1982) Schooling in Babylon, in Centre for Contemporary Cultural Studies (ed.) *The Empire Strikes Back: Race and Racism in 70s Britain*, Hutchinson, London.

Centre for Contemporary Cultural Studies (Education Group) (1981) *Unpopular Education: Schooling and Social Democracy in England since 1944*, Hutchinson, London.

Chevannes, M. (1979) The Black Arrow Supplementary School Project, *The Social Science Teacher*, Vol. 8, no. 4, pp. 136–7.

Chevannes, M. and Reeves, R. (1987) The Black voluntary school movement: definition, context and prospects, in B. Troyna (ed.) *Racial Inequality in Education*, Tavistock, London.

Coard, B. (1971) *How the West Indian Child is made ESN in the British School System*, New Beacon Books, London.

Corrigan, P. (1979) *Schooling the Smash Street Kids*, Macmillan, London.

Cronin, A. (1984) Supplementary schools: their role in culture maintenance, identity and underachievement, *New Community*, Vol. 11, no. 3, pp. 12–14.

Dale, R. (1989) *The State and Education Policy*, Open University Press, Milton Keynes.

Dhondy, F. (1978) Teaching young blacks, *Race Today*, Vol. 10, no. 4, pp. 80–6.

Eggleston, S. J., Dunn, D. and Anjali, M. with the assistance of Wright, C. (1985) *The Educational and Vocational Experiences of 15–18 Year Old Young People of Ethnic Minority Groups* (report to the DES), University of Warwick.

Gilroy, P. (1981) You can't fool the youths...race and class formation in the 1980s, *Race and Class*, Vol. 23, no. 2/3, pp. 207–22.

Griffin, C. (1985) *Typical Girls? Young Women from School to the Job Market*, Routledge & Kegan Paul, London.

Hall, S., Critcher, C., Jefferson, T., Clarke, J. and Roberts, B. (1978) *Policing the Crisis: Mugging, the State and Law and Order*, Macmillan, London.

Hall, S. and Jacques, M. (eds.) (1983) *The Politics of Thatcherism*, Lawrence & Wishart/Marxism Today, London.

Hilton, S. (1989) School rumpus blacks opt out, *Birmingham Evening Mail*, p. 3, 2 December.

John, G. (1989) Clean up the Act, *The Teacher*, p. 10, 29 May.

Jones, V. (1985) *We are Our Own Educators*, New Beacon Books, London.

Lawrence, E. (1982) In the abundance of water the fool is thirsty: sociology and black pathology, in Centre for Contemporary Cultural Studies (ed.) *The Empire Strikes Back: Race and Racism in 70s Britain*, Hutchinson, London.

Mac an Ghaill, M. (1988) *Young, Gifted and Black: Student-Teacher Relations in the Schooling of Black Youth*, Open University Press, Milton Keynes.

Mac an Ghaill, M. (1989) Coming-of-age in 1980s England: reconceptualizing black students' schooling experience, *British Journal of Sociology of Education*, Vol. 10, no. 3, pp. 273–86.

McLean, M. (1985) Private supplementary schools and the ethnic challenge to state education in Britain, in C. Brock and W. Tulasiewicz (eds.) *Cultural Identity and Educational Policy*, Croom Helm, London.

Rampton Report (1981) *West Indian Children in Our Schools*, HMSO, London.

Reeves, F. and Chevannes, M. (1981) The underachievement of Rampton, *Multiracial Education*, Vol. 10, no. 1, pp. 35–42.

Reynolds, Z. (1987) The third force, *The Times Educational Supplement*, p. 20, 20 March.

Sivanandan, A. (1983) Challenging racism: strategies for the 80's, *Race and Class*, Vol. XX, no. 1, pp. 1–11.

Stone, M. (1981) *The Education of the Black Child in Britain*, Fontana, London.

Tomlinson, S. (1985) The 'black education' movement, in M. Arnot (ed.) *Race and Gender: Equal Opportunities Policies in Education*, Pergamon Press/Open University Press, Oxford.

Wellum, J. (1981) *Survey of Library Needs of Black Supplementary Schools*, North London Polytechnic.

Weston, C. (1990) Home life is key to top marks, *Guardian*, p. 10, 9 March.

Willis, P. (1977) *Learning to Labour: How Working-Class Kids get Working-Class Jobs*, Saxon House, Farnborough.

Wright, C. (1985) School processes: an ethnographic study, in S. J. Eggleston, D. K. Dunn and M. Anjali, op. cit.

10
FROM ASSISTED PLACES TO CITY TECHNOLOGY COLLEGES

Tony Edwards, Sharon Gewirtz and Geoff Whitty

City technology colleges (CTCs), subsequently described by Margaret That-cher as 'state-funded independent schools' (McCulloch, 1989), were originally announced by Kenneth Baker at the 1986 Conservative Party Conference. Their origins have been variously located – for example, in the advice of Professor Brian Griffiths, head of the Downing Street Policy Unit and an advocate of the energizing effects on educational performance of greater diversity and competition; in the directly government-funded comprehensive schools canvassed before the 1983 election as a remedy for the alleged failure of urban LEAs; in the 1982 threat that LEA hostility to the government's 'new institutional arrangements for Technical and Vocational Education' might force the Manpower Services' Commission to found its own 'purely technical' schools for pupils aged 14–18; or in a century of unsuccessful at-tempts to promote secondary technical education (McLeod, 1988; McCulloch, 1989; Morrell, 1989). Although *The Sunday Times* (22 December 1985) had referred, while Sir Keith Joseph was still at the DES, to a plan to create 16–20 directly funded technological schools that would be outside LEA control, that leak or prediction seemed to have been largely forgotten when Joseph's successor promised twenty CTCs by 1990. The promise was interpreted at the time as a personal initiative by a new and notably ambitious Secretary of State. Subsequent difficulties in finding sites and sponsors, especially in the same places, suggested that it had been neither thought through nor properly planned. Indeed, the view attributed to the chairman of the CTC Trust that the DES had 'woefully underestimated' the start-up costs of CTCs might be interpreted as a criticism of instant policy-making (Nash, 1988). Yet the enthusiastic Conservative Party Conference response to Baker's announce-ment, made in the course of a general attack on 'producer interests' and LEA 'monopolies', reflected the confidence of a party expecting another election victory and a third, more radical, administration. The CTCs could therefore

be regarded approvingly as harbingers of the much more diversified and privatized educational provision to which the party was increasingly committed.
They could also be regarded disapprovingly in the same way. Although no
more than twenty were promised, they have been described as the 'centre-
piece' of a new deal for the users of education (*Guardian*, 8 October 1986);
as 'a fundamental attack on comprehensive education' (NUT, 1989); and as
'a spearhead of Tory hopes of resurrecting a semi-independent sector outside
the control of LEAs' (*The Financial Times*, 25 February 1987).

In examining such broad interpretations of the initiative by advocates and
critics, we refer for comparison and contrast to an earlier Conservative policy
that has also caused controversy out of all proportion to its modest scale. The
Assisted Places Scheme was attacked from the outset as an offensive declar-
ation of no-confidence in the capacity of comprehensive schools to cater for
able children, as a government-sponsored withdrawal of parental support
from the sector for which the government itself is responsible and as a deliberate enhancement of private education. Unlike the CTC initiative, however,
its sources are relatively clear. It originated in moves from within the private
sector, first to improve the direct-grant arrangements by making the subsidizing of places less indiscriminate, and then to restore a 'scholarship ladder'
from the public sector when the Labour government ended the direct-grant
schools intermediate position between private and public education. The
scheme was then taken up by the Conservative Party as part of the counter-
attack against 'egalitarianism', and in the context of mounting concern about
the 'denial' of academic opportunities to able working-class children brought
about by the rapid disappearance of maintained grammar schools. It was
certainly not 'instant policy-making'. Energetic canvassing within the private
sector had assured it of considerable support before its formal announcement
in June 1979 as the new government's first educational initiative. It was then
implemented to a tight timetable, with none of the setbacks that have been
experienced in establishing CTCs (Edwards, Fitz and Whitty, 1989).

The preceding paragraphs may seem to illustrate a contrast between 'old
right' and 'new right' educational policy – a conservative restoration of educational opportunity as traditionally defined, and a radical, neo-liberal innovation with characteristics of 'pure Thatcherism' (David, 1990). In exploring
the significance of CTCs and their radical potential, we consider whether that
contrast is quite so sharp and whether Conservative policy-making as illustrated in the two initiatives is so neatly divisible into discontinuous strands.
There is certainly some obvious common ground in the justifying rhetoric
used by their respective proponents. Both are presented as responses to alleged failures in comprehensive secondary education, especially in the inner
cities. From this perspective, independent schools and CTCs are seen as
providing maintained schools with the spur of competition, while also representing examples of 'excellence' to be emulated or at least imitated. But
the two initiatives reflect and reinforce very different definitions of secondary education, and it is with these differences that our analysis begins.

DEFINITIONS OF EXCELLENCE AND OPPORTUNITY IN SECONDARY EDUCATION

The Assisted Places Scheme represents the private sector at its most merito-cratic. It was intended to give 'able children from our poorest homes. . . the opportunity of attending academically excellent schools' as excellence has traditionally been defined (*Daily Mail*, 25 June 1979). The schools selected in 1981 for 'Assisted Place status' included almost all the former direct-grant schools that had opted for 'full' independence in 1976, eight former voluntary-aided grammar schools and fourteen Headmasters' Conference day-schools, such as Dulwich College and St Paul's. Nearly 80 per cent of the places avail-able to children aged 11–13 were allocated to these three categories of school. Many of the rest went to other market leaders in a sector that has become markedly more academic in orientation since the early 1960s, and that has been conspicuously successful in associating 'academic excellence' with in-dependence in its publicity (ISIS, 1974, 1976, 1981). Indeed, it is a useful reminder of how the leading independent schools throw a halo around the rest of the private sector that some of the schools invited to apply for allo-cations of assisted places, and many of those that initially declared themselves interested in doing so, had to be discouraged or rejected as unsuitable. For if assisted places were to be defended as a sponsored escape-route for academi-cally able children from comprehensive schools assumed to be incapable of providing properly for them, then the independent schools allowed to offer those places had to have demonstrably high academic standards themselves. That obvious requirement determined the criteria used to select appropriate schools – namely, size of sixth form, range of A-level subjects (which were expected to include three sciences and at least two modern languages), the quality of A-level results and the number of pupils going on to higher edu-cation. The scheme therefore sustains the assumption that access to a tradit-ionally academic education, and to the high-status careers to which academic success gives access, is the ideal form of educational opportunity.

In its resolute traditionalism, the scheme connects with a main strand in conservative 're-appraisals of progressive assumptions', to borrow a phrase from the Black Papers' opening statement of intent – namely, the strong de-fence of traditional academic subjects traditionally taught and rigorously examined (Cox and Dyson, 1969). Indeed, some of those associated with the New Right have also attacked what they regard as an over-emphasis on 'rel-evance', seeing it as a reprehensible rejection of traditional educational values because it risks 'imprisoning the children of the urban poor' in their disad-vantaged environment by denying them access to the 'literate culture and broader horizons', which secondary schools should make available (Sher-man, 1988). From such perspectives, independent schools and the remaining grammar schools are exempted from blame for the ill-effects of 'progress-ivism', and identified as oases of traditional values and academic standards. Assisted places are then defended as enabling their holders to attend schools

in which a 'real' academic education is still available, and which thereby confer real occupational advantages of which the parents of those children are
well aware. Presented in this way, the scheme is easily aligned with other
government policies that seem to defend provision for a traditional academic
élite – for example, the continuing resistance of any significant broadening
of 18+ examinations because A-level is regarded as a guarantee of high
academic standards and an objective regulator of entry to higher education,
and the rejection of LEA schemes for re-organizing post-16 provision where
these are judged to be damaging to schools of 'proven worth' (the proof
usually being the possession of a large, traditional sixth form).

It is here that a contrast becomes apparent, not only between the specific
initiatives we are comparing but also between the 'policy sets' to which they
belong. For the kind of academic education the Assisted Places Scheme so
explicitly promotes has also been attacked by some commentators on the
right as an anachronism – even for the academic élite, perhaps, but certainly
when offered in diluted form down the ability range. Successive Conservative
administrations have carried on from their immediate Labour predecessor
the criticism that secondary schools have been unresponsive to the needs
of modern industry, that too much of what they teach is unrelated to the
demands of working life, that technology of all kinds is being persistently
neglected and that too many of the country's ablest children are being
diverted away from industrial employment by a system still biased against
'trade' and against 'useful knowledge'.

The consequence of all this is judged to be a workforce seriously under-
skilled, at all levels from manager to labourer, in comparison with industrial
competitors. Among the remedies sought through reforming secondary education have been the promotion of courses with an explicitly vocational or
pre-vocational orientation, of work experience and other direct links with
industry to produce greater industrial awareness, and of information technology and design and technology within the curriculum itself. While it is
unclear why the creation of a new kind of school was also judged to be necessary when TVEI was supposed to be reshaping the whole of secondary education, it is clear that the CTCs are intended to embody all those remedies.
They therefore reflect the 'modernizing' tendency Richard Johnson (1989)
identifies as a continuing strand in contemporary Conservative ideology,
and as a powerful influence on the Baker reforms. The schools accepted for
assisted-place status, however, have not been required to incorporate any of
these modernizing reforms. In so far as they set an example to the maintained
system, a matter we explore in the following section, it is as a stimulus to
return to old educational paths. Their exemption from the statutory requirements of the National Curriculum, despite the presence in many of large
numbers of publicly funded pupils, is defended as respecting their independent
status. It is also argued that since they already teach what sensible parents
want, then legislative prescriptions are unnecessary – a defence seized on by
those still inclined to see the National Curriculum as the old grammar-school

curriculum writ large, but presumably a defence not available to those convinced of that curriculum's considerable irrelevance to an advanced industrial society. CTCs are certainly required by their funding agreements to adhere to 'the substance of' the National Curriculum. But their relative freedom from detailed prescription is a licence for curriculum innovation and curriculum differentiation, and for being especially responsive to the requirements of sponsors and other employers. The official intention is that they should offer 'a broadly-based secondary education' (DES, 1986); the highlighting of science and technology, or of technology as applied to the performing and creative arts, is to be made possible by a longer working day and specially targeted resources rather than by large reductions in other areas of the curriculum. There is also to be a pervading emphasis on 'qualities of enterprise, self-reliance and responsibility' (*ibid.*).

As the colleges take shape, rather different working definitions of technology seem to be operating. Information technology still predominates, as is evident not only in CTC publicity but in the allocation of resources. But the original image of schools with a mission task of producing technologists and other applied scientists has been modified to include serving the technological needs of the performing arts. It is also unclear whether the products of such schooling are intended to join a technological élite or whether they represent part of that 'next 15% to 45%' of the ability range Lord Young described at the outset of TVEI as being 'the bright and able' who, unattracted by traditional academic subjects, would be the technicians of the new industrial age (Chitty, 1987). But if an explicit curriculum bias is an obvious distinguishing mark of the colleges, they were also described by the Chief Executive of the CTC Trust (*Guardian*, 12 September, 1989) as being ideally placed to 'trial and evaluate' new modes of learning because of their freedom from LEA control. For example, the colleges already open or well underway with their curriculum planning display a public determination to cross conventional curriculum boundaries, to integrate pupils' studies wherever possible, to use information technology to give pupils' more control over the pace and sequence of what they learn and to encourage collaborative learning and problem-solving. It might be argued, of course, that these are innovations for pupils outside that élite for whom a traditional academic curriculum transmitted in traditional ways is still thought appropriate. It is interesting, nevertheless, that they resemble aspects of that 'progressivism' that is regularly deplored from the neo-conservative right in its defence of traditional learning. That the Solihull CTC is considering the replacing of A- levels (the embodiment of traditional academic standards) by a choice between the International Baccalaureate or BTEC vocational qualifications as alternative sixth-form routes could be seen as compounding the offence.

The different definitions of secondary education sustained by the two initiatives lead to different notions of who the appropriate recruits should be. Assisted places were attacked from the time of their first announcement as returning the 11-plus 'by the back door'. Justified as a restoration of opportunities to attend 'academically excellent' independent schools, the scope of the scheme is necessarily restricted to children who are academically 'meritorious' as such merit is identified through the schools' normal selection procedures. Given the supporting rhetoric about rescuing 'embers from the ashes' of urban secondary education, some priority might be expected to be given to children of acceptable rather than exceptional ability who are judged to be especially disadvantaged. In practice, many of the schools able to pick and choose among their financially eligible applicants seem to follow a straight-forward order of academic merit. Certainly, the scheme's publicizers have regularly drawn attention to conspicuous academic successes, and there is now evidence of the relatively superior A-level performance of assisted-place holders compared with their 'full-fee' – paying contemporaries (*The Times Educational Supplement*, 1 December 1989). The main argument about the take-up of places has been about whether it matters that working-class children appear to be under-represented in comparison with the scheme's initial presentation as a lifeline for the 'bright working-class child', or whether the high proportion (around 40 per cent) entitled to free places and the many more from families with incomes below the national average are sufficient evidence of the scheme's success in matching opportunity with need.

In so far as CTCs are selective, it is not in traditional academic ways. Each is supposed to serve 'a substantial catchment area', large enough to contain the 1,000 or so children aged 11 from whom it should recruit about a fifth. There is an obvious conflict here with 'open enrolment' to maintained schools, and there is already pressure to free the CTCs from a constraint that is il-logical in the context of the Education Reform Act 1988. But while they are clearly not to be neighbourhood schools taking all-comers, they are not sup-posed to be academically selective technological high schools either. Their intakes are intended to be from the full ability range, and to be representative of the 'catchment' population in ethnic and social-class composition. Yet where applications exceed the places available, as is already the case with the first colleges opened, then the criteria for choosing among the applicants include the children's aptitude for and interest in a technologically oriented curriculum, and their parents' acceptance of the distinctive ethos of the col-lege and willingness to support their child's education there until the age of 18. Since very few pupils holding assisted places leave school before the age of 18, this might seem an important similarity between the two initiatives. But in those independent schools 'with assisted-place status', progression through A-levels to higher education can safely be assumed as the normal pupil career. It will be a very different matter to establish a seven-year norm in schools with a wide ability intake, often located in areas with traditionally low staying-on rates. The CTCs may well wish to achieve that social rep-resentativeness to which they are formally committed. But a question asked when the colleges were first announced will have to wait some time to be answered: 'In depopulated inner cities, is it likely that a thousand "accept-able" pupils will be flushed from the high-rise flats and depopulated buildings', or will many of those pupils be found in families wanting 'a subsidized grammar school in high technology clothes?' (Glazier, 1986).

PARENTAL CHOICE AND
THE SPUR OF COMPETITION

It has become a familiar neo-liberal diagnosis that the complacency of entrenched producer interests – teacher unions, LEAs and their various allies within the 'education business' – carries much of the blame for 'falling' educational standards and for a persistent unresponsiveness to the legitimate demands of consumers. Of particular concern from this perspective are those many consumers of education who are denied an effective 'voice' in their children's schooling because they cannot exercise the right to 'exit' from schools they judge to be unsatisfactory by buying or moving their way out. Much greater parental choice has therefore been advocated from the neo-liberal right, not only as an embodiment of individual rights but also as the only effective way of making schools accountable. It is argued that as long as many maintained schools are protected from the full consequences of their unpopularity – namely, that they should lose resources in proportion to their loss of custom – then they escape the real pressure of market forces to improve or perish. Advocates of educational vouchers as the best mechanism for creating that pressure remain disappointed, but much of the Education Reform Act 1988 is devoted to securing greater competition between schools through the encouragement of opting out, open enrolment and devolved budgets determined largely by pupil numbers. Taken together, these changes are intended to constitute a stern test of market popularity. The CTCs are also intended to serve that over-riding objective. They introduce more diversity into secondary education, while their presence is supposed to challenge comprehensive schools in and around their catchment areas to improve or suffer the consequences. In considering the claim that they thereby enhance parental choice, we again make some initial comparisons with the Assisted Places Scheme.

That scheme was included in an Education Act (1980) that also strengthened parents' right to challenge LEA-allocated secondary places, and that required maintained secondary schools to publish examination results, which could then be used as evidence for a more informed parental choice. The arrangements by which fees are paid or partly paid by the Exchequer mean that parents of successful applicants for assisted places bring a means-tested government subsidy (worth on average nearly £2,000 in 1988–9) to the independent school of their choice. There is, at least in the English version of the scheme, enough resemblance to voucher proposals to have some appeal for the neo-liberal right – for example, because parents are enabled to 'trigger off an incremental portion of the private school grant by his/her decision to choose one independent school in preference to others or to state schools'

(West, 1982, p. 15). But as the subsidies are limited to parents of academically able children, they are largely irrelevant to those wanting a radical enhancement – on principle and in the interests of subjecting all schools to the 'discipline' of unremitting consumer pressure – of *all* parents' power of choice. As an Education Minister during its introduction, Rhodes Boyson supported the scheme as a 'life-belt' for able inner-city children who would otherwise 'go down' with failing comprehensive schools. But he soon noted its illogicality from a radical perspective: if effective parental choice is such a powerful mechanism for improving schools, then the whole public sector needs galvanizing in this way (Albert, 1982). A New-Right explanation of how the Conservative government in 1983 lost its nerve about vouchers in the face of DES advice that they were impractical, makes little mention of assisted places as a model or trial run for what might be done (Seldon, 1986). And our own initial report on the scheme's implementation up to 1986 noted that it had not been expanded since its inception five years earlier, offered no scope for significant expansion on its strictly academic terms and had not yet been followed by more radical initiatives involving (for example) 'private funding for educational experiments in inner-city areas' (Fitz, Edwards and Whitty, 1986). The subsequent addition of 50 schools to the scheme in 1989 was an attempt to ameliorate regional and gender inequalities in the availability of places; even then, only five places were allocated to each school.

Although not similarly restricted by traditionally academic terms of reference, and although they offer a free education to a much wider range of recruits, the CTCs in their 'pilot' form make an even less significant numerical contribution to increasing parental choice. When fully grown, the twenty CTCs promised by 1991 will contain some 20,000 pupils compared with the 35,000 assisted places intended for the 276 English independent schools now participating in the scheme. Even in the locations identified by the DES in its 1986 promotional publication, there was no equivalent to the still-unrealized ambition off putting an assisted place within geographical reach of any interested parent with an eligible child. The indirect effects of CTCs, however, may be considerable. Unlike the somewhat esoteric academic examples offered by independent schools with assisted places, they are presented as alternative *comprehensive* schools – catering for similar intakes in ability (and cultural background) but enabled to do a much better job by their more relevant curricula, greater capacity for innovation and a productive partnership with industry promising better employment opportunities for pupils. It is likely that comprehensive schools around them will watch their development with concern as competitors in the same market, even while being tempted to write off any relative advantages as a simple consequence of better resources. LEAs affected by their actual or projected appearance certainly deplore the disruptive effects on their own attempts to reorganize secondary provision, seeing the CTCs as putting back places they have tried to remove through the painful processes of school mergers and closures. It is argued, of course, that any short-term disruption will be justified in the long run if these 'beacons of excellence' shed new light across the system. Yet a large part of the case against them is that they offer nothing – in uses of information technology, emphasis on collaborative learning and cross-curricular links, work experience, even 'compact' arrangements with local employers – that cannot be found within existing comprehensive schools at considerably less cost, and that their introduction merely adds to the pressure on maintained schools to divert scarce resources into marketing themselves more effectively.

A similar argument was advanced against assisted places – that they drew able pupils away from comprehensive schools without any firm evidence that their publicly sponsored withdrawal was necessary (Rae, 1981). But while that scheme was also defended as challenging maintained schools to improve their own academic standards so as to avoid being 'creamed' by competitors, its main justification has been that it gives access to a *kind* as well as to a *quality* of academic education not otherwise available to its participants. It is therefore much harder to see *how* its exemplary influence is supposed to be exerted. If it encouraged maintained schools to return to traditional academic paths, it would be in conflict with other government policies and with the substantial 'rewards' those policies have brought to schools willing to give greater priority to (for example) developing technological competence, vocational relevance and industrial awareness, and to catering more imaginatively for lower-attaining pupils. Such direct competitive pressure on schools faced with a loss of able entrants is in any case mitigated by the geographically dispersed intakes to academically prestigious independent schools – a fact often cited by defenders of the scheme to deny that significant damage is being done to individual comprehensive schools – and above all by evidence that most of the place-holders do not come from those inner-city areas where comprehensive schools are most often accused of failure (Edwards, Fitz and Whitty, 1989). That evidence adds weight to a concern expressed even in the house journal of the Headmasters' Conference (February 1980) – that a scheme designed to 'save' able children from poor comprehensives may 'simply attract middle class children who would otherwise go to a good comprehensive'.

ORIGINS, INTENTIONS AND OUTCOMES

In many ways, the introduction of assisted places was an example of successful pressure-group politics. The main pressure group was conservative in its view of academic standards, and traditionally liberal in its commitment to educational opportunity. Subsequent reinterpretations of the scheme as being consistent with neo-liberal principles are largely unconvincing, apart from its direct subsidizing of parental choice (Fitz, Edwards and Whitty, 1989). It originated in attempts by the Direct-Grant Schools Joint Committee, first to produce a more politically defensible scholarship system by ending the provision of free places without reference to parents' capacity to pay fees, and then to replace opportunities thought to be lost through the ending of the direct-grant system. The scheme gained support within the private sector once it became clear that it would extend well beyond the former direct-grant schools, whose relative protection from the full rigours of market forces had long caused some resentment among more market-dependent members of that sector. It also benefited from the growing tendency to justify the position of independent schools as bastions of traditional academic standards and so as a necessary complement (or even antidote) to public-sector provision. It was a defence well adapted to win political support. For as the Labour Party became more intent on 'reducing and eventually abolishing' the private sector, so the Conservative Party became much more responsive to the strenuous campaigning through which that sector organized its defences. And in its reaction against the so-called 'progressive consensus', and against 'egalitarianism' in particular, the remaining grammar schools (a high proportion of them now independent) were defended for retaining real academic opportunities and so making a necessary contribution to training the country's future élite.

In reporting how assisted places originated, we commented that we could see no significant contributions to the scheme's formulation from the ideologies actively engaged in preparing the ground within the Conservative Party for radical policies by a new-style Conservative government (Whitty, Fitz and Edwards, 1989). In retrospect, that may misrepresent the role of Stuart Sexton in promoting the scheme politically and in canvassing likely schools. Given his subsequent emergence as Director of the Education Unit for the Institute of Economic Affairs, and his evident enthusiasm for reconstructing the entire education system as an open market, he may well have seen more radical possibilities in the scheme than were visible to (or indeed wished for) by its main supporters within the private sector. In his contribution to the last collection of Black Papers, he had argued for the removal of any 'bureaucratic direction' that got in the way of parental choice, and of all constraints that 'seek to distort the pattern of educational supply and demand' (Sexton, 1977). His alternative was a system in which choice was 'open' and power devolved, with maintained schools also given independence from LEA control by various forms of direct funding (Sexton, 1987). Assisted places represented a small step in that direction, in so far as they encouraged some of the remaining grammar schools to opt out and so enlarge the 'network' of independent schools. But the main motivation for the scheme lay elsewhere, notably in the desire to restore a scholarship ladder to traditionally excellent schools.

In contrast, the CTCs seemed from the time of their announcement to constitute a more radical initiative. They were greeted from the neo-liberal right as inaugurating a much more determined government policy of extending parental choice incrementally – of introducing State-funded alternatives gradually rather than through a root-and-branch system of vouchers (Hillgate Group, 1987). Even so, the 'modernizing' aspects of the policy as presented by Kenneth Baker were at least as evident as its neo-liberal market orientation. For by providing public subsidies directly to the institutions rather than directly to the individual consumer, and by requiring intakes representative of defined catchment areas, the initiative might even be described as distorting the market. In this respect at least, the Assisted Places Scheme might appear the more radical. But it is the later initiative that has the wider scope, despite that uncertainty about its origins we noted earlier and the continuing difficulty of identifying its primary purposes. Are the CTCs a 'radical' attempt, much more sharply focused than the 'reformist' TVEI, to give technologically oriented secondary education the status (and resources) it has lacked in this country, and by so doing help to reshape the curriculum for all? (McCulloch, 1989). Are they becoming a more broadly based attempt to create centres for real innovation in curriculum and learning, free from the 'shackles' of LEA control? Are they an attempt to bring greater diversity, but a *stratified* diversity in which assisted places would still contribute to producing the 'trained élite' while the CTCs helped to produce the officer-technologists? Is the undoubted disruption of LEA planning as well as LEA provision intended to accelerate the emergence of varied, fragmented and highly competitive educational provision, as the attribution of 'parentage' to Professor Brian Griffiths might suggest? And how far should CTCs be seen as part of the 'Action for Cities' programme, a government strategy of working in 'partnership' with business to privatize public services and end the domination of Labour-controlled councils?

Whatever its varied ideological attractions, the initiative has certainly lacked the momentum given to the Assisted Places Scheme by the 'secret élite negotiations' that preceded its announcement (Tapper and Salter, 1986). Indeed, preparatory negotiations are hardly evident at all. The DES document (DES, 1986), which promptly followed the Secretary of State's announcement, located the places most in 'need' of colleges without having established whether suitable sites might be available either for new building or for the rebuilding of empty or redundant schools. The most specific locations – Moss Side in Manchester, Chapeltown in Leeds, Highfields in Leicester and St Paul's in Bristol – are therefore still without colleges or even firm projects. As exemplifications of the policy, however, they were intended to indicate the priority to be given to areas 'suffering acute social deprivation', where (in the Secretary of State's words) 'the education is at present under most serious pressure' (DES, 1986). Although some of them were already benefiting from urban-aid projects, there was no reference to their also being areas of exceptionally high unemployment or of intense skill shortages. And there was no reference whatsoever to consultations with LEAs, even though those describable as being under the severest educational pressure were also likely to be responding to sharply falling school rolls. The response of LEAs to the appearance of a 'new choice of school' in areas where they were seeking to rationalize provision, often through contentious plans for closing or merging existing schools, was certain to be hostile except where political loyalty to the government was the paramount consideration. Nor was there a queue of eager sponsors, equivalent to that queue of independent schools that had been so willing to offer assisted places six years earlier.

Among the consequences of the initial failure to identify practicable sites have been an expedient redefinition of the 'inner-city' to include areas adjacent to it, and an extension of where CTCs might 'rise from the ashes' to include taking over from LEAs 'their most deprived or failing schools' even in circumstances where that definition is strenuously and justifiably rejected. The latest list of colleges, which are either open or 'certain' to be so by 1991, is therefore considerably different from the original DES map, leaves some of the then-designated areas unexploited, and bunches the CTCs projected for the south east so as to site three of them within a few miles of each other. The Chairman of the CTC Trust blames LEA fears of competition for their apparent preference for keeping schools 'empty and vandalised rather than selling the site for a hefty capital receipt' (*The Times Educational Supplement*, 2 October 1988). But the failure to attract sufficient private capital has been no less a problem.

Difficulties in finding sponsors have brought large changes in funding the colleges. As initially presented, the DES was to meet the recurrent costs of each college at the level needed to match the resources allocated to comprehensive schools in the catchment area. Capital costs were to be 'wholly or substantially' the responsibility of the sponsors. In practice, the DES proved to have over-estimated the willingness of industry and business to 'invest' in the new ventures, and 'woefully under-estimated' the start-up costs. As a result, the 'whole or substantial' contributions of their sponsors to the already existing colleges at Solihull, Nottingham and Teesside represent 22, 15 and 25 per cent respectively of their capital costs, to which the Exchequer has already contributed altogether some £21 million. Recent official estimates indicate that Exchequer contributions to launching CTCs will amount to £93 million by 1991 compared with £31 million from industrial sponsors – a ratio moving towards the government's 85-per-cent contribution to the capital costs of voluntary-aided schools, and high enough to support those who argue that business-supported aided schools within the public sector may constitute the next, much larger step forward towards a fragmented system.

As things stand, the political necessity of bailing out the initiative with public money provides its political opponents with an obvious objection at a time when the deteriorating fabric of maintained schools brings repeated (if discreetly worded) warnings from HMI, and when the £7 million of public money invested in the Nottingham CTC can be polemically compared with the £2.4 million spent by the Nottinghamshire LEA on all its 500 schools (NUT, 1989). Such comparisons are met by counter-arguments that spending on CTCs is 'new' money not otherwise available for public-sector education (that same argument having been used in 1980–1 in defence of the public funding of assisted places); that it represents positive discrimination in favour of urban areas badly in need of regeneration; and that spreading the money around the country's secondary schools would produce additional resources averaging only £1,800 per school and lose the galvanizing effects of a properly funded innovation. That argument is double-edged. For if the emphasis on information technology, to take the most obvious example, requires 'hardware and software on a scale more extensive than is normal in the maintained sector' (as the original DES brochure asserted, DES, 1986), then it is open to that sector to claim that nothing is being done that is not achievable by maintained schools if they were similarly funded. Indeed, that claim seemed to be anticipated in a display at the DES in February 1990, which presented the 'beacon' effects of CTCs as being dependent on their being equipped 'to no higher level than can be attained by any state secondary school within its existing budget'.

The extent to which, in practice, CTCs help to develop a distinctive approach to educational provision or to pioneer new directions for the system as a whole remains to be seen. Despite the national framework represented by the work of the CTC Trust and the CTC Unit within the DES, considerable divergences in curriculum emphasis and ethos are already apparent in the emerging colleges. From a neo-liberal perspective, this is no doubt how things should be. What is looked for from that perspective is a highly diversified market with competing suppliers offering 'real' alternatives, in place of homogeneous near-monopoly *systems* of schools. Although CTCs are not able to expand as they might wish to meet demand, they are seen from the right as inaugurating (or trialling) developments that will eventually make secondary education as 'open' as a fully fledged voucher scheme would do (Hammer and Flude, 1989). Yet this, in turn, creates considerable uncertainties about whether they will be able to fulfil the 'modernizing' mission Kenneth Baker has ascribed to them.

The colleges are certainly intended to socialize their pupils into a 'market culture' very different from the 'literary-moral tradition' still prominent in independent schools. In this respect they seem to represent a clear strand in the continuing conflicts within the right between its modernizing, utilitarian, even anti-intellectual components and surviving neo-conservative exponents of 'traditional culture and values' (Musgrove, 1987). Preparing pupils for the demands of a modern industrial society is to be achieved through the technologically oriented curriculum, the special links with employers and their frequent presence, an overt emphasis on enterprise and self-reliance and the various 'messages' carried in the organization of the colleges (for example, in the adoption of an 08.30 to 17.00 'industrial day').

Yet the history of English education (and especially of technical and technological education) suggests that quite different outcomes are possible. The lack of parity of esteem, both in secondary and higher education, has often led vocationally oriented secondary schools and technologically oriented higher-education institutions to drift in curricula and selectiveness towards the model embodied in traditional high-status institutions (Banks, 1955; Couper and Harris, 1970; McCulloch, 1989). It remains possible that the

CTCs will emerge as surrogate grammar schools rather than as the beacons of 'modernism' claimed in the rhetoric that surrounds them. Indeed, neo-liberal and neo-conservative influences on government policy may combine in this instance and frustrate the 'modernizing' aspects of Baker's initiative and any chance that CTCs could help to 'break the mould' of English secondary education (Johnson, 1989). Both the exercise of parental choice (embodying a ladder of opportunity reconstructed to suit the 'well-motivated' rather than the academically able) and the constraining effects of broad conformity to the National Curriculum could lead to a much more conservative style of schooling than that originally proposed (Whitty, 1989). The CTC initiative would then be an experiment that produced a new choice of school without producing a new type of school. If so, it would be no more radical in its outcomes than the Assisted Places Scheme.

NOTES

This is an edited version of a paper delivered to the ERA Research Network at King's College London on 12 March 1990. It draws upon an evaluation of the Assisted Places Scheme funded by the Economic and Social Research Council (research grant no. C00230036) and identifies some of the issues currently being explored in a study of CTCs, also funded by the Economic and Social Research Council (research grant no. C00232462).

REFERENCES

Albert, T. (1982) The cheapest way to help the brightest and best, *Guardian*, 23 November.

Banks, O. (1955) *Parity and Prestige in English Secondary Education*, Routledge & Kegan Paul, London.

Chitty, C. (1987) The commodification of education, *Forum*, Vol. 29, no. 3, pp. 66–9.

Couper, M. and Harris, C. (1970) CAT to university: the changing student intake, *Educational Research*, Vol. 12, no. 2, pp. 113–20.

Cox, C. and Dyson, A. (eds.) (1969) *Fight for Education: A Black Paper*, Dent, London.

David, T. (1990) Down and almost out, *Education*, p. 13, 5 January.

DES (1986) *A New Choice of School*, London.

Edwards, T., Fitz, J. and Whitty, G. (1989) *The State and Private Education: An Evaluation of the Assisted Places Scheme*, Falmer Press, Lewes.

Fitz, J., Edwards, T. and Whitty, G. (1986) Beneficiaries, benefits and costs: an investigation of the Assisted Places Scheme, *Research Papers in Education*, Vol. 1, no. 3, pp. 169–93.

Fitz, J., Edwards, T. and Whitty, G. (1989) The Assisted Places Scheme: an ambiguous case of privatisation, *British Journal of Educational Studies*, Vol. 37, no. 3, pp. 222–34.

Glazier, J. (1986) CTCs – so what's new? *Education*, 5 December.

Hammer, M. and Flude, M. (1989) 'Grant-maintained schools are nothing to do with party politics': an interview with Andrew Turner, Director of the Grant-Maintained Schools Trust, *Journal of Education Policy*, Vol. 4, no. 4, pp. 373–85.

Hillgate Group (1987) *The Reform of British Education*, Claridge Press, London.

ISIS (1974) *The Case for Independence*, London.

ISIS (1976) *Selection: Modern Education's Dirty Word*, London.

ISIS (1981) *The Case for Collaboration*, London.

Johnson, R. (1989) Thatcherism and English education: breaking the mould or confirming the pattern? *History of Education*, Vol. 18, no. 2, pp. 91–121.

McCulloch, G. (1989) *The Secondary Technical School: A Usable Past?*, Falmer Press, Lewes.

McLeod, J. (1988) CTCs – a study of the character and progress of an educational initiative, *London Government Studies*, Vo. 14, no. 1, pp. 75–82.

Morrell, F. (1989) *Children of the Future*, The Hogarth Press, London.

Musgrove, F. (1987) The Black Paper movement, in R. Lowe (ed.) *The Changing Primary School*, Falmer Press, Lewes.

Nash, I. (1988) CTCs forced to change tack, *The Times Educational Supplement*, 17 June.

NUT (1989) *CTCs – No Thanks*, London.

Rae, J. (1981) *The Public School Revolution*, Faber & Faber, London.

Seldon, A. (1986) *The Riddle of the Voucher*, Institute of Economic Affairs, London.

Sexton, S. (1977) Evolution by choice, in C. B. Cox and R. Boyson (eds.) *Black Paper 1977*, Temple Smith, London.

Sexton, S. (1987) *Our Schools: A Radical Policy*, IEA Education Unit, Warlingham.

Sherman, A. (1988) Relevant steps in the wrong direction, *Guardian*, 20 September.

Tapper, T. and Salter, B. (1986) The Assisted Places Scheme: a policy evaluation, *Journal of Education Policy*, Vol. 1, no. 4, pp. 315–30.

West, E. G. (1982) Education vouchers – evolution or revolution?, *Journal of Economic Affairs*, Vol. 3, no. 1, p. 15.

Whitty, G. (1989) The New Right and the National Curriculum: state control or market forces?, *Journal of Education Policy*, Vol. 4, no. 4, pp. 329–41.

Whitty, G., Fitz, J. and Edwards, T. (1989) Assisting whom?, in A. Hargreaves and D. Reynolds (eds.) *Controversies and Critiques: Issues in Education Policy*, Falmer Press, Lewes.

11

CITY TECHNOLOGY COLLEGES: A PRIVATE MAGNETISM?

Geoffrey Walford

INTRODUCTION

It is often difficult to trace the origins of particular educational policy initiatives. The previous chapter by Edwards, Gewirtz and Whitty has shown that the decision to establish a network of twenty city technology colleges (CTCs) is no exception, and that there was a range of somewhat competing ideas and pressures that led to the final proposal. This chapter concentrates on two of the major arguments used to justify CTCs and examines the extent to which the first CTC at Kingshurst, Solihull, acts in accord with these justifications. The two aspects are, first, the private-school status and nature of the colleges and, second, the magnet school concept, which originally developed in the USA.

The CTC announcement was made by Kenneth Baker, then Secretary of State for Education and Science, on 7 October 1986, at the Conservative Party Annual Conference. In front of the enthusiastic audience, the colleges were presented as 'breaking the grip' of left-wing LEAs, and offering new opportunities to children in the inner cities where the LEAs were said to be failing to provide effective education. They were to serve 11–18-year-olds within specific areas, some of which were already designated as part of the government's Inner City Initiative. In part, the CTCs were also intended to help solve the perceived national shortage of qualified scientists, technicians and engineers, for they were to offer a curriculum rich in science and technology, and pupils were to pledge to stay in full-time education or training until the age of 18.

What was most unusual about the CTC idea was that the colleges were to be independent or private schools, run by educational trusts established specifically for the purpose and heavily supported by industry and commerce. The colleges were to be registered charities and receive regular donations from sponsors. They were to charge no fees but to have some current expenditure provided directly by the DES in line with per-capita spending in similar LEAs. However, it was expected that the initial capital expenditure and major contributions to the extra current expenditure required to run a highly technological school would be provided by industry and commerce. The plan thus extended the government's ideology of reducing public expenditure and encouraging charitable giving by sponsors to cover the shortfall (Robson and Walford, 1989).

Further details of the plan were given in a glossy brochure published by the DES a week after Kenneth Baker's speech (DES, 1986). It was sent to about 2,000 leading industrial and commercial organizations asking them to support the new venture. According to the booklet, it was in the cities that the education system was under the most pressure and where the government's aims and parents' aspirations 'often seem furthest from fulfilment':

> There are many examples of good schooling offered by committed teachers in the cities. But the families living there who seek the best possible education for their children do not have access to the kind of schools which measure up to their ambitions. The government believes that there is, in the business community and elsewhere, a widespread wish to help extend the range of choice for families in urban areas.
>
> *(Ibid.* p. 3)

It was planned that each CTC would serve a substantial catchment area, with the composition of the student body being representative of the community served. These catchment areas were to be defined in such a way that places would be available for about one in five or six children from within the area. It was made clear that the CTCs would not be academically selective, but that selection would still be an important feature. They were not to be neighbourhood schools taking all-comers, but the head and governing body were to select from applicants on the basis of

> general aptitude, for example as reflected in their progress and achievements in primary school; on their readiness to take advantage of the type of education offered in CTCs; and on their parents' commitment to full-time education or training up to the age of 18, to the distinctive characteristics of the CTC curriculum, and to the ethos of the CTC.
>
> *(Ibid.* p. 5)

It is now well known that industry and commerce has shown itself extremely reluctant to take on the funding of this part of secondary education. The government's belief that there was a 'widespread wish to help' was misplaced, and sponsors have only gradually come forward over a four-year period in response to specific government overtures. Moreover, those who have been persuaded to become sponsors have been only prepared to donate on a scale far smaller than was originally envisaged, leaving the government to provide the major part of the capital and current expenditure.

Such lack of support from British industry for new private-education ventures could have been easily predicted by considering the fate of the University of Buckingham. Margaret Thatcher and the Conservative government have strongly supported the idea of private higher education and gave a Royal Charter to Buckingham in 1983 so that it could award its own degrees (Walford, 1988). However, more than twenty years after the plan was first mooted, the University of Buckingham still has only about 600 students, who study a limited range of subjects, on a small campus with facilities few would consider to be of university standard (Shaw and Blaug, 1988). Nevertheless, no serious research on industry and commerce's support for the CTC project appears to have been conducted, and the lack of support came as a surprise to the government. It seemed to anticipate that local industrialists would rush to become sponsors for a CTC in their area but, in practice, the government had to take a more active role. Both sites and sponsors were difficult to find and the government eventually helped to establish the City Technology Colleges Trust to push the policy through.

The first CTC to be announced was at Kingshurst, in Solihull, one of the metropolitan boroughs of the West Midlands. The borough sold a long lease on what had previously been Kingshurst Secondary School, and the first intake of about 180 children were admitted in September 1988. This college has been the subject of intensive case-study research (Walford and Miller 1991). Local headteachers, LEA administrators, politicians and others concerned with the college were interviewed between 1988 and 1990, and a mini-ethnographic study was conducted within the college itself during the autumn term of 1989. During that term, teaching and other activities were observed, documents collected, a sample of 45 second-year students and some teachers were interviewed and the majority of other pupils completed a questionnaire. Fuller details of the research methods are given in Walford (1991). This chapter will discuss features of the City Technology College, Kingshurst, in relation to the college's private and magnet statuses.

CTCS AS PRIVATE SCHOOLS

It is worth remembering that the British State's involvement in education is relatively recent. Before 1870 all schools were private schools, for it was only then that the government of the day began to establish State-owned and maintained elementary schools to fill the gaps in private, voluntary and charitable provision. Over the years the Church schools became increasingly dependent upon government funding and have been largely regarded as part of the maintained sector since the establishment of the equivalent of LEAs in 1902. Since that point, the private sector of education rapidly shrank, reaching a low of 5.8 per cent in England in 1976.

This process of gradually increasing government involvement and expenditure on schooling was not without its critics. Throughout the 150 years of growing government concern with education, each new change requiring further expenditure has been subject to severe disapproval from those who felt they would have to foot the bill. More recently, however, there have been growing strictures about government responsibility and control of education as well as funding, and the Conservative governments since 1979 have been ideologically committed to the privatization all public services wherever possible. Over the last decade or more, the Conservatives have shown strong support for the private sector of education, and have sought to help and extend private schooling in competion with the maintained sector (Walford, 1990).

There have been numerous articles, books and pamphlets that have argued for less direct control of education by government, but of particular importance have been those by Stuart Sexton, who was educational adviser to Mark Carlisle and Sir Keith Joseph when they were Secretary of State for Education and Science. As indicated in the last chapter, Sexton was a firm advocate of the Assisted Places Scheme, and a long-standing supporter of selective education, grammar schools and of a fully privatized and differentiated educational system. He was a contributor to the 1977 Black Paper (Cox and Boyson, 1977), where he argued for schools to have specialisms and for devolution of administration to schools such that maintained schools would become 'independent units as in the private sector' (Sexton, 1977). The Assisted Places Scheme that developed was more restricted than he had planned, but Sexton has continued to strive for a fully privatized educational system, possibly supported by vouchers (Sexton, 1987).

As the 1980s progressed, the calls from the political right for increased privatization and differentiation between schools became more widely spread. Dennison (1984), for example, called for the establishment of new private schools, and recommended that these might be encouraged by handing over the premises of LEA schools due for closure to private trusts. He also considered the possibility of capital grants and further subsidies to private school to cover such items as salaries or capital expenditure. The *No Turning Back* group of Conservative MPs (Brown *et al.*, 1985, 1986) argued for parents and teachers to be able to start their own private schools funded by central government.

Many commentators on the political right saw private schools as more responsive to the desires of parents, and less likely to be influenced by left-wing ideas, which they saw as prevalent in many LEAs. They wished to see less emphasis on the social and community aspects of education and more on the education and training of a future workforce. Many on the right believed that private schools would be more efficient and effective in terms of value for money and traditional examination successes. Some critics of the maintained sector also saw the possibility of private schools breaking the power of teacher unions within schools, giving the possibility of payment based on geographical area, on a teacher's competitive position in the labour market and on evaluations of the effectiveness of individual teachers. Others saw private schools as a way by which government might be able to reduce gradually its responsibility for an expenditure on education, and hand both back to parents.

CTCs can be seen as one of the results of a long campaign for more private schools, for they are officially registered as independent schools, and DES statistics now include CTC staff and student numbers within the totals for independent schools (DES, 1990). Moreover, there was actually no necessity for CTCs to be included as part of the Education Reform Act 1988. Although the government encouraged sponsors to establish these new private CTCs by promising to pay for their current expenditure at a level broadly comparable to that of schools in similar locations, the Secretary of State was initially only using existing powers in the Education Act 1944 to give grants to private schools. CTCs were included in the Education Reform Act 1988 mainly to ensure that any future government would have to pass legislation (rather than simply change regulations) to cease to fund them. The 1988 Act ensured that the Secretary of State entered into an individual agreement with each of the CTCs to provide payments. Section 105 (4) provided for continued funding according to the terms of that agreement for at least seven years, while section 105 (6) indemnified the sponsors against any loss caused by the Secretary of State terminating the agreement. The Act also made it clear that any capital expenditure from the government would have to be repaid if the governors decided to discontinue the school or changed its characteristics away from those that define it as a CTC. It is these agreements that the CTCs sign with the DES that make them different from other private schools, but they enter into these agreements voluntarily.

THE CTC KINGSHURST AS A PRIVATE SCHOOL

Each CTC is a separate independent school with its own governing body, charitable trust and trustees. Their official position is very similar to that of any other private school with charitable status, and the principal and governors take many decisions about the colleges without recourse to any higher body. The DES, HMIs or the City Technology Colleges Trust do not have control over the day-to-day organization of any of the college or act to see that the decisions of individual CTCs are co-ordinated. Over time, each college is expected to develop in its own way, and this diversity is seen as an essential part of the experiment. This means that any discussion of the City Technology College, Kingshurst, is limited to just that one example. What has occurred there may or may not occur elsewhere, and what is reported in this chapter about Kingshurst is not necessarily generalizable to the other CTCs.

At Kingshurst the procedure adopted for establishing the college had much in common with that used by Victorian churchmen, such as Nathaniel Woodard or William Sewell, in founding private boarding schools to support their own particular theological opinions. There were the same small gatherings of supporters, uncertainties about the sufficiency of future funding, and *ad hoc* arrangements to ensure the school opened on time. Parents had little idea what they were entering their children for, but they took the future schools on faith and signed up just the same. The difference between the foundation of Kingshurst and, for example, Lancing College (Kirk, 1937) or Radley College (Boyd, 1948) was that the government was one of the small band of backers for the project, and Kenneth Baker's personal reputation was in part tied to its success. The government has shown itself to be a far more generous supporter than any that the Victorian founders had access to.

One of the first tasks supporters of any new private school have is that of appointing a first head. The Principal of the CTC Kingshurst, Mrs Valerie Bragg, was appointed by the sponsors before any governing body was in place, or a funding agreement worked out with the DES. In common with other private-school heads, she has played a fundamental role in shaping the organizational structure of the college, and has a very high level of personal responsibility for the running of the college. The composition of the governing body was decided in consultation between the Principal and the sponsors. In December 1989 there were 13 members, with a number of vacancies. Seven of those so far appointed were representatives of sponsoring industries and commercial organizations. The Chairman of Governors was Divisional Chairman of T & N, the Vice Chairman was Director of Hanson plc. Also represented at director level were Hardy Spicer Ltd, Deloitte Haskins and Sells, Arlington Business Parks Ltd, IMI and Lucas Industries plc. The DES had one representative on the governing body, who was actually the local Education Liaison Officer for Engineering Employers and was previously Project Director for the college. The other governors included Miss S. J. Browne, Principal of Newnham College, Cambridge, Mr John Lewis, formerly Senior Science Master, Malvern College, Dr J. Sharp, Chairman of the Independent Schools Joint Council Inspection Service and formerly Head of Rossall School, Mr G. Verow, Director of Training for the Incorporated Association of Preparatory Schools and Miss B. A. Simpson, Governor of Hereford Sixth Form College and former head of a State comprehensive school. Being a charity, the college cannot have teachers as members of the governing body and there are no parent governors.

Within this governing body, the bishops, deans and field-marshals evident within major private schools such as Radley or Lancing College are omitted (Walford, 1986, p. 212), and the industrialists (which are now common within private-school governing bodies) are there by virtue of their companies rather than because they are former pupils of the college. However, there is a similar firm Oxbridge link, and a surprisingly large contingent with links to other private schools. The inclusion of the Chairman of the Independent Schools Joint Council Inspection Service and the Director of Training for IAPS is particularly noteworthy. Again, in most major private schools, there are no parent governors and there can be no teacher governors.

The highly prestigious people who compose the governing body act in a way similar to the governing bodies of most leading private schools. In this case the governing body has also given the Principal full powers of appoint-

ment of other staff and full powers over day-to-day organization of the college
and of the budget. This degree of control is unusual in maintained schools
but usual for heads of private schools, and may become more common with
the introduction of local management of schools. The governing body meets
regularly about twice each term and, while it is not simply a rubber-stamping
body, is unlikely to overrule the Principal's decisions. Traditionally, private-
school governing bodies only act against the head if disaster looms.

At the CTC is within the private sector it has developed its own organizational structure, salary scales and conditions of service for all staff, rather
than having to accept those currently imposed within the maintained sector.
The organizational structure is modelled on industry with (currently) six area
managers supervising large areas of the curriculum. There are no heads of
department or deputy principals, and area managers report directly to the
Principal. Each member of teaching staff is within one of the six areas, with
no further levels in the hierarchy. The details of this organizational structure
are unusual for any school, but the short command structure is typical of
private schools. Unlike most private schools, the pastoral structure is based
upon tutor groups, and tutors retain the same group of children throughout
their time at the college. Area managers provide pastoral support to tutors
within their own areas, and there is no separate pastoral hierarchy. A further
important feature of the organizational structure is that there is a Director of
Administration and Finance who is responsible for much of the routine
administration of the college as well as having budgetary control. This is a
role larger than that of the traditional private-school bursar, but holds a
similar level of prestige. Secretarial and administrative staff are responsible
to the Director of Administration and Finance.

Additional funding from sponsors allows the salaries of staff to be slightly
higher than they would be in maintained schools, but the major difference is
that, instead of incremental scales, there are two broad continuous salary
bands – one for area managers and the other for other teaching staff. In
practice this simply means that there is a top and bottom point to each band,
and a teacher can be paid anything between the two points. Broadly, the
bottom of the teachers' band is slightly higher than the minimum for State
schools and the band rises to very slightly above the top salary available for a
classroom teacher. The crucial decision as to where a teacher is positioned
within either band is made by the Principal according to the teacher's experience and previous salary. The other major difference between the Kingshurst
salaries and State-school salaries is that increments are given on the basis of
performance, and no teacher automatically gains an increment just for getting
older. All staff automatically receive an inflation-related increase, but any
real increase is based on performance as judged by the Principal and/or area
managers. This salary structure is based upon salaries in industry, and differs
from that in most other private schools. However, it is similar to that used in
private schools in the degree of personal discretion given to the Principal in
salary negotiations with individual staff. At Kingshurst, teachers can be

members of trades unions and some are, but these unions have not yet been involved in salary negotiations.

The CTC also has its own appraisal system, in which most teachers are appraised by their area manager each year. This is seen as separate from performance-related payments, which are linked to activities above and beyond a teacher's everyday job. Performance-related payments are made to teachers who take on special responsibilities in areas of the curriculum or in organizing and developing special extra-curricula activities. The private-school status of the college means that it can appoint teaching staff without qualified teacher status. One such teacher has been appointed so far, but four of the technicians are also involved in some small-group teaching and industrialists also occasionally teach some groups of children.

Teachers are expected to be flexible. There is no set limit to the number of hours to be worked in the year. The school-day for staff starts at 8.10 a.m. and goes on until 4.00 p.m. on most days, 4.30 p.m. on Wednesdays and 3.00 p.m. on Fridays. Staff are often involved in CTC-related activities at the college beyond these hours, and some staff are still at the college some hours after the official close. This length and flexibility of working hours is a common feature of private schools, both day and boarding, but there is usually a slight compensation in that the term is shorter than in State schools. At the CTC the term is actually longer than in State schools.

Language is an important indicator of ideology. The CTC is a school for 11–18-year-old children but is called a college. It is unusual in the State sector for this term to be used for children under 16, but many of the major public schools call themselves colleges rather than schools. Kingshurst also uses the term 'students' rather than pupils, and has a 'lecture theatre' which is a large, flat room. Such language use is part of making pupils feel special and more adult, but it is also the language used within the private sector more than the State sector.

Perhaps one of the most important ways in which pupils are made to feel special in any school is for them to be selected for it. In the private sector 12-year-old pupils work with a passion to 'pass' the common entrance examination to the public school of their choice (Walford, 1986, p. 187). At Kingshurst, selection is not based upon academic ability, as the college accepts a span of abilities roughly representative of the range that apply. However, children are interviewed with their parents (much as in private schools) and are selected on such criteria as progress and achievement in primary school, their parents' commitment to the CTC and the pupils' positive qualities, which will help them to succeed (DES, 1986, p. 5). As with entry to other private schools, personal qualities, skills or attributes, such as being a good athlete or playing a musical instrument, can act in the child's favour. One of the greatest similarities between the CTC Kingshurst and most private schools is this feature of selectivity. Parents do not, in this case, pay for their children's schooling, but they are chosen from among those who apply. Moreover, if the child (or the parents) do not keep their side of the bargain, in terms of keeping up with work for example, the child can be removed. Kingshurst has not yet expelled any child, but this ultimate possibility is an important one.

On a more positive note, the atmosphere of trust that pervades the CTC Kingshurst is also a feature it shares with the major private schools. The college is well equipped'with televisions, video-players and tapes, computers and various forms of software. This expensive equipment is not locked away, but is available for any child to use at lunch and break times. Children are trusted to remain within the college buildings at all times if they wish to do so and to treat the equipment with care and respect. They are free to use the building, with its classrooms, social areas and other specialist rooms in a reasonable way. While there are some restrictions, of course, the degree of trust given to the children is high, and echoes the level of trust given to pupils in the major private schools (Walford, 1986). Here, though, the children are predominantly from working-class homes, in contrast to the affluent backgrounds of the children in most other private schools.

The influence of the CTC's private-school status on the curriculum is fascinating. Private schools do not have to follow the National Curriculum, but the funding agreements with the DES ensure that the CTCs follow 'the substance' of the National Curriculum. Exactly what this form of words means is open to question, but the CTC Kingshurst has decided to follow the National Curriculum as closely as possible. In practice, this is likely to be the same decision that other private schools will make, for most would not wish to be seen to offer less than the National Curriculum, and would present this coverage as the minimum on which they would wish to build.

The longer school hours and term for the CTC enable it to cover the National Curriculum and add various other non-standard extras. These additions include lessons on Business and Economic Awareness for all pupils and three sessions given to 'Enrichments', where pupils chose from a range of cultural, aesthetic and sporting options designed to broaden their interests. While some other private schools may wish to include Business and Economic Awareness as an extra course, it is more likely that they will wish to continue to offer such subjects as Latin, Greek and extra modern languages. Most private schools also have a range of enriching activities run either as extra-curricular activities or, particularly in boarding schools, as afternoon activities. The CTC also has sufficient time available to suspend the timetable for about seven days each term so that pupils can work on group projects related to a general theme, such as health, survival or time. These project weeks are an important feature of the CTC, which are not directly echoed in the curriculum of most private schools, but some of the major private schools do suspend the curriculum for an annual week of cultural activities.

The CTC Kingshurst branches away from the traditional curriculum of both private and maintained schools in its proposed post-16 provision. The intention is that all pupils at the CTC will remain in full-time education or training until they are 18, which means that the CTC must offer a range of post-16 courses that will cater for the whole of the ability range. The narrowly specialist and academic curriculum of the A-level has been rejected and replaced by Business and Technicians Education Council (BTEC) First and National Certificates and the International Baccalaureate (IB). The BTEC qualifications have, until recently, only been available through colleges of further education, for they involve extended periods of work experience, close contact with industry and commerce and the availability of extensive teaching equipment and facilities. Some schools have recently been able to offer their own independent courses, but the CTC Kingshurst is the first school to offer such a wide range of BTEC courses, and to make them the main post-16 offering.

The IB is designed for above-average ability pupils as a two-year international pre-university curriculum and university entrance examination. It was developed within the private-sector international schools, which were established to provide education for children of internationally mobile business people, administrators, diplomats and similar. These schools aim to provide an education overseas for parents who wish their children to return to their own country for higher education. Students follow six subjects – one chosen from each of six groups – such that they must study a social science and a second language together with the natural sciences and mathematics. Students also follow a Theory of Knowledge course, write an extended essay on a piece of personal research and spend at least one half day in some form of creative aesthetic activity or active social service.

The IB course is taken by about 400 schools in 56 countries, both private and state maintained. Within the UK, however, it is mainly to be found within the private sector, with such well-known schools as Sevenoaks School and the United World College of the Atlantic being prominent. It is also available in several private sixth-form colleges, but the total number of UK schools and colleges offering IB is less than 20. The CTC's choice of the IB as its main higher-education entry course thus represents a distinct break with the majority of both private and maintained schools. Moreover, the CTC wishes to offer the course to a far wider ability range than is usual in other schools, in an attempt to show that average and above-average ability children are able to be successful in the correct environment. The decision not to offer A-levels was not an easy one, with governors and the DES expressing severe doubts about this move away from the traditional curriculum. Parents were not consulted about the decision, and had expected that the CTC would be offering A-level courses rather than IB.

In summary, there are many decisions that have been made in the CTC Kingshurst that are related to the college's private status. It has been able to institute its own staff salary and appraisal scheme, conditions of work and organizational structure. It has a governing body closer in the nature of its membership and method of working to that of private schools than to that of the maintained sector. However, this does not necessarily mean that the CTC has consciously tried to follow the example of existing private schools.

Decisions have been made on the basis of what was considered best for the pupils, and that some of these decisions follow those made in other private schools could be simply that those schools are operating on the same basis. Further, since the passing of the Education Reform Act 1988, many schools have been given some of the greater freedom of action private schools have. Already, the private nature of Kingshurst CTC is less exceptional now than it was when it opened in 1988.

Thus, the private status of the CTC is important, but it should not be overstated. There is an obvious ambiguity in status with a school that is predominantly funded by the State, but that is formally independent. Indeed, the CTC's *Mission Statement* claims that the CTC 'remain[s] within the State education system...'. This ambiguity would have been less if business and industry had decided to support the colleges at a higher level, but as the DES has reluctantly become the major sponsor, it has had a larger influence on decision-making than might have at first been envisaged. As the major sponsor, the DES has sought to restrict its expenditure and, for example, tightly defines the maximum number of pupils that can be admitted each year. The DES also has a representative on the governing body, and HMIs have made regular visits to the college. Equally importantly, although some aspects of the atmosphere and culture of the CTC are similar to those within private schools, practically all teachers have had their major experience of teaching within the maintained sector, and only a minute number of children have been to private-sector preparatory or primary schools. The social-class distribution of the parents of children is also highly unusual for a private school, as it is heavily weighted towards the working class, and is representative of the generally poor neighbourhood the CTC serves. The CTC Kingshurst may be a private school, but it is also an unusual one.

THE CTCS AS MAGNET SCHOOLS

The first magnet schools were designated in the USA in the early 1970s, and federal funding of magnet schools designed to reduce racial segregation through voluntary means started in 1976. The number of magnet schools in the USA has since risen dramatically, such that in 1989 Rolf Blank could claim that at the high-school level about 20 per cent of pupils were in magnet schools in the average urban district. The Federal Magnet Schools Grants Program supported about 40 district programmes in 1989, at a total cost of $114 million (Blank, 1989).

A magnet school is one that specializes in a particular academic, aesthetic or cultural subject area and that is designed to attract pupils who wish to specialize in that particular area. The full curriculum is usually covered in each of these schools, but there is an additional enrichment specialization that may be, for example, science, mathematics, technology, sport, art, drama, dance or music. In the USA some magnet schools even specialize in preparation for military careers, or in highly specific vocational areas such as aeronautical engineering. In Britain, the idea is perhaps most popularly known through the television programme 'Fame', which was based on the New York High School for the Performing Arts.

As with any educational innovation, proponents see a range of different advantages for magnet school. Cooper (1987) argues that magnet schools raise academic standards by providing increased choice for parents and pupils, and by promoting competition between schools for pupils. Magnet schools are seen as a way of opening schools to the free market, and are said to produce a diversity of schools, each of which can then provide a curriculum better suited to the children it serves. Diversity and choice are seen as desirable in themselves. However, the magnet-school concept has developed over time. Originally, it referred to little more than a school system with a few élite special schools, rather similar to grammar schools acting as 'academic magnets' within the British selective system. From the mid-1970s, however, the concept has been closely linked to methods of desegregating American school districts on a voluntary basis, and whole school systems have been magnetized. In practice, the majority of magnet schools have been introduced in order to attract pupils from a variety of neighbourhoods (and thus from a variety of ethnic groups and social classes) into areas that otherwise would be ethnically and socially segregated. The legal requirement for desegregated schooling can thus be achieved without resorting to assigning pupils to specific schools according to ethnic group and its associated bussing of pupils.

At the time of writing Cooper (1987) reported that over 1,800 school systems in the USA had established one or more magnet schools, and that many were attempting to magnetize the entire local system. He gives details of the system adopted in Kansas City, where the US court found the city to be operating a two-tier system, and recommended that the education authorities implement a total system of magnet schools to desegregate the city. At the secondary level, eight magnet high schools were created with a range of specialisms including Law and Public Service, Business Technology, International Studies and even Air Force Reserve Officer Training Corps. Cooper warns that the extra costs of establishing such a system may be very high.

In Britain, the idea of having specialisms within different schools is far from new. The tripartite system that developed after the Education Act 1944 might be seen as a peculiar form of the magnet-school concept, where selection was based on ability to pass tests rather than the child's interest in what a particular type of school had to offer. As the number of selective schools decreased and comprehensive schools increased, many on the right called for greater diversity between schools. Sexton (1977), for example, argued that parents should be able to seek out schools for their children where particular subject expertise existed. Pupils and parents should be able to select schools and the schools should also be selective about whom to accept from the children who applied. More recently, Caroline Cox (1986) called explicitly for magnet schools to be introduced into Britain as a way of improving what she perceived to be declining standards in schools.

In September 1987, Kenneth Baker visited some magnet schools in Washington and New York, and came back with a new justification for the CTCs. The educational Press was filled with pictures of him talking to teachers and pupils in the specialist New York schools, on to which he heaped praise, and claimed that magnet schools were models the CTCs would emulate. So that the message got through to those directly involved, the DES later paid for Valerie Bragg and some others to visit similar magnet schools in New York and Washington. The Secretary of State's visit also led to an expansion of an already-planned conference, such that in the autumn of 1988 a group of about 50 British educationists, including seven HMI, spent about three weeks in New York City schools.

The New York City system is particularly interesting for it provides for a population that is predominantly poor and from ethnic minorities. The few remaining white and middle-class parents rarely use the State system. In response, New York has created the largest magnet system in the USA. More than 90 of the 116 high schools have at least one magnet programme (Cooper, 1987). In practice, though, the New York system is not all that it seems. Three of the most prominent high schools (some of which Kenneth Baker visited and highly praised) are schools that are more than 40 years old. The Bronx High School of Science, Stuyvesant High and Brooklyn Technical High use their own admission tests as the main test of admission. They draw their pupils from all over New York City and are highly selective. This is also true of the High School for the Performing Arts, which holds auditions or reviews a portfolio of past work. Only the most able few per cent gain a place.

Admission to the bulk of the magnet schools, which are more recent in origin, is more open to a range of abilities. Selection used to be on the basis of a set percentage from each of three ability levels; however, a strongly critical report on magnet schools, *Lost in the Labyrinth* (Educational Priorities Panel, 1985), argued that this led to schools selecting the most able pupils within each category and pupils being unfairly treated. The entry procedure has since been replaced by randomly chosen admissions from those children who apply to fill 50 per cent of the places, with the remaining places being selected by the schools on their own criteria (which include test scores and attendance and punctuality records). Nevertheless, the costs of travel are still not provided, which must act as a considerable disincentive to children from poor families.

While the Secretary of State saw the magnet-school concept as worthy of emulation, it was not without its critics on both sides of the Atlantic. For example, in her case study of an unnamed city system, Metz (1986) shows that, in contrast to the rhetoric, magnet schools had only played a small part in desegregating that city's schools. The major change had been achieved by closing inner-city schools and bussing black children to neighbourhood white schools. Few parents had actually made a choice of school on the basis of magnet specialism. Other commentators have argued that selectivity and competition discriminate against less able pupils and against children from poor homes (Rowan, 1988). There is also growing concern in the USA that where magnet schools thrive, this could be to the detriment of nearby neighbourhood schools, and that magnet schools could produce a two-tier education system with special opportunities for selected students in one set of schools and lower-quality education for the remaining students in the non-magnet schools (Moore and Davenport, 1989). The particular concern here is not just about inequality of provision, but about the social class and ethnic groups that might benefit or be disadvantaged by such a system. In their study of four city districts, Moore and Davenport (*ibid.*) found that very few 'at-risk' students were enrolled in magnet schools compared with the proportion in non-magnet schools. As proponents such as Cooper (1987) recognize, there is a fundamental conflict between the desire for equitable access and the schools' need to retain their unique magnetic quality. He argues, 'self selection and some admissions criteria are at the very heart of most special schools' (*ibid.* p. 40). In Britain, Caroline Cox shows herself to be aware of similar problems, but argues that the majority of magnet schools are only 'somewhat moderately selective' (1986, p. 199). She seems unperturbed that the main type of selection is self-selection, and sees this as an indication of enthusiasm and a contributory factor to strong motivation in school. She quotes the findings of an unnamed research team, which is said to have found that 'the extent of creaming is only minor'.

Anthony Green (1988), from the University of London, who retraced the footsteps of Kenneth Baker on his tour of New York, was far more critical of the effect of magnet schools on the schools that remain as neighbourhood schools. He argues that the magnet schools have a broad political role of helping to maintain the interest of the middle class and the aspirant working class in State education, but that they recruit an unfair share of the best pupils and damage other schools. He could find no evidence that they provided a competitive spur to other schools but found that they generated much resentment.

The delegation of 50 educationalists who visited New York schools at Kenneth Baker's behest did not restrict its inquiries to the magnet schools but watched lessons in a large number of schools covering the full range of children. The resulting report from the HMI (1990) has several critical passages, and reports that 'many educationists and lay people in New York City believe that the high school system has become too diverse, too specialised, and too hierarchical in its structure. Several principals and administrators claim that the selective and optional arrangements favour the more advantaged' (*ibid.* 9). They argue further that taking highly able pupils out of their neighbourhood schools leaves fewer students who can give academic, creative and pastoral leadership, and that the admissions arrangements are too complicated for many parents to understand. They report that a daily exodus of pupils from neighbourhood schools weakens those schools and leave some schools that now 'serve very deprived areas, largely populated by an "underclass" with few opportunities to get on' (*ibid.*).

It is strange that at a time when within the USA there is a significant lobby of opinion that believes that 'excellence has been pursued at the expense of equity and that the challenge now is to restore fair measures of equality of opportunity in all schools' (*ibid.*), Britain is heading in the opposite direction, with the growth of CTCs, grant-maintained schools and at least one LEA moving towards a complete magnet system.

THE CTC KINGSHURST AS A MAGNET SCHOOL

After his visit to New York and Washington, Kenneth Baker often presented the CTCs in terms of their magnet status, but in practice they differ considerably from the American model. This can be seen through a close study of the CTC Kingshurst. The most important difference is that the catchment area for Kingshurst is comparatively small, and was originally drawn to include a fairly homogeneously working-class area, and explicitly to exclude more middle-class areas (see Walford and Miller 1991, for further details). It is a roughly circular boundary with a diameter of less than four miles, which includes some of the poorest districts of north Solihull and east Birmingham. This original catchment area was only used for the first intake of pupils in 1988 and has been modified since that time. During this first year the CTC could act as a magnet for pupils from within this limited catchment area, but this could only remove well-motivated pupils from the seven other neighbourhood schools, with little opportunity for any increase in social-class or ethnic-group mixing. For the second and subsequent entry years the catchment area has been extended to include two adjacent areas where there is a slightly higher proportion of middle-class families, and the admission regulations have been changed such that 5 per cent of the intake (nine pupils each year) can be taken from outside the enlarged catchment area. This change gives a greater possibility of social mixing.

During the last weeks before Christmas 1989, 80 per cent of the first intake of pupils to the CTC and 60 per cent of the second intake were either interviewed or completed a questionnaire. One of the questions gathered information about their parents' occupations. While children's knowledge about their parents' jobs is limited, and their answers should not be taken too seriously, there are some interesting differences between the social-class composition of the first and second intake years as described by the pupils. For both years, the percentage of parents in social classes IV and V (partly skilled and unskilled) (Registrar General's classification) outweighed the percentage in social classes I and II (professional and intermediate), but the second intake year had a higher proportion of social class I and II parents than did the first intake year. There was also a higher proportion of ethnic-minority children in the second intake year than in the first intake year. This is exactly what would be expected as a result of the catchment area changes, and might be seen as the CTC Kingshurst acting more similarly to the American magnet schools in the second year of operation than it did in the first. Of particular importance here are three children in the second intake year who stated that they would have attended a private school had they not been accepted by the CTC. All three appear to have benefited from the catchment area changes, with two being accepted as part of the 5 per cent outside the boundary.

There is a fascinating tension here, for while the CTC might now be seen to be acting more like a magnet school by having an intake that has a greater social-class and ethnic-group diversity, this also means that some children from more affluent homes are benefiting from a college originally designed to serve inner-city children. The social aspect of the magnet concept was not a part of the original CTC proposals and, indeed, the DES (1986, p. 5) booklet stated that CTCs would not be expected to admit children from outside the catchment area. Kingshurst's moves to take on more of the social-engineering characteristics associated with magnet schools are thus in conflict with the original CTC plan to provide education only for specific inner-city children.

There are further tensions when the nature of the magnetism is discussed. If the CTC Kingshurst is a magnet school, it is presumably a magnet for technology. Yet, far from all the pupils saw it in this way. In interviews and in the questionnaires, pupils were asked why they had applied to enter the CTC. The range of replies was wide, but could be classified roughly into four groups of reasons:

1. Those concerned with computing, technology and the facilities of the college.
2. Those linked to the idea of 'good education' or 'better education'.
3. Those concerned with obtaining a job or a 'better' job.
4. Those cases where it was important that the college was new or different.

There was overlap between these categories and some pupils gave more than one reason, but an unexpected finding was that less than a quarter of the pupils mentioned computing, science, technology or related aspects. Nearly half expressed their desire to come to the college in terms of it offering a 'better education' or similar broad terms. While these general expressions might include aspects of technology and computing, it is of note that so few pupils discussed their desire to enter the CTC in terms of its supposed magnetic specialism.

In the interviews, pupils were explicitly asked whether the fact that it was a *technology* college had been important. Less than half claimed that it had been an important reason for their choice of school. While this group were prepared to enthuse about technology and often had their own computers at home, many others stated clearly that they had not felt technology or computing had been what had drawn then to the college. They felt the fact that it was new and different had been more important, or saw it as a chance to go to a 'better' school than their existing nearby LEA schools. Some pupils even

said that they originally had no interest in the computing aspects, but that
they were enjoying using the technology now.

CONCLUSION

It has been shown that the CTC Kingshurst does not readily fit into existing
categories of school, or mesh neatly with the various justifications used for its
existence. As a private school it has been able to introduce several innovations (such as those concerned with staff salaries and conditions of service)
that would be impossible in the State sector and, as a magnet school, it has
been able to attract well-motivated students, yet there is a fundamental
conflict between its role as a magnet school and its private status. The government's original intention was that industry and commerce would pay for a far
greater proportion of expenditure than has actually occurred, and the establishment of CTCs could be seen as part of a wider privatization strategy for
education (Walford, 1990).

Fundamentally, the CTCs were designed to attract selected pupils *away
from* LEA schools into a newly developed private sector, and to help establish a hierarchy of differentiated schools. This aim is in direct conflict with the
desire for social-class and ethnic-group integration, which was one of the
main reasons for introducing magnet schools in the USA. There, magnet
schools were supported by government in order to attract more white and
middle-class pupils *back into* the State sector and produce a more integrated
and egalitarian society.

In its changes to the catchment area and admissions policies, the CTC
Kingshurst has moved slightly towards becoming more like this original
model for a magnet school. It has provided the means for a little more social-
class and ethnic-group integration, and has encouraged a few potential
private-school users to use a school in a relatively poor neighbourhood.
However, it appears to attract many pupils for reasons other than that of its
advertised technological specialism, and is the choice of many simply because
it is seen as being at the top of the local hierarchy of schools. A similar
development of a hierarchy of schools, with the most highly motivated
children being selected for the leading schools, is exactly what has occurred in
many American cities, where magnets have been introduced. In the USA,
élitism has occurred as something of a by-product of many of the magnet
schemes, while in Britain it was central to the strategy. The CTC is thus in a
cleft stick. It cannot be both a magnet school that is part of an egalitarian
social-engineering programme, and also a selective private school forming a
part of the Conservative government's élitist objectives. It will be interesting
to follow the course of events to see which of these models eventually predominates, but unfortunately, at present, it seems most likely that the
attractiveness of magnetism as a justification for CTCs will fade with time.

ACKNOWLEDGEMENTS

My sincere thanks go to Mrs Valerie Bragg and the staff and students of the City Technology College, Kingshurst, for allowing me to enter their world and to experience their kindness and hospitality. Although this chapter could not have been completed without their generous help, the responsibility for its content is mine alone.

This study was funded by the Social Innovation Research Group at Aston Business School, and through a consultancy to an ESRC-funded research project on City Technology Colleges directed by Professors Tony Edwards and Geoff Whitty (Grant no. C00232462). I am also most grateful to Henry Miller who worked with me on the wider CTC project.

REFERENCES

Blank, R. K. (1989) Educational effects of magnet high schools (paper given at the Conference on Choice and Control in American Education), University of Wisconsin-Madison, Wis., 17–19 May.

Boyd, A. K. (1948) *The History of Radley College, 1847–1947*, Blackwell, Oxford.

Brown, M., Chope, C., Fallon, M., Forsyth, M., Hamilton, N., Howarth, G., Jones, R., Leigh, E., Lilley, P., Maude, F., Portillo, M., Rumbold, A. and Twinn, I. (1985) *No Turning Back*, Conservative Political Centre, London.

Brown, M., Chope, C., Fallon, M., Forth, E., Forsyth, M., Hamilton, N., Howarth, G., Jones, R., Leigh, E., Lilley, P., Portillo, M. and Twinn, I. (1986) *Save Our Schools*, Conservative Political Centre, London.

Cooper, B. S. (1987) *Magnet Schools*, Institute of Economic Affairs, London.

Cox, C. (1986) Specialist comprehensives: one answer to curriculum problems, in D. O'Keeffe (ed.) *The Wayward Curriculum*, Social Affairs Unit, London.

Cox, C. B. and Boyson, R. (eds.) (1977) *Black Paper 1977*, Temple Smith, London.

Dennison, S. R. (1984) *Choice in Education* (Hobart Paperback 19), Institute of Economic Affairs, London.

DES (1986) *City Technology Colleges, A New Choice of School*, London.

DES (1990) *Statistical Bulletin: Statistics of Schools in England – January 1990*, London.

Education Priorities Panel (1985) *Lost in the Labyrinth: New York City High School Admissions*, New York, NY.

Green, A. (1988) The power of magnets, *The Times Educational Supplement*, p. 23, 6 May.

HMI (1990) *Teaching and Learning in New York City Schools*, HMSO, London.

Kirk, K. E. (1937) *The Story of the Woodard Schools*, Hodder & Stoughton, London.

Metz, M. H. (1986) *Different by Design. The Context and Character of Three Magnet Schools*, Routledge & Kegan Paul, London.

Moore, D. and Davenport, S. (1989) *The New Improved Sorting Machine*, National Center on Effective Secondary Schools, Madison, Wis.

Robson, M. and Walford, G. (1989) Independent schools and tax policy under Mrs Thatcher, *Journal of Education Policy*, Vol. 4, no. 2, pp. 149–62.

Rowan, P. (1988) The huge gap between reality and rhetoric, *The Times Educational Supplement*, p. 13, 25 November.

Sexton, S. (1977) Evolution by choice, in C. B. Cox and R. Boyson (eds.), op. cit.

Sexton, S. (1987) *Our Schools – A Radical Policy*, Institute for Economic Affairs, London.

Shaw, G. K. and Blaug, M. (1988) The University of Buckingham aften ten years: a tentative evaluation, *Higher Education Quarterly*, Vol. 41, no. 2, pp. 72–89.

Walford, G. (1986) *Life in Public Schools*, Methuen, London.

Walford, G. (1988) The privatisation of British higher education, *European Journal of Education*, Vol. 23, no. 1/2, pp. 47–64.

Walford, G. (1990) *Privatization and Privilege in Education*, Routledge, London.

Walford, G. (1991) Researching the City Technology College, Kingshurst, in G. Walford (ed.) *Doing Educational Research*, Routledge, London.

Walford, G., and Miller, H. (1991) *City Technology College*, Open University Press, Milton Keynes.

AUTHOR INDEX

SUBJECT INDEX